RUSSIA: MARKET APPROACHES

The Definitive Business Digest

Published by
David Cant

THE RUSSIA HOUSE LTD

STEPTOE & JOHNSON  CONTAINERSHIPS

TNG

ISBN 5-901003-10-1   Media-Press Ltd. (Moscow)

CONTENTS

7.   SETTING UP IN RUSSIA

PREFACE

A message from HM Ambassador to Russia
His Excellency, Sir Anthony Russell Brenton, KCMG

Russia's economy is growing impressively and its booming capital, Moscow is visibly, colourfully and dramatically becoming more prosperous with no sign of a slowdown. To those who have not witnessed this dynamism for themselves and only seen a Russia making the headlines for all too often the wrong reasons in the UK media this may come as something of a shock. But the fact that Russia, and Moscow, in particular, is packed with opportunities for UK business is undeniable.

Many UK companies – more than 400 at the last count – are finding out for themselves with notable success. UK exports to Russia in 2007 increased by more than 37% from 2006 to some £2.9bn. The Russian government ranked the UK as the biggest investor in Russia in 2007 at around £13bn.

The largest investors into Russia, BP and Shell, have vital relationships in Russia and are here for the long run. Financial services companies are also booming with a long and impressive queue of Russian companies looking to use London's financial markets and international expertise as a springboard for going global. But there is also a new focus on Russia from large, medium-sized and small UK firms.

Russia, in common with other emerging markets, is not always the easiest place for foreign companies to do business. There are still market access issues and developing the long-term relationships necessary to do business in Russia requires time, effort and patience. Most in the UK business community in Russia will be able to tell a story or two about the complexities of dealing with Russian bureaucracy but most, if not all, will in the next breath tell of high profit margins and hard-working, capable and well-educated Russian colleagues.

Helping UK companies break into the market is, in particular, where my colleagues in UK Trade and Investment (UKTI) in the Moscow Embassy and Consulate Generals in St Petersburg and Ekaterinburg can make a difference. How can they do this? My UKTI colleagues start by trying to find out what the strengths of the UK company are and how it likes to operate. They then research the specifics of Russian market for the company, advise on first steps, find potential partners – the key to doing business in Russia – and then talk to them about the UK company and report back. Ultimately, making a business breakthrough in Russia needs the UK company to visit the market several times.

For those UK companies which do decide to come to Russia or who are already here I wish you every success. In Russia, you will find opportunities across virtually all sectors and industries, in a dynamically growing economy that is very much open for business and welcoming to UK companies. But more than that, visitors to Russia will find an endlessly fascinating and vast country going through one of the most exciting and vibrant periods of its history. It is an opportunity not to miss.

Anthony Brenton CMG
HM Ambassador to the Russian Federation

FOREWORD

Adam Greaves, Partner, Steptoe & Johnson

As many of the developed economies head towards leaner and more difficult times, the growth of the emerging market economies are now even more likely to be considered for investment opportunities. Given Russia's growth over the last ten years, with GDP having risen by over four times in that period, it is likely to be one of the first markets that is considered.

Having personally spent a great deal of time in Russia in recent years, I have witnessed this tremendous growth and with it the opportunities that this brings. In the last year, the Russian economy has shown no sign of slowing down, growing at a rate of 7% and is now measured at $1.3 trillion. Moreover, contrary to popular opinion, that growth is not just limited to Moscow but throughout Russia with several sectors booming and no more so than the spectacular 20% growth of the construction industry.

Of course great opportunity does bring problems and as a lawyer who has encountered some of these it would be naïve for new investors to ignore some of the pitfalls of investing in Russia but careful and diligent planning can often help minimise these risks. Western investors frequently discover that Russian businesses are not familiar with Western standards of due diligence and expect a deal to be done quickly. Many Russian businesses themselves have been caught out by insufficient attention to the details of their acquisitions. So sophisticated Western investors should insist on full and detailed due diligence, which can sometimes prove a slow process in an economy which is still getting used to Western standards of business and transparency, but is an important step in the investment process.

As we enter a new era with the beginning of Medvedev's government, Russia has the third largest foreign reserves. This should place it well for internal investment programmes but inflation is currently running in early double digits so the administration has to be careful not to stoke inflation further by spending its reserves too quickly but given the difficult market conditions elsewhere in the world, this may be the greatest time to invest in Russia.

Adam Greaves, Partner, Steptoe & Johnson

INTRODUCTION

Thank you for your purchase of this publication.

This fifth edition of "Russia: Market Approaches" has again been expanded to include more up to date facts, figures, contact details and background information.

Russia has changed immeasurably since we first put this book together in 1994. Since the default of the Rouble in 1998, Russia has enjoyed consistent and robust growth. Today, Russia is one of the largest economies in the world; compare this to just a few years ago, when the size of its economy was on a par with that of Portugal.

Some point out the factor in this growth of a high oil price, which rose in that period from ten Dollars to one hundred Dollars per barrel. True; yet a strong bank balance is a strong bank balance, whatever the reasons behind it.

Russia already has overtaken many large economies and economists predict this position to become stronger in the foreseeable future.

It may be unsurprising that Russia now wishes to stake its claim at the world's table. We should encourage Russia to join in a spirit of cooperation.

Business is one area in which nations cooperate. Despite areas where the two do not see eye to eye, the economic ties between Russia and the United Kingdom continue to rise. One constant in all this period of dynamic change in Russia, is our belief that companies can still enjoy good business in this market.

The nature of this potential has changed. Gone are the days of exporters to Russia being "pioneers". With the growth in the infrastructure in Russia, comes a growth in competition, and a reduction in the number of easy opportunities. It is less easy simply to sell goods and services to Russia. Not only are Russians increasingly self-sufficient in many sectors, but where sales opportunities exist, the competition forces us to consider ways of making ourselves more viable, through price, an increased range of products, credit facilities, service levels, proactive engagement with Russia's regions and so on. This is very welcome.

Russia has gone from being a widely disregarded "basket case", then an emerging market, to being now a high-growth economy.

There still exist many challenges to doing business in Russia. But the business in Russia is very real, and opportunities remain.

It is not too late to enter this market. I hope this book might play a small role in assisting companies to realise these opportunities.

My thanks as always go to my good friend and Editor, Harris Rosenberg, and to those companies which help to put this publication together, Antal International, Steptoe & Johnson LLP and GSL Law & Consulting. They also support this book's sister initiative, the London conference, "Russia: Practical Solutions". Other supporters of both

projects whom I would like to thank include BMI, O'Grady Air Services, PBN, The Russia House, SGS, Containerships, TNG. And of course, we are always to UKTI and the British Embassy and Consulates General in Russia and to the Russo-British Chamber of Commerce for their continued support of these projects, and of businesses operating with Russia.

I wish you, the reader, all the best for your success in Russia.

David Cant

ACKNOWLEDGEMENTS

This fifth edition of Russia: Market Approaches has received support and advice from many specialists with vast experience and knowledge of doing business in Russia. Thanks must be given to my sponsors, without whose support and backing, this new edition of my book would not have been possible. My deep gratitude goes to:

Brian Robertson and Mick Essex of UK Trade & Investment
Tremayne Elson of Antal
Gary O'Grady of O'Grady Air
Barry Martin and Margaret Rowse of The Russia House
Charlie Fleming of SGS (GOST) United Kingdom Ltd
Aniko Sebok of GSL Taxation
Adam Greaves and Lisa Wong of Steptoe and Johnson
Paul Wolstencroft of TNG
Julie Jones of British Midland Airways
Trevor Barton of PBN Company

A special word of thanks must also be extended to my editor and friend, Harris Rosenberg. My gratitude also goes to his wife Michelle for helping with proof reading on this revised edition of my book and to Ruth Jennings and Emanuel Dor-chay for assisting in the research.

Abacus Factoring Consultants – Barry Rogers
Aid-Funded Business Service – Claire Gamage
Albion (Overseas) Limited – Marcin Laszczewski, Evgeniya Baranovskaya, Anna Velichkina, Mikhail Kondrashov
Antal International Russia – Alexandra Zheryadina
Atradius – Simon Groves
British Chambers of Commerce – Steph Rushmere
British Council – Giles Morris
British Council, BOND – Jan Schraibman
British Library – Business & IP Centre – Peter O'Reilly
British Midland Airways – Emily Walton
Bureau Veritas – Lesley Thrift
Business Monitor International – David Snowdon – James Key
Containerships Group – Ken Menikou
ECGD – Bubola Kolawole
Eureka – Pete Munday
Export Marketing Research Scheme – Robin Godfrey
Factors Chain International – Jeroen Kohnstamm
Foreign & Commonwealth Office – Patrick Haughey
Import Licensing Branch – Andrew Cobby
N.A.G. Consulting Co – Nick Chernov
National Statistics Library – Gillian Bowen
Northern Ireland Public Centre Enterprises – Graeme McCammon
Norwegian Centre for International Cooperation in Higher Education – Arne Haugen
Overseas Trade – Janet Tibble
Russian Trade Delegation in the UK – Fedor Takhtamanov
Steptoe and Johnson – Egishe Dzhazoyan, Robert Harris
Templeton Thorp – Chris Gilbert
UK Trade and Investment – Wayne Lewis
UK Trade & Investment, Russia & Turkey – Bob Packard
UK Trade & Investment, Trade Development & Services Unit – Suzanne Youd
Willis Limited – Simon Aubrey Jones

KEY FACTS

RUSSIAN FEDERATION

Capital – Moscow

Head of State (President) – Dmitry Medvedev
Prime Minister – Vladimir Vladimirovich Putin

Area	17,075,200 km² (76.2% of Soviet Union)
Population	141.3m – July 2007 est. (a decline of nearly 8m since 1992) 78% of the population live in European Russia. 14.4% of the population consists of people older than 65 years of age. 55% of the population is female. 81.5% of the population are ethnic Russians, 3.8%Tatars and 3% Ukrainian. There are more than 100 nationalities in all.
Life expectancy	65.9 years (59.1 years for men, 73 years for women) – 2007
Average family size	3 people
Labour force	75.1m (2007 est)
Unemployment rate	5.9m (7.8%) There is also considerable underemployment. (2006)
Average wage	7,500 Roubles ($250) per month
Official language	Russian (Russian alphabet – Cyrillic)
Adult literacy rate	99.4%
Currency	Rouble = 100 Kopecks
Exchange rate	£1 = 47.39 Roubles and $1 = 23.63 Roubles (25th March 2008) For up to date exchange rates visit www.xe.com
Weights and measures	Metric system
Climate	Ranges from continental to Arctic
Holidays	7 January – Russian Orthodox Christmas 23 February – Dyen Zashitnikov (Army day) 8 March – International Women's Day 1–2 May – Spring Holiday 9 May – Victory Day 12 June – Independence (Russia) Day 4 November – Day of National Unity 12 December – Constitution day 30 December – 2 January – New Year Where a holiday falls on a weekend the statutory holiday moves forward to the Monday. Many Russians take holidays from July to mid-September and in late December. Holiday entitlement is generally four weeks per annum.
Hours of business	09.00 to 18.00, Monday – Friday

Flying time to Moscow	3 hrs 35 minutes from London, Heathrow; 4 hrs from London, Gatwick.
Time zones	GMT +3 Moscow, St Petersburg GMT +4 Samara GMT +5 Ekaterinburg GMT +6 Novosibirsk GMT +8 Irkutsk GMT +10 Vladivostock Clocks change, by one hour, to summer and winter time at the end of March and at the end of September, respectively.
Weather	Winter (October-April) – Down to minus 30 degrees Celsius Summer (May-Sept) – Up to 30 degrees Celsius
International telephone code (To Russia)	007 (codes for many regions and major cities may be found at the front of British Telecom's telephone directories).
(To the UK)	8 – 1044 (UK code minus 0 at the beginning)

KEY FACTS

Economic Statistics

GDP ($tn)	1,286 (2007) – up from 975.3 in 2006, making the Russian Federation the 10th largest economy in the World.
GDP growth	8.1% (2007) – up from 6.9% in 2006.
Industrial production rate	6% (2007 est)
Inflation rate	11.9% (2007) 9.8% per annum (2006)
World imports ($bn)	260.4 (2007 est).
Main import partners	Germany 13.9%, China 9.7%, Ukraine 7%, Japan 5.9%, South Korea 5.1%, USA 4.8%, France 4.4%, Italy 4.3%, UK 2%
World exports ($bn)	365 (2007 est). Some 80% of exports are oil, gas, metals and timber.
Main export partners	Netherlands 12.3%, Italy 8.6%, Germany 8.4%, China 5.4%, Ukraine 5.1%, Turkey 4.9%, Switzerland 4.1%
Total direct foreign investment ($bn)	45 (2007) – Total 271.6 (2006)
Total foreign investment abroad ($bn)	209.6 (2006)

UK direct foreign investment ($bn)	The UK has been one of the largest foreign investors in Russia for many years, with a direct investment total of $7 (2006). Nearly half of UK investment in Russia was in wholesale/retail trade sectors (47.7%), with processing industries, transport and communications, and coke and oil goods production accounting for the main portion of the remaining investment (45.1%).
Foreign debt ($bn)	287.4 (2006 est) – decreasing as Russia has had trade surpluses since 2003.
Foreign reserves ($bn)	470 surplus
Business with UK (£m)	Import to UK – 5,464 (2007) 5,820 (2006) Export to Russia – 2,810 (2007) 2,058 (2006)

Figures are latest available as at 31ˢᵗ March 2008.

UK INVESTMENT IN RUSSIA 2006

UK's Invesment to Russia by Sector, 2006

Country	Million USD	% of total
Wholesale/retail trade	3,658	40.3
Processing industries	1562	17.2
Real estate	944	10.4
Transport & communications	807	8.9
Coke and oil goods production	642	7.1
Metallurgy/metal production	269	3.0
Chemical production	200	2.2
Other	994	11.0
Total	9,076	100.0
Source: UK Trade & Investment 2006		

PRINCIPAL IMPORTS AND EXPORTS (NON CIS)

	ALL GROUPS OF PRODUCTS	Export (%) from Russia	Import (%) to Russia
1	Food Products and Agricultural Raw Materials	1.1	17
2	Mineral Goods (Gas, Oil, Petrol, Ores, Coal etc.)	67.5	0.9
3	Chemical Products and Rubber	5.5	17.9
4	Leather Raw Materials, Furs and their products	0.1	0.3
5	Wood, Timber, Pulp and Paper Goods	3.4	3.4
6	Textiles and Footwear	0.2	3.3
7	Precious Stones and Precious Metals	3.2	0.3
8	Ferrous and Non-Ferrous Metals and Products	14.5	5.1
9	Machinery, Equipment and Transport Equipment	3.6	48.2
10	Other goods (which are not mentioned above)	0.9	3.6
	TOTAL	**100%**	**100%**
Source NAG Consulting Co. (London) 2007			

Trade Statistics to end 2007

UK exports to Russia increased by 36.6% in 2007 to £2.8b
UK imports from Russia decreased by 6.1%% in 2007 to £5.5b

Russia is the UK's 16th largest export market (2007)
Russia is the UK's 14th largest source of imports (2007)

Main UK exports to Russia
by value during 2007 (with changes over 2006)

	2007 £ million	% change 2007/2006
1. Road vehicles	893	87.7
2. Miscellaneous manufactured articles	244	32.8
3. Specialised industrial machinery	205	59.8
4. Essential oils, perfumes, cleaning preps.	137	24.5
5. Power generating machinery	132	18.4

Main UK imports from Russia
value during 2007 (with changes over 2006)

	2007 £ million	% change 2007/2006
1. Petroleum & petroleum products	2,780	-13.6
2. Coal, coke & briquettes	836	-2.7
3. Non-ferrous Metals	577	22.0
4 Inorganic chemicals	275	22.4
5. Non-metallic mineral manufactures	254	-24.9
Source: BERR analysis of data from H M Revenue and Customs		

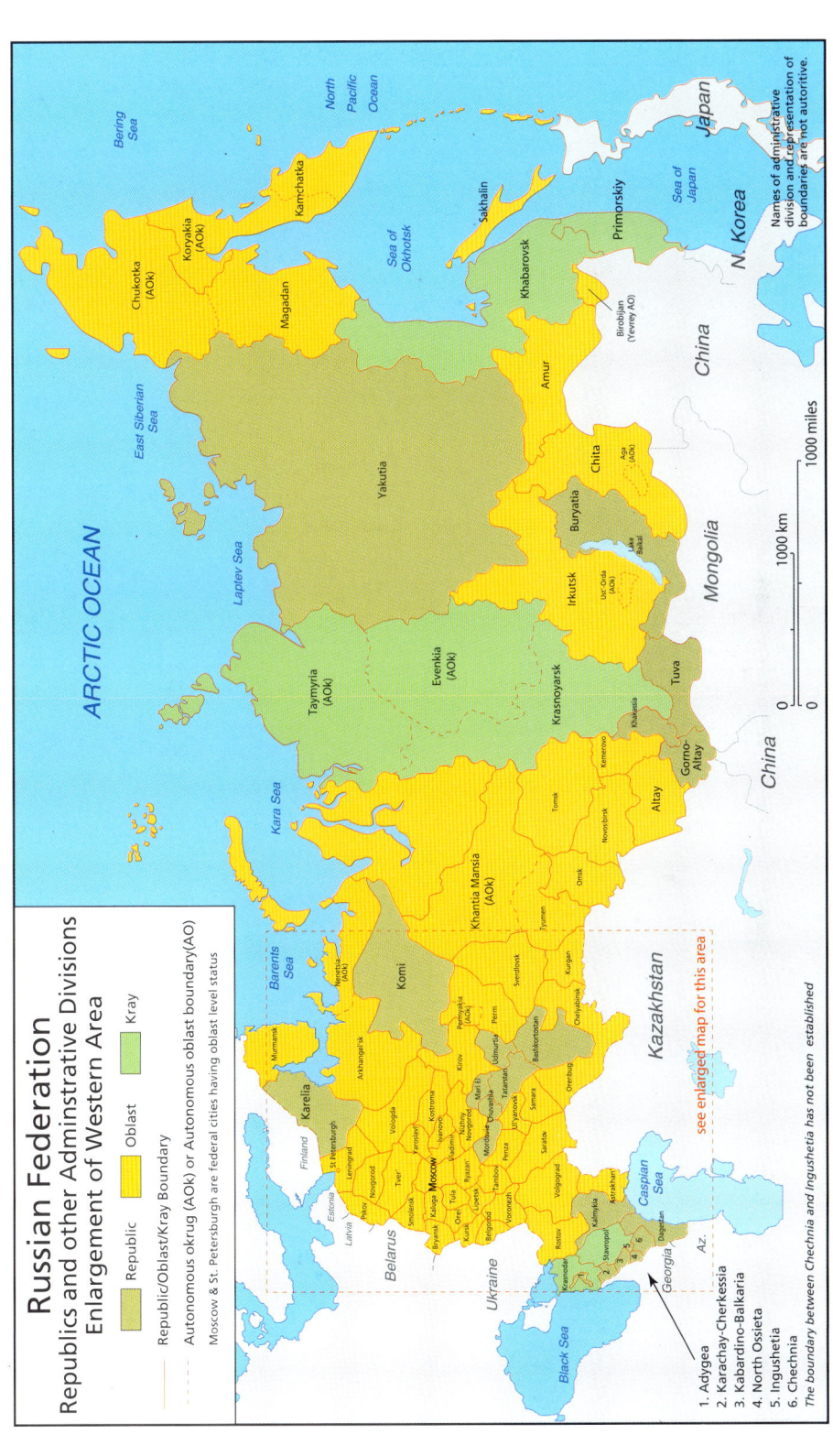

Russian Federation
Republics and other Adminstrative Divisions
Enlargement of Western Area

Republic

Oblast

Kray

Republic/Oblast/Kray Boundary

Autonomous okrug (AOk) or Autonomous oblast boundary(AO)

Moscow & St. Petersburgh are federal cities having oblast level status

1. Adygea
2. Karachay-Cherkessia
3. Kabardino-Balkaria
4. North Ossieta
5. Ingushetia
6. Chechnia

The boundary between Chechnia and Ingushetia has not been established

Names of administrative
division and representation of
boundaries are not autoritive.

1000 miles

1000 km

see enlarged map for this area

ARCTIC OCEAN

Bering
Sea

North
Pacific
Ocean

East Siberian
Sea

Sea of
Okhotsk

Laptev Sea

Kara Sea

Barents
Sea

Black
Sea

Caspian
Sea

Sea of
Japan

Japan

China

Mongolia

China

N. Korea

Kazakhstan

Ukraine

Georgia

Az.

Belarus

Finland

Estonia

Latvia

Chukotka
(AOk)

Koryakia
(AOk)

Kamchatka

Magadan

Yakutia

Khabarovsk

Amur

Primorskiy

Birobijan
(Yevrey AO)

Chita

Aga
(AOk)

Buryatia

Irkutsk

Ust-Orda
(AOk)

Lake
Baikal

Taymyria
(AOk)

Evenkia
(AOk)

Krasnoyarsk

Khakassia

Tuva

Gorno-
Altay

Altay

Tomsk

Kemerovo

Novosibirsk

Omsk

Tyumen

Khantia Mansia
(AOk)

Kurgan

Sverdlovsk

Chelyabinsk

Komi

Nenetsia
(AOk)

Murmansk

Karelia

Arkhangel'sk

St Petersburg

Leningrad

Vologda

Perm

Kirov

Udmurtia

Bashkortostan

Orenburg

Pskov

Novgorod

Tver

Yaroslavl

Kostroma

Ivanovo

Nizhny
Novgorod

Mari El

Chuvashia

Tatarstan

Samara

Saratov

Volgograd

Moscow

Smolensk

Kaluga

Tula

Mordovia

Penza

Ul'yanovsk

Bryansk

Orel

Kursk

Lipetsk

Tambov

Voronezh

Belgorod

Rostov

Krasnodar

Stavropol

Kalmykia

Astrakhan'

Dagestan

0   1000 miles

0   1000 km

Russian Federation
Republics and other Adminstrative Divisions
Enlargement of Western Area

Republic Oblast Kray

— Republic/Oblast/Kray Boundary

- - - Autonomous okrug (AOk) or Autonomous oblast boundary(AO)

Moscow & St. Petersburgh are federal cities having oblast level status

Barents
Sea

Finland

Estonia

Latvia

Belarus

Ukraine

Murmansk

Karelia

St Petersburgh

Nenetsia
(AOk)

Leningrad

Pskov

Novgorod

Arkhangel'sk

Tver'

Vologda

Komi

Smolensk

Yaroslavl'

Bryansk Kaluga Moscow

Kostroma

Ivanovo

Orel Tula

Vladimir

Kirov

Permyakia
(AOk)

Kursk

Ryazan'

Nizhny
Novgorod

Lipetsk

Mari El

Udmurtia

Perm

Belgorod

Mordovia

Chuvashia

Tambov

Penza

Tatarstan

Sverdlovsk

Voronezh

Ul'yanovsk

Samara

Bashkortostan

Saratov

Kurgan

Rostov

Volgograd

Orenbug

Chelyabinsk

Krasnodar

1

Kalmykia

2 Stavropol'

Astrakhan'

3

5

Caspian
Sea

Kazakhstan

4

6

Dagestan

1. Adygea

2. Karachay-Cherkessia

3. Kabardino-Balkaria

4. North Ossieta

5. Ingushetia

6. Chechnia

The boundary between Chechnia and Ingushetia has not been established

Names of administrative
division and representation of
boundaries are not autoritive.

THE RUSSIAN ALPHABET

Printed Letter	Name of Letter	Pronunciation
А а	ah	like **a** in father
Б б	beh	like **b** in box
В в	veh	like **v** in voice
Г г	geh	like **g** in get
Д д	deh	like **d** in day
Е е	yeh	like **ye** in yet
Ё ё	yo	like **yo** in your
Ж ж	zhe	like **s** in pleasure
З з	ze	like **z** in zoo
И и	ee	like **ee** in need
Й й	ee kratkoye	not pronounced but like **y** in boy
К к	keh	like **k** in key
Л л	el	like **l** in love
М м	em	like **m** in men
Н н	en	like **n** in nose
О о	o	like **o** in not
П п	peh	like **p** in put
Р р	er	like **r** in arrow
С с	she	like **s** in miss
Т т	teh	like **t** in take
У у	oo	like **oo** in pool
Ф ф	ef	like **f** in fat
Х х	kha	like **kh** in khan
Ц ц	tse	like **ts** in its
Ч ч	cha	like **ch** in chance
Ш ш	she	like **sh** in ship
Щ щ	shche	like **shch** in fresh cheese
Ъ ъ	tvordy znak (hard sign)	not pronounced
Ы ы	eih	**eih** in the throat
Ь ь	myaki znak (soft sign)	not pronounced
Э э	eh	like **e** in end
Ю ю	you	like **u** in use
Я я	ya	like **ya** in yard

THE REPUBLICS, AREAS, TERRITORIES AND REGIONS OF THE RUSSIAN FEDERATION

The Russian Federation comprises 21 constituent republics, 1 autonomous region (Avtonomnaya oblast), 4 autonomous areas (Okrugs), 9 territories (Krais), 46 regions (Oblasts) and two federal cities – Moscow and St Petersburg. It remains as true today as it was in 2005 that "Russia's regions have the largest potential for attracting foreign investments into the Russian economy" with many tangible privileges for investors to encourage this. RIA – Novosti.

THE CONSTITUENT REPUBLICS

ADYGHEYA REPUBLIC

Location	Adygheya is in the foothills of the Caucasus in South West Russia.
Area KM²	7,600
Population	447,109
Capital City	Maikop
Main Airport	Maikop
Principal seaport	Landlocked
Natural Resources:	Oil, natural gas, gold, silver, mercury, wolfram, iodine, bromide, zinc cobalt, barite, coloured marble, granite, timber
Industry:	Maikop "white" oil and gas, timber, brick, cement, glass
Light Industry:	Medicines, ceramic pipes, pottery and other ceramic products, furniture, woodworking, washing machines, food processing and in particular, macaroni, wine, vodka
Other Commerce:	Horse breeding, tourism
Agriculture, fisheries and food	Livestock, poultry, fish, fruit, vegetables, grain, rice, edible oils
Useful Websites	http://research.rencap.com/eng/government/region_detail0103.asp www.kommersant.com/t-88/r_5/n_432/Republic_of_Adygea/ www.adygheya.ru/ (Web pages in Russian) www.angelfire.com/co/adygheya/ http://en.wikipedia.org/wiki/Adygeya

ALTAI REPUBLIC

Location	The Altai Republic is in South Central Russia bordering on Mongolia, China and Kazakhstan.
Area KM2	92,600
Population	202,947
Capital City	Gorno-Altaisk
Main Airport	Barnaul
Principal seaport	Landlocked
Natural Resources:	Gold, molybdenum, tungsten, bismuth, cobalt, lithium, tantalum, mercury, granite, iron, brown and bituminous coal, marble, timber
Industry:	Hydro-electricity, metallurgy
Light Industry:	Machine building, mechanical engineering, chemicals and petrochemicals, food processing, mining, cotton, knitted fabrics

Other Commerce:	Tourism
Agriculture, fisheries and food	Grain, livestock
Other information:	1. The republic suffers from after-effects of nuclear testing in neighbouring Kazakhstan. 2. Approximately one third of the hydro-energy produced for Western Siberia comes from this republic.
Useful Websites	http://eng.altai-republic.ru/index.php?newlang=eng http://research.rencap.com/eng/government/region_detail0601.asp www.kommersant.com/t-82/r_5/n_426/Altai_Territory/ http://en.wikipedia.org/wiki/Altai_Republic

BASHKORTOSTAN REPUBLIC

Location	The Bashkortoston Republic is situated in Southern Russia, due east of Moscow.
Area KM2	143,600
Population	4,104,000 inc Ufa 1.1 m
Capital City	Ufa
Main Airport	Ufa Airport
Principal seaport	With the Byelaya, the Kama and the Volga rivers the republic possesses the Ways out to five seas. It is the largest river port in the Urals (Three of five Russia latitudinal railways between the East and the West cross Bashkortostan Republic)
Natural Resources:	Oil
Industry:	Oil extraction and refining, petrochemicals including polyethylene, polypropylene and rubber, oil-field equipment, soda and other chemicals, herbicides, machine building, cables, timber
Light Industry:	helicopters, tip-trucks, aircraft-motors, electric pumps, communication devices, machine-tools, optics, snow-vehicles, binoculars, medicines, motors, electrical equipment, milk products, plywood, mineral fertilisers
Other Commerce:	aircraft engineering, machine building, biology, solid structure physics
Other information:	Bashkortostan is the premier region for oil processing in Russia. Annually 20 percent of the whole oil processing in Russia is carried out here. Production of plastics and synthetic rubber is less expensive here than in Russia on an average. The production value of this highly developed sector is nearly 3 million cubic meters of timber annually.
Credit Rating	S&P Local currency: B+ stable Foreign currency: B+ Stable Moody's Local currency bonds: Ba3 Issuer rating: Ba3
Useful Websites	www.bashkortostan.ru/ (Web pages in Russian) http://research.rencap.com/eng/government/region_detail0401.asp www.bashkortostan-export.com/eng/about.html www.ufacity.info/english_version/index.shtml http://en.wikipedia.org/wiki/Bashkortostan http://en.wikipedia.org/wiki/Ufa

BURYATIA REPUBLIC

Location	The Republic of Buryatia is in Southern Russia, bordering Mongolia and the East of Lake Baykal.
Area KM2	351,300
Population	981,238
Capital City	Ulan-Ude
Main Airport	Ulan-Ude
Principal seaport	Landlocked
Natural Resources:	Tungsten, coal, gold, bitumen, molybdenum, lignite, beryllium, tantalum, strontium, uranium, timber
Industry:	Machine building, metal working, non-ferrous metallurgy
Light Industry:	Wood processing , pulp and paper
Agriculture, fisheries and food:	corn, potatoes and other root vegetables, dairy and meat cattle, sheep, goats
Other information:	Navigation is on the Baikal, the Selenga and Barguzin Rivers. Many health resorts in the region. Some Western joint venture operations have been established. Total reserves of timber are estimated at 1,850 million cubic meters
Useful Websites	http://egov-buryatia.ru/eng/ http://research.rencap.com/eng/government/region_detail0609.asp www.kommersant.com/t-91/r_5/n_435/Buryat_Republic/ www.buryatia.ru/buryatia/index_e.html http://en.wikipedia.org/wiki/Buryatia

CHECHENIYA REPUBLIC (CHECHNYA)

Location	Checheniya is in South West Russia bordering on Georgia.
Area KM²	19,300
Population	1,103,686
Capital City	Grozny
Principal seaport	Landlocked
Natural Resources:	Oil, natural gas, limestone, gypsum, sulphur
Industry:	Oil, petroleum refining and petrochemicals
Light Industry:	Building materials
Agriculture, fisheries and food:	Fruit, grapes, vegetables, wheat, barley, corn, rice, sunflowers, sugar beets
Other information:	Checheniya is currently in a state of turmoil owing to its seeking secession from the Russian Federation. This problem has spilled into other parts of Russia. Major attacks blamed on Chechen separatists include: the deadly siege at a school in Beslan; North Ossetia; the mid-air destruction of two Russian civilian airliners; the bombing of a Moscow metro train as well as the seizing of a Moscow theatre in October 2002.
Useful Websites	http://news.bbc.co.uk/1/hi/world/europe/country_profiles/2565049.stm http://chechnya.gov.ru/ (Web pages in Russian) http://geography.about.com/library/maps/blchechnya.htm http://news.bbc.co.uk/1/hi/world/europe/country_profiles/2565049.stm http://en.wikipedia.org/wiki/Chechnya

CHUVASHIA (CHAVASH) REPUBLIC

Location	Chuvashia is situated in the middle of the Volga Valley bordering the Southern frontier of Nizhny-Novgorod.
Area KM2	18,300 KM2
Population	1,346,300
Capital City	Cheboksary
Main Airport	Cheboksary
Principal seaport	Volga down river connects to the Black and Caspian Sea basins, and via the Danube – Europe; up the river in connects to Moscow
Natural Resources:	Gypsum, anhydrite, dolomite, clay and loam for the manufacture of bricks, tripoli suitable for the manufacture of heat-insulation materials
Industry:	Industrial tractors, electro-technical and measuring equipment, physical devices, trailers, shuttle less looms, cables; chemical industry is famous for production of caustic soda, dyes, pesticides, tanning extracts, plastics; light industry produces
Light Industry:	Cotton fabrics, threads, yarn, knitted wear, socks and stockings, Electrical and telecommunications equipment, cables, cardboard, woodworking, food processing
Other Commerce:	Exports from Chuvashia are sold to over 60 countries.
Agriculture, fisheries and food:	Wheat, barley, rye, buckwheat, potatoes
Other information:	Navigation on the Volga and the Sura rivers.
Useful Websites	www.cap.ru/cap/main.asp?id=103 http://en.wikipedia.org/wiki/Chuvashia

DAGESTAN REPUBLIC

Location	Dagestan is situated in the Northern Caucasus and borders Georgia and Azerbaidjan.
Area KM²	50,300
Population	2,576,531
Capital City	Makhachkala
Principal seaport	Makhachkala Sea Trade Port
Natural Resources:	Hydro-electric power, natural gas
Industry:	Food processing, machine building, light industry
Light Industry:	Carpets, textiles
Other Commerce:	Oil, domestic crafts, jewellery, art
Agriculture, fisheries and food:	Grain, wheat, rice. grapes, fruit and vegetables
Other information:	Dagestan is a major source of phosphates for the Russian Federation. It is the main conduit for Russia's oil exports from the Caspian Sea Violence in the Caucasus has, at times, spilled over to this Republic
Useful Websites	http://news.bbc.co.uk/1/hi/world/europe/country_profiles/3659904.stm www.e-dag.ru/ (Web pages in Russian) http://research.rencap.com/eng/government/region_detail0104.asp http://en.wikipedia.org/wiki/Dagestan

INGUSHETIA REPUBLIC

Location	Ingushetia and Chechnya (see above) was a United Republic until 1991.
Area KM²	19,300
Population	467,294
Capital City	Magas
Principal seaport	Landlocked
Natural Resources:	Oil
Industry:	Oil extraction and refining, machine building
Light Industry:	food processing
Agriculture, fisheries and food:	Vegetables, fruit and grain. Rice is grown in irrigated fields. Sheep and goats are raised
Other information:	Like Chechnya, Ingushetia is not totally free from political and civil disruption. In June 2004, several dozen people, including an Ingush minister, were killed in attacks reported to have involved hundreds of armed fighters loyal to the Chechen warlord Shamil Basayev.
Useful Websites	http://news.bbc.co.uk/1/hi/world/europe/country_profiles/3829691.stm www.ingushetia.ru/ (Web pages in Russian) http://en.wikipedia.org/wiki/Ingushetia

KABARDINO-BALKAR REPUBLIC

Location	Kabardino-Balkar is situated in South West Russia bordering on Georgia.
Area KM²	12,500
Population	900,500
Capital City	Nalchik
Principal seaport	Landlocked
Natural Resources:	Soil made up from chernozen
Industry:	Non-ferrous metals, hydro-metallurgical plants, machine building, high-voltage electrical equipment. ferrous metals
Light Industry:	Instrument making, engineering, footwear and clothing
Other Commerce:	Mountaineering
Agriculture, fisheries and food:	Grain, fruit and vegetables, cattle breeding and meat production, milk, eggs
Other information:	The area is not totally free of political unrest, including the spill over of violence from Chechnya
Useful Websites	http://news.bbc.co.uk/1/hi/world/europe/country_profiles/4338292.stm www.nalnet.ru/ (Web pages in Russian) http://reference.allrefer.com/encyclopedia/K/Kabardin.html http://en.wikipedia.org/wiki/Kabardino-Balkaria

KAINYKAI-KHALM TANGSH (KALMYKIA) REPUBLIC

Location	The Kalmykia Republic is situated to the North of the Caspian Sea.
Area KM²	76,100
Population	316,000
Capital City	Elista
Principal seaport	Kaspiyskiy
Natural Resources:	Oil, natural gas, bishophite (magnesium chloride), raw materials
Industry:	Oil refining, construction, concrete
Light Industry:	Food processing, textiles
Other Commerce:	Fishing, horse breeding
Agriculture, fisheries and food:	Wheat, dairy and meat cattle, caracul and fat tail sheep
Other information:	1. The Republic's industrial base is at an early stage of development and it is heavily dependent upon exports. 2. Plans are being implemented to develop the Republic's power, telecommunications, food and fishing industries.
Useful Websites	http://news.bbc.co.uk/1/hi/world/europe/country_profiles/4580467.stm http://kalm.ru/en/ www.kalmykiaembassy.ru/html/eindex.html www.bobiverson.com/kalmykia/links.htm http://en.wikipedia.org/wiki/Kalmykia

KARACHAEVO-CHERKESS REPUBLIC

Location	Karachaevo-Cherkess is situated in South West Russia bordering on Georgia and the Black Sea.
Area KM²	14,100
Population	436,100
Capital City	Cherkessk
Natural Resources:	Coal, non-ferrous metals
Industry:	Chemical, oil processing, acrylics, enamels, paint
Agriculture, fisheries and food:	Dairy farming, grain, horticulture
Other information:	Astronomy and space science
Useful Websites	http://news.bbc.co.uk/1/hi/world/europe/country_profiles/5381570.stm www.kchr.info/ (Web pages in Russian) relay.sao.ru/Doc-en/index.html http://en.wikipedia.org/wiki/Karachay-Cherkessia

KARELIA REPUBLIC

Location	Karelia lies on the Southern border with Finland
Area KM²	172,400
Population	716,281
Capital City	Petrozavodsk
Main Airport	Petrozavodsk connects to Joensuu and Helsinki in Finland.
Principal seaport	Waterways connect to Barents, Baltic, Black and Caspian Seas
Natural Resources:	Iron, chromium, titanium-magnetite, vanadium, molybdenum, gold, quartze, granites, mineral rocks, marble
Industry:	Pulp and paper, ferrous metallurgy, titanium, nickel, copper, semi-precious metals, phosphate based fertilisers, construction, electricity, timber
Light Industry:	Machine building
Other Commerce:	Fishing, tourism
Agriculture, fisheries and food:	Milk and meat cattle
Other information:	Finland, Germany, Great Britain, Sweden and Turkey, constitute over 60% of external commodity exchange. Lakes Ladoga, Onega, Belmoro and the Baltiyski Channel make the area a very accessible location to neighbouring Finland. 80% of paper bags in Russia come from Karelia
Useful Websites	www.gov.karelia.ru/index_e.html www.karelia.ru/ http://en.wikipedia.org/wiki/Republic_of_Karelia

KHAKASSIA REPUBLIC

Location	Khakassia is situated in South Central Russia.
Area KM²	61,900
Population	575,400
Capital City	Abakan
Principal seaport	Landlocked
Natural Resources:	Coal, marble, limestone, clay, bitumen, gold, iron, molybdenum, timber
Industry:	Electricity, ferrous and non-ferrous metals, electrical energy, wood, mining, railway cars
Light Industry:	Wool, food processing
Other Commerce:	Production of Sayanmramor (objects carved from stone and marble).
Agriculture, fisheries and food:	Livestock, dairy cattle breeding
Other information:	Large industrial complex located in Komi. Main granary of Eastern Siberia.
Useful Websites	http://en.wikipedia.org/wiki/Khakassia

KOMI REPUBLIC

Location	Komi is situated in North West Russia.
Area KM²	415,900
Population	158,000
Capital City	Kudymkar
Principal seaport	Landlocked
Natural Resources:	Bauxite, titanium, materials for the construction industry, coal, oil, sulphur, diamonds, rubies, amethysts, timber
Industry:	Aluminium, ship building and repairing, pulp and paper.
Light Industry:	Timber products
Agriculture, fisheries and food:	Dairy cattle breeding
Other information:	Large industrial complexes are situated in this Republic. A number of joint ventures have been established.
Useful Websites	www.rkomi.ru/ (Web pages in Russian) www.parma.ru/~emin/ http://reference.allrefer.com/encyclopedia/K/KomiRepu.html http://en.wikipedia.org/wiki/Komi_Republic

MARI EL REPUBLIC

Location	The Republic of Mary El borders the Southern Frontier of Nizhny-Novgorod.
Area KM²	23,200
Population	764,300
Capital City	Yoshkar-Ola
Principal seaport	Landlocked
Natural Resources:	Sulphate-chloride mineral water, diatomite, marly-chalk rocks, clays, timber
Industry:	Bricks, pulp and paper
Light Industry:	Engineering and metal processing, canning, brewing, wood and clay working, sheepskin clothing, bicycles. radio electronics, mirrors
Other Commerce:	Tourism
Agriculture, fisheries and food	Grain, livestock and animal husbandry, orchards.
Other information:	Located in the middle current of the Volga.
Useful Websites	http://gov.mari.ru/ (Web pages in Russian) http://en.wikipedia.org/wiki/Mari_El

MORDOVIA REPUBLIC

Location	Mordovia is situated in the centre of the Eastern European plain.
Area KM²	26,200
Population	888,766
Capital City	Saransk
Principal seaport	Landlocked
Natural Resources:	Natural gas, timber
Industry:	Machine building, machine making, automobiles, excavators and dump trucks, chemical and oil tankers, metal working, penicillin.
Light Industry:	Electric lighting, textiles, knitted goods, instrument making, televisions, electronic engineering, telecommunications equipment
Other Commerce:	Vodka
Agriculture, fisheries and food	Buckwheat, wheat, rye, potatoes, sugar beet, livestock
Other information:	Mordovia is a major producer of export goods, particularly for the Far East. It is the largest synthetic rubber, electric lighting producing area in Russia. A number of joint ventures have been started in this Republic.
Useful Websites	http://whrm.moris.ru/ http://en.wikipedia.org/wiki/Mordovia

NORTHERN OSSETIA-ALANIA REPUBLIC

Location	Northern Ossetia-Alania lies in South West Russia bordering Georgia.
Area KM²	8,000
Population	709,900
Capital City	Vladikavkaz
Principal seaport	Landlocked
Natural Resources:	Timber
Industry:	Electricity, non-ferrous metallurgy
Light Industry:	Woodworking, machine building, electronics, food processing
Agriculture, fisheries and food	Potatoes, sugar beet, vegetables, sunflower seeds, grapes broad-leaf forests, poultry, dairy and meat cattle, eggs, honey
Other information:	As with many Republics in this region, it is not free of political unrest and friction with neighbouring Ingushetia. Ingush fighters were part of the siege force that held more than 1,000 hostages at Beslan in 2004 There have also been moves to unite North Ossetia with South Ossetia, currently part of Georgia.
Useful Websites	http://news.bbc.co.uk/1/hi/world/europe/country_profiles/3621698.stm http://president.osetia.ru/ (Web pages in Russian) www.therussiasite.org/conflicts/ossetia.html www.osetia.ru/~toma/ http://en.wikipedia.org/wiki/North_Ossetia-Alania

SAKHA (YAKUTIA) REPUBLIC

Location	The Republic of Sakha is the largest of the autonomous republics in the Russian Federation. It lies in Russia's Far East.
Area KM²	3,103,200
Population	949,280
Capital City	Yakutsk
Principal seaport	Tiksi
Natural Resources:	Gold, diamonds, coal, natural gas, tin, aluminium, lignite, timber
Industry:	Diesels
Light Industry:	Woodworking, food processing
Other Commerce:	Tourism, hunting
Agriculture, fisheries and food:	Reindeer breeding, sable and other fur, dairy and meat cattle, pigs, horses, potatoes and other vegetables, fishing
Other information:	Permafrost covers most of this region
Useful Websites	www.spri.cam.ac.uk/resources/rfn/sakha.html www.turkiye.net/sota/yakut.html www.yakutiatravel.com/eng/main.htm http://en.wikipedia.org/wiki/Sakha

TATARSTAN REPUBLIC

Location	Tatarstan is based in Central West Russia.
Area KM²	68,000
Population	3,763,200
Capital City	Kazan
Main Airport	Kazan Airport
Principal seaport	Landlocked
Natural Resources:	Oil, gypsum, sandstone, limestone, combustible shale, copper, bauxite, bitumen, natural gas, peat, brick clay, coal, phosphates
Industry:	Automobiles, trucks, aeroplane, helicopter, engine, compressors, vacuum production, chemicals, petrochemicals, synthetic rubber, tyres, cranes
Light Industry:	Electronics, radios, hosiery, clocks, footwear, mechanical engineering, food processing, leather, perfume, optical and medical instruments, heat resistant glass, plywood, furs, felt boots, sanitary equipment, porcelain, medicines, glass, detergents, beverages, tobacco, recording tapes, catgut, domestic gas appliances, varnish
Agriculture, fisheries and food:	Poultry, meat and dairy cattle breeding, sheep, pigs, fur farming, bee keeping, grain, fodder, vegetables
Other information:	Beginning of petroleum pipeline "Druzhba" (Friendship) in Tatarstan. Tatarstan contributes the following to the Russian economy: 100% of photo/cinema film, catgut; 95% of gas turbines; 75% of styrene; 50% of axifugal electric pumps for oil extraction; 50% of diesel trucks, thermoplastic tubes and pipeline units
Credit Rating	**S&P** Foreign Currency CCC+/Positive/-- **Moody's** Issuer Rating: Ba3
Useful Websites	www.tatar.ru/english/index.htm http://en.wikipedia.org/wiki/Tatarstan

TUVA REPUBLIC

Location	The Republic of Tyva borders Mongolia.
Area KM²	170,500 km2
Population	310,200
Capital City	Kyzyl
Principal seaport	Landlocked
Natural Resources:	Gold, iron, cobalt, coal, asbestos, timber
Industry:	Food processing (meat packing, flour and cereals), plants, wood and woodworking, coal, electrical energy, wood processing
Light Industry:	Leather making, building materials, metal working
Agriculture, fisheries and food:	Meat cattle, sheep, goats, horses, reindeer, camels
Other information:	Connected with railway stations: Abakan and Abaza.
Useful Websites	http://gov.tuva.ru/ (Web pages in Russian) www.sokoltours.com/destination.phtml?m=148 www.rusnet.nl/encyclo/t/tuva.shtml http://en.wikipedia.org/wiki/Tuva

UDMURDIA REPUBLIC

Location	Udmurdia Republic is on the foothills of the Urals.
Area KM²	42,100
Population	1,635,700
Capital City	Izhevsk
Main Airport	Izhevsk
Principal seaport	The Kama and Vyatka rivers enable river shipment to the Volga River and to the sea.
Natural Resources:	Timber, oil, peat, coal, lignite, construction materials
Industry:	Sporting and hunting guns, structural, alloy and stainless steel rolled stock, rocket and space equipment, microelectronics and communications manufacturing, medical equipment, machines for cellulose and paper industry, various reduction gearboxes, geological survey equipment, drilling and other equipment for the oil industry, various bearings, consumer goods, automobiles, motorcycles, plant for the oil industry, oil refining, machine manufacturing, and roller bearings
Light Industry:	Mechanical engineering, microwave ovens, computers. garments, cassette recorders, motorised units
Other Commerce:	Mud baths
Agriculture, fisheries and food:	Cattle-breeding, grain, eggs, potatoes and other vegetables, flax.
Other information:	Part of the Ural Economic region. The port of Sarapul located in the region. There are many joint ventures in this Republic. About a third of the people involved in the economy of the republic are experts with higher and specialised secondary education.
Useful Websites	www.udmnet.ru/udmitem/ www.udm.ru/ http://en.wikipedia.org/wiki/Udmurtia

THE JEWISH AUTONOMOUS REGION

Location	This region lies in Russia's Far East.
Area KM²	36,000
Population	190,915
Capital City	Birobidzhan
Principal seaport	Landlocked
Natural Resources:	Tin, iron, gold, silver, manganese, dolomite, opal, chalcedony, coal, oil and natural gas.
Industry:	Mining, metallurgy, chemical, construction
Light Industry:	Food processing equipment, food processing, textile machinery, building materials and construction equipment, wood processing equipment, mining exploration and equipment
Other Commerce	Telecommunications services, engineering consulting
Agriculture, fisheries and food:	Livestock, vegetables, dairy and meat cattle, pigs, soya, cereal, vegetables, potatoes
Other information:	Despite the region's name, only 1.2% of the population is Jewish.
Useful Websites	www.eao.ru/eng/ http://en.wikipedia.org/wiki/Jewish_Autonomous_Oblast

AUTONOMOUS AREAS (OKRUGS)

AGA BURYATIA

Location	This Okrug lies within the Chita Oblast which itself borders North East Mongolia.
Area KM²	19,000
Population	72,213
Capital City	Aginskoye
Principal seaport	Landlocked
Natural Resources:	Lead, zinc, ores, coal, timber
Industry:	Mining extracts, gold, molybdenum, tin, coal
Light Industry:	Woodworking, machine building, food processing
Agriculture, fisheries and food:	Reindeer husbandry, fur animals, dairy and meat cattle, wheat, oat, barley and fodder
Other information:	Borders China and Mongolia.
Useful Websites	http://en.wikipedia.org/wiki/Aga_Buryatia

CHUKOTKA AUTONOMOUS AREA

Location	The Chukchi Autonomous Area is based in Russia's Arctic Tundra. It is the closest Russian territory to the United States.
Area KM²	737,700 km2
Population	55,000
Capital City	Anadyr'
Principal seaport	Beringovsky Sea Trade Port
Natural Resources:	Gold, tin, black and brown coal
Industry:	Electricity, nuclear power, mining
Light Industry:	Machine building, metal working
Agriculture, fisheries and food:	Reindeer breeding, fur
Other information:	Main means of transport via the sea and six major ports. Air traffic and automobile routes are developed in this area. Lake El'gygytgyn, an important site for scientific research on climate change, is located in Chukotka. This region is home to Roman Abramovitch, the owner of Chelsea FC.
Useful Websites	http://members.tripod.com/~argun/anadyr.htm http://en.wikipedia.org/wiki/Chukotka

KHANTY MANSIYSK AUTONOMOUS AREA

Location	Khanty Mansiysk lies in Russia's Central Plain.
Area KM²	523,100
Population	1,456,000
Capital City	Khanty-Mansiysk
Main Airport	Surgut
Principal seaport	Surgut and Hanty-Mansijsk ports by river to the North
Natural Resources:	Oil, natural gas, gold, vein quartz brown and black coal iron-ore deposits, copper, zinc, lead, niobium, tantalum, bauxite, decorative stone, brick clays, construction sands, timber
Industry:	Oil and gas extraction, logging (pine, cedar, larch, fir and deciduous woods including aspen and birch), electric power, gas processing, building materials
Light Industry:	Metal working, machine-building, metal cutting
Other Commerce:	Mineral (iodine-bromide) waters
Agriculture, fisheries and food:	Dairy and meat cattle, fur animals
Other information:	The area, owing to the richness of its fuel deposits, has attracted much foreign investment There are 13. Ventures with foreign investment from the UK
Credit Rating:	S&P rating BB
Useful Websites	www.hmao.wsnet.ru/english/index.htm http://en.wikipedia.org/wiki/Khantia-Mansia

NENETS AUTONOMOUS AREA (MENETS REPUBLIC)

Location	Nenets Autonomous Area lies just below the Arctic Circle bordering the Barents Sea.
Area KM²	176,700
Population	41,546
Capital City	Naryan-Mar
Natural Resources:	Oil, natural gas, cobalt, lead, zinc, gold, diamonds, titanium, clay and sand
Industry:	Power engineering, wagon building, instrument making, paper, chemical and petroleum refining
Light Industry:	Ferrous and non-ferrous metallurgy, woodworking
Agriculture, fisheries and food:	Fodder crops, grain cultures, reindeer, fishing and hunting, fur animal husbandry
Other information:	Main river: The Neva
Useful Websites	http://reference.allrefer.com/encyclopedia/N/NenetsAu.html http://en.wikipedia.org/wiki/Nenetsia

UST-ORDA BURYATIA AUTONOMOUS AREA

Location	This Okrug is situated entirely within Irkutsk in South Eastern Siberia.
Area KM²	22,400
Population	130,000
Capital City	Ust-Ordynsky
Principal seaport	Landlocked
Natural Resources:	Iron, gold, silver, diamonds, nickel, aluminium, coal and other mineral deposits, timber
Industry:	Steel, chemical factories, hydroelectric power
Light Industry:	Hydroelectric power
Agriculture, fisheries and food:	Grain, wheat, potatoes and vegetables, dairy and meat cattle, wool
Other information:	A referendum is to be held on 16 April 2006 on the merger of Irkutsk Oblast and Ust-Orda Buryatia.
Useful Websites	http://en.wikipedia.org/wiki/Ust-Orda_Buryatia

YAMAL-NENETS AUTONOMOUS AREA

Location	Yamal-Nenets is situated in North Western Russia bordering the Arctic Ocean.
Area KM²	750,300
Population	550,000
Capital City	Salekhard
Principal seaport	Sevakha
Natural Resources:	Natural gas, oil, non-ferrous metals, rare earth metals, bauxite, copper, iron, gold, timber
Industry:	Oil and gas extraction, chemicals
Light Industry:	Machine building, metal working, plastics
Agriculture, fisheries and food:	Fishing
Other information:	Numerous lakes and swamps in the region.
Useful Websites	http://en.wikipedia.org/wiki/Yamalia

THE TERRITORIES (KRAIS)

ALTAI TERRITORY

Location	Altai Krai borders Western Kazakhstan.
Area KM²	169,100
Population	2,600,000
Capital City	Barnaul
Principal seaport	Landlocked
Natural Resources:	Semi-precious metal, iron
Industry:	Medicines, chemicals, petrochemicals
Light Industry:	Light engineering, machinery, food processing, diesel engines, generators, tractors, fabrics
Other Commerce:	Cotton
Agriculture, fisheries and food:	Livestock, grain, vegetables
Other information:	The territory is Russia's fifth largest producer of agricultural products and is famous for its fatty cheeses.
Useful Websites	http://en.wikipedia.org/wiki/Altai_Krai

KAMCHATKA TERRITORY

Location	The Kamchatka peninsula lies on Russia's Pacific coast.
Area KM²	472,300
Population	358,801
Capital City	Petropavlovsk-Kamchatsky
Main Airport	Petropavlovsk-Kamchatsky – Yelizovo Airport
Principal seaports	Petropavlovsk-Kamchatsky, Olyutorskiy
Natural Resources:	Coal, gold, oil and natural gas, timber
Industry:	Mining, oil and gas, ship repair
Light Industry:	Fish and food processing
Other Commerce:	Salmon and other fishing, eco-tourism and hunting
Agriculture, fisheries and food:	Corn, deer ranching, livestock, vegetable production
Other information:	On 23 October 2005, a referendum was held on the merger of Kamchatka Oblast and Koryakia to form Kamchatka Krai. This took place on 01 January 2007. It is the easternmost region in Russia, almost separated from the mainland by the sea of Okhotsk. Kamchatka hosts Eurasia's most active volcano (Kluchevskoy) and its highest concentration of bears.
Useful Websites	www.kamchatkapeninsula.com/ http://en.wikipedia.org/wiki/Kamchatka_Oblast

KHABAROVSK TERRITORY

Location	This territory is in Eastern Siberia bordering the Sea of Japan and Pacific Ocean.
Area KM²	788,600
Population	1,420,200
Capital City	Khabarovsk
Main Airport	Khabarovsk
Principal seaport	Sovied Skaya Gavan, Nikolaevsk on Amur Sea Port
Natural Resources:	Oil, gold, black and brown coal deposits, tin, copper, vanadium, iron, silver, tungsten, bismuth, beryllium, zirconium and indium, feldspar, phosphates, complex ores, timber
Industry:	The Khabarovsk Oil Refinery and Komsomolsk Oil Refinery are crucial to the local and national economy. 64% of its export revenue, in 2006, was petroleum based. The territory also manufactures aircraft engines, pulp and paper. Other industries include metallurgy, chemical processing, wood products
Light Industry:	Precision machine building, electronics, food processing, clothes, footwear and knitted goods, leather haberdashery
Other Commerce:	Fishing
Agriculture, fisheries and food:	Medicinal plants, grain, soybeans, Alaskan Pollock and other fish, seaweed, crab, shrimp, squid
Other information:	1. The Port of Sovied Skaya Gavan is Russia's largest on the Pacific Ocean. 2. The territories main trading partner is China, which attributed for 64.2% of exports and 56.8% of imports in 2006
Useful Websites	www.adm.khv.ru/invest2.nsf/folders/Welcome-en.htm http://en.wikipedia.org/wiki/Khabarovsk_Krai

KRASNODAR TERRITORY

Location	Krasnodar Krai lies on the Black Sea. Its principle cities include Novorossisk, Sochi, Armavir and Toupse.
Area KM²	76,000
Population	5,125,221
Capital City	Krasnodar
Main Airport	Krasnodar airport
Principal seaport	Port of Novorossisk
Natural Resources:	Natural gas, oil
Industry:	Cement
Light Industry:	Electronics, machine building, metal working, building materials and wood processing, canning, food processing, wine making, wool, cotton, leather and fur
Other Commerce:	Health farms, tourism
Agriculture, fisheries and food:	The region produces approximately 6% of meat and dairy products, 10% of all-Russian grain, 30% of fruit production, 60% of oilseed production, 90% of rice production and 97% of wine production Durum wheat, sugar beet, sunflowers, dairy farming, market gardening, tea, tobacco, grapes, rice
Other Information:	In former times, this territory was referred to as the "bread basket of Russia". Novorossisk is a main oil pipeline and terminal point for Russia's oil fields. Much of the oil is piped from wells within the territory. It also supplies Russia with much of its cement. The City of Krasnodar is the home of Russian champagne. Multinational companies in the region, include Cargill, Petrak, Conagra, Monsanto, Tetra-Pak, Danone, Coca Cola, Phillip Morris, Boyuges, Radisson and LaRoute. The krai's Black Sea coast, often called the "Russian Riviera," includes the resort city of Sochi, which attracts over one million tourists each year. 43% of the food processing industry of the Russian Federation is in this region.
Useful Websites	http://en.wikipedia.org/wiki/Krasnodar_Krai http://en.wikipedia.org/wiki/Krasnodar http://en.wikipedia.org/wiki/Sochi http://en.wikipedia.org/wiki/Novorossisk

KRASNOYARSK TERRITORY (KRASNOYARSK KRAI)

Location	This territory stretches from Russia's Arctic North to its Southern Republic of Tyva and borders East and West Siberia
Area KM²	2,339,700
Population	3,023,525
Capital City	Krasnoyarsk
Main Airport	Krasnoyarsk Airport
Principal seaports	Dikson Sea Trade Port, Dudinskiy Sea Trade Port, Igarka
Natural Resources:	Coal, oil, natural gas, zinc, copper, nickel, molybdenum, manganese, poly-metallic ores, iron, gold, silver, germanium, tellurium, titanium, mercury, hallium, indium, phosphates and nephelines – (the main raw material used for the production of aluminium), marble, graphite, fluorite, salt, phosphates, talc, timber
Industry:	Mining, gas extraction, ferrous metallurgy, heavy engineering and machine building, tyre production, wagons and containers, canning, pulp and paper, cardboard, combine harvesters, synthetic rubber, chemical fibres, hydro-electric power, helium, building materials, heavy, electric mobile cranes
Light Industry:	Woodworking, machine building, metal working, food processing
Other Commerce:	Fishing and fish farming
Agriculture, fisheries and food:	Siberian sturgeon and other fish, grain, potatoes and other vegetables, dairy and meat cattle, sheep, fur farming, reindeer, game, poultry, bees
Other information:	On January 1, 2007 the Evenk and Taimyria (Doljan-Nenets) Autonomous Areas were merged into Krasnoyarsk Krai, making it the second largest Russian region after Sakha Republic (Yakutia). Nearly 50% of Russia's domestic timber production comes from this territory. Of great importance are the metal resources found and produced around the Arctic City of Norilsk. In this area over 50% of the world's nickel (80% of Russia's), 40% of its copper (70% of Russia's), and 90% of its platinum are found. Norilsk also has significant natural gas deposits. In addition to the above the krai produces 75% of Russia's cobalt, 16% of its coal and 10% of its gold Much of Siberia's timber is exported through the deep sea port of Igarka.
Credit Rating:	**Moody's** Issuer rating: Caa1
Useful Websites	www.kgtu.runnet.ru (Web pages in Russian) http://en.wikipedia.org/wiki/Krasnoyarsk_Krai www.spri.cam.ac.uk/resources/rfn/evenki.html http://en.wikipedia.org/wiki/Evenkia http://en.wikipedia.org/wiki/Taymyria

MARITIME TERRITORY (PRIMORSKY KRAI)

Location	Primorsky Krai lies in South East Russia bordering the Sea of Japan, North Korea and China. Its major city is Vladivostock. Vladivostock is the Eastern terminal of the Trans-Siberian Railway.
Area KM²	165,900
Population	2,301,700inc Vladivostock 591,800
Capital City	Vladivistock
Main Airport	Vladivostock Airport
Principal seaport	Vladivostock Port, Nakhodka Marine Commercial Port
Natural Resources:	Coal, tin, lead, boron, tungsten, fluoride, lead, zinc, gold, copper, building materials, timber
Industry:	Shipping, mining
Light Industry:	Food processing, machine building
Other Commerce:	Fishing, banking
Agriculture, fisheries and food:	Livestock, rice, buckwheat, honey
Other information:	The Krai is an important fishing and shipping area catching one third of the country's fish.
Useful Websites	www.primorsky.ru/ (Web pages in Russian) http://en.wikipedia.org/wiki/Primorsky_Krai http://en.wikipedia.org/wiki/Vladivostock

PERM KRAI

Location	Perm Krai is situated in the Urals.
Area KM²	193,370
Population	2,956,000
Capital City	Perm
Principal seaport	Landlocked
Natural Resources:	Oil, coal, iron, chromium, copper, lead, zinc, tin, aluminium, gold, manganese, nickel, platinum, pine and birch forests
Industry:	Metals, fertilisers, mining, logging, paper making, machine building, turbo generators, electrical engineering, mining and drilling equipment, plywood, cellulose, aircraft engines, Proton rockets, space control systems
Light Industry:	Silk, clothing, footwear, woodworking
Other Commerce:	Cultural activity, especially ballet
Agriculture, fisheries and food:	grain, potatoes, fodder, livestock, market gardening, furs
Other information:	On December 1, 2005, Perm Oblast and Permyakia merged to form Perm Krai One quarter of the world's potassium deposits are in this area, producing 98% of Russia's potassium-based fertilisers. Perm Krai produces 30 percent of Russia's paper 50% of Russia's magnesium and most of Russia's titanium ore come from Perm Krai. Substantial Joint Venture operations have taken place in this region.
Useful Websites	http://krai.perm.ru/ (Web pages in Russian) http://perm.ru/eng/ www.parliament.perm.ru/main/index.php# http://en.wikipedia.org/wiki/Permyakia http://en.wikipedia.org/wiki/Perm_Oblast http://en.wikipedia.org/wiki/Perm

STAVROPOL TERRITORY

Location	This Krai lies on the Northern Caucasus.
Area KM²	66,500
Population	2,671,800
Capital City	Stavropol
Principal seaport	Landlocked
Natural Resources:	Natural gas, petroleum, non-ferrous ores, coal.
Industry:	Machine building, metal processing, electric power stations, automobiles, oil and gas, chemical fertilisers, chemical reagents, polyethylene
Light Industry:	Wool, food processing, wine making, furniture
Other Commerce:	Mineral water.
Agriculture, fisheries and food:	Speciality crops including winter wheat, cereals, legumes, oats and plant oils. Livestock including chickens
Other information:	This territory is one of the main grain producing areas of Russia.
Useful Websites	www.stavropol.ru/ (Web pages in Russian) http://en.wikipedia.org/wiki/Stavropol_Krai http://en.wikipedia.org/wiki/Stavropol

THE REGIONS (OBLASTS)

AMUR REGION

Location	The Amur Oblast borders North East China.
Area KM²	363,700
Population	1,031,700
Capital City	Blagoveshchensk
Main Airport	Blagoveshchensk
Principal seaport	Landlocked
Natural Resources:	Natural gas, coal, gold, timber
Industry:	hydro-electric power, machine building, ferrous and non-ferrous metals, building materials
Light Industry:	Mechanical work, clothing, shoes, cotton industry, electrical engineering, food processing (meat packing plant)
Agriculture, fisheries and food:	Soya beans, grain, dairy cattle breeding, bee keeping
Other information:	Two forest reserves.
Useful Websites	www.amurobl.ru/ (Web pages in Russian) http://en.wikipedia.org/wiki/Amur_Oblast

ARCHANGELSK REGION

Location	Archangelsk Region is in North West Russia.
Area KM²	587,400
Population	1,336,539
Capital City	Archangelsk
Main Airport	Archangelsk – Talagi Airport Vaskovo Airport
Principal seaport	Archangelsk Port, Naryan-Mar Port
Natural Resources:	Oil, natural gas, diamonds, dolomite, gypsum, agates, bauxite, building rocks, raw materials for cement production, iodine waters, jewellery
Industry:	Logging, woodworking, pulp and paper, oil refining
Light Industry:	Machine building
Agriculture, fisheries and food:	Poultry, Fishing, pedigree, dairy and meat cattle, reindeer husbandry, vegetables
Other information:	Archangelsk is a large sea and river port.
Useful Websites	http://en.wikipedia.org/wiki/Arkhangelsk_Oblast http://en.wikipedia.org/wiki/Arkhangelsk

ASTRAKHAN REGION

Location	Astrakhan lies to the North of the Caspian Sea.
Area KM²	44,100
Population	1,005,276
Capital City	Astrakhan
Principal seaport	Astrakhan Sea Commercial Port
Natural Resources:	Oil, natural gas, limestone, building sands and clays.
Industry:	Heavy engineering and metal-working including ship building and repair, compressors for household refrigerators, pulp and paper, boats, chemicals
Light Industry:	Clothing, fish processing and canning, wool, consumer goods
Other Commerce	Hunting and fishing
Agriculture, fisheries and food:	Grain crops, melons, fodder, vegetables, livestock for meat and dairy farming, sheep breeding
Other information:	The region's most famous product is Caviar
Useful Websites	www.astrobl.ru/ (Web pages in Russian) www.zagrantour.ru/ (Web pages in Russian) http://en.wikipedia.org/wiki/Astrakhan_Oblast

BELGOROD REGION

Location	Belgorod lies on Russia's Western border with Ukraine.
Area KM²	27,100
Population	1,511,620
Capital City	Belgorod
Principal seaport	Landlocked
Natural Resources:	Iron
Industry:	Machine building, iron working, building materials, mining
Light Industry:	Beer, food processing, including sugar refining
Agriculture, fisheries and food:	Fruit and vegetables, dairy and meat cattle, poultry, bees
Other information:	A number of preserves in the region
Useful Websites	http://en.wikipedia.org/wiki/Belgorod_Oblast

BRYANSK REGION

Location	Bryansk lies in Western Russia and borders both the Ukraine and Belarus.
Area KM²	34,900
Population	1,398,941
Capital City	Bryansk
Main Airport	Bryansk
Principal seaport	Landlocked
Natural Resources:	Peat, phosphates, limestone, clays and sands
Industry:	Engineering, metalworking, chemical industry, petro-chemical, pulp and paper, diesel and other engine production, bicycles, cargo wagon production, bulldozers, irrigation machines
Light Industry:	Wool and carpets, dairy products, cereals, furniture. Crystal glass
Other Commerce:	Food processing (alcohol, meat, food canning)
Agriculture, fisheries and food:	Pine, Birch, Oak, alder, ash, maple, lime Grain, flax, potatoes, sugar beet, fruit and vegetables, livestock
Other information:	Part of the Central Economic Region
Useful Websites	http://en.wikipedia.org/wiki/Bryansk_Oblast

CHELYABINSK REGION

Location	Chelyabinsk is in South West Russia bordering Kazakhstan.
Area KM²	87,900
Population	3,603,339 inc Chelyabinsk 1,078,300
Capital City	Chelyabinsk
Main Airport	Chelyabinsk – Balandino Airport
Principal seaport	Landlocked
Natural Resources:	Coal, iron, graphite and fire clay, gold, copper, nickel, rare earth metals, marble, gemstones
Industry:	Nuclear power, ferrous metal-working, rolled stock, tractors, excavators, bulldozers, non-ferrous metals, chemicals, coke
Light Industry:	Mining extracting
Other Commerce:	Watch production and metal casting
Agriculture, fisheries and food:	Grain, vegetables, livestock, poultry
Other information:	This is one of the main areas for metal-working in the Russian Federation. Many Joint Ventures are undertaken in this Oblast. The Mayak Nuclear reactor accident occurred in this Oblast. The city of Magnitogorsk has one of the world's largest iron and steel integrated works. Magnitogorsk also produces 70% of the regions metal exports.
Useful Websites	http://info.abaara.com/pac/Chelyabinsk_Oblast http://en.wikipedia.org/wiki/Chelyabinsk_Oblast http://en.wikipedia.org/wiki/Chelyabinsk

CHITA REGION

Location	Chita is situated in Eastern Siberia bordering on Mongolia and China.
Area KM²	431,500
Population	1,155,346
Capital City	Chita
Principal seaport	Landlocked
Natural Resources:	Lead, zinc, molybdenum, rare metals, coal, timber
Industry:	Engineering, mining equipment, elevators, agricultural machinery, ferrous and non-ferrous metals including steel, railway equipment
Light Industry:	Textiles, wool worsted, footwear, sheepskin coats, woodworking, machine building, refrigeration plants
Other Commerce	Scientific research
Agriculture, fisheries and food:	Livestock, grain, potatoes and other vegetables
Other information:	The main source of livelihood in the mountains is hunting
Useful Websites	http://en.wikipedia.org/wiki/Chita_Oblast

IRKUTSK REGION

Location	Irkutsk lies in East Siberia.
Area KM²	767,900
Population	2,784,900
Capital City	Irkutsk
Main Airport	Irkutsk Airport
Principal seaport	Landlocked
Natural Resources:	Coal, water, gold, timber
Industry:	Non-ferrous metallurgy, chemicals and pharmaceuticals, heating, paper and electricity, aluminium
Other Commerce:	Sable fur, tourism
Other information:	A referendum is to be held on 16 April 2006 on the merger of Irkutsk Oblast and Ust-Orda Buryatia. Joint Ventures with many companies, in particular those from Japan. The City of Bratsk contains the world's largest hydro-electric power station.
Credit Rating S+P	Foreign Currency B-/Positive/--
Useful Websites	www.irkutsk.org/fed/title_eng.html http://en.wikipedia.org/wiki/Irkutsk_Oblast

IVANOVO REGION

Location	Ivanovo is situated in Western Russia, south east of Moscow.
Area KM²	21,800
Population	1,148,329
Capital City	Ivanovo
Main Airport	Ivanovo International Airport
Principal seaport	Landlocked
Natural Resources:	Clay, sand, gravel and limestone, timber, mineral and medicinal-table waters
Industry:	Peat industry equipment, cranes
Light Industry:	Woodworking and furniture, hosiery and knitted goods, high quality fabric production, food processing, alcohol-free beer, macaroni, cured meats
Other Commerce:	It is highly regarded for its mineral water. Palekh boxes are a major product of the area as are small painted toys, embroidery
Agriculture, fisheries and food:	dairy and meat cattle, pigs, poultry
Other information:	Navigation is on the Volga and Klyazma. Also located 300 km (170 miles) from Moscow
Useful Websites	http://ivadm.ivanovo.ru/ (Web pages in Russian) http://en.wikipedia.org/wiki/Ivanovo_Oblast

KALININGRAD REGION

Location	This Oblast is unique in that it is not situated within the Russian Federation but is an enclave bordered by Poland, Lithuania and the Baltic Sea.
Area KM²	15,100 km2
Population	968,200
Capital City	Kaliningrad
Principal seaport	Port Authority of Kaliningrad
Natural Resources:	Salt, building materials, oil, peat, amber, pulp and paper, brown coal, timber
Industry:	Electrical equipment, carriages, dump trucks, equipment for the food and fishing industries
Light Industry:	Furniture
Other Commerce:	Fishing, health resorts
Agriculture, fisheries and food:	Meat and dairy products, vegetables and fodder
Other information:	Kaliningrad operates a Free Economic Zone which offers a wide range of tax exemptions and other privileges to investors (See Chapter 3) More than two thirds of the world's amber is found here.
Useful Websites	http://news.bbc.co.uk/1/hi/world/europe/country_profiles/6177003.stm http://gov.kaliningrad.ru/ (Web pages in Russian) http://en.wikipedia.org/wiki/Kaliningrad_Oblast

KALUGA REGION

Location	Kaluga is located in the Central Region of Western Russia bordering Moscow, Tula, Orel, Bryansk and Smolensk.
Area KM²	29,900
Population	1,095,900
Capital City	Kaluga
Principal seaport	Landlocked
Natural Resources:	Coal, quartz, limestone, phosphorous, soils, timber
Industry:	Engineering and metal-work, machine building, electricity, construction materials
Light Industry:	Textiles, cotton, wool, flax, food processing, wood by-products woodworking
Agriculture, fisheries and food:	Grain, berries, potatoes, fodder, fruit and vegetables, dairy cattle, pigs, poultry, plants
Other information:	Many Joint Ventures have been attracted to this Oblast by its liberal tax regime The first atomic power station in the world was built here.
Useful Websites	www.admobl.kaluga.ru/ (Web pages in Russian) http://en.wikipedia.org/wiki/Kaluga_Oblast

KEMEROVO REGION

Location	Kemerovo is based in Western Siberia.
Area KM²	95,500
Population	2,899,142
Capital City	Kemerovo
Main Airport	Kemerevo has two principle airports, Kemerovo and Novokuznetsk
Principal seaport	Landlocked
Natural Resources:	Coal, iron, poly-metal ores, methelines, phosphates and construction materials
Industry:	Cast iron, ferrous metal, steel, chemical industry, plastics, synthetic resins, chemical fibres and threads, building materials, coal extraction
Light Industry:	Cloth
Agriculture, fisheries and food:	Livestock, grains, vegetables
Other information:	It produces over 38% of Russia's coal. Substantial assistance from the British Government has been given to this area.
Useful Websites	www.kemerovo.ru (Web pages in Russian) http://en.wikipedia.org/wiki/Kemerovo_Oblast

KIROV REGION

Location	The Kirov Oblast lies in the Eastern European, or Volgo-Vyatsky, part of the Russian Federation.
Area KM²	120,800
Population	1,503,529
Capital City	Kirov (also known as Vyatka)
Principal seaport	Landlocked
Natural Resources:	Phosphates, peat
Industry:	Mechanical engineering, metal-working, lifting and conveying equipment, ship building, farming and timber machinery, washing machines, pulp and paper, chemical, petro-chemical, tyres
Light Industry:	Woodworking, food processing, measuring equipment, leather, fur
Other Commerce:	Timber
Agriculture, fisheries and food:	Livestock, meat, milk, wool, eggs, grains, flax, potatoes and other vegetables
Other information:	Many Joint Ventures have established themselves in this Oblast.
Useful Websites	www.ako.kirov.ru/ (Web pages in Russian) http://en.wikipedia.org/wiki/Kirov_Oblast

KOSTROMA REGION

Location	Kostroma is situated in the Volga Region of Western Russia, north east of Moscow.
Area KM²	60,100
Population	736,641
Capital City	Kostroma
Principal seaport	Landlocked
Natural Resources:	Limestone, marl, quartz, sands, peat, clay, fertilisers, mineral water
Industry:	Electric power generation, engineering, metalworking, timber, pulp and paper, petrochemicals, fuel, construction materials, polymers processing machinery, excavators
Light Industry:	Fur, leather, footwear, clothing particularly using linen, technological machinery, plywood, woodworking products, food processing, cheese
Other Commerce:	Mineral water, tourism
Agriculture, fisheries and food:	Livestock, crop cultivation including rye, wheat, barley, oats, flax, potatoes, berries, fruit and vegetables
Other information:	Saint Spring Water Company based in Kostroma. Also the Volga runs through the region
Useful Websites	http://kos-obl.kmtn.ru/ (Web pages in Russian) www.kostroma.net/eng/ http://en.wikipedia.org/wiki/Kostroma_Oblast

KURGAN REGION

Location	Kurgan Region is situated in the Urals and West Siberian Plain. To the south it borders Kazakhstan.
Area KM²	71,000
Population	1,019,532
Capital City	Kurgan
Principal seaport	Landlocked
Natural Resources:	Clay, sands, gypsum, iron, peat and minerals
Industry:	Road and bridge building equipment, buses, printing equipment, farm machinery
Light Industry:	Clothing, leatherwear, footwear, carpets, furniture and other wood products, food processing including fats, butter, cheese, flour, canned meat, medicines, medical equipment
Other Commerce:	Famous traumatology and orthopaedics centre
Agriculture, fisheries and food:	Grains, especially wheat, livestock farming
Other information:	Many Joint Ventures are taking place in this Oblast.
Useful Websites	www.admobl.kurgan.ru/ (Web pages in Russian) http://en.wikipedia.org/wiki/Kurgan_Oblast

KURSK REGION

Location	Kursk borders the Ukraine.
Area KM²	29,800
Population	1,235,091
Capital City	Kursk
Principal seaport	Landlocked
Natural Resources:	Iron, peat, phosphates, construction materials
Industry:	Mechanical engineering, chemicals, petrochemicals, rubber, tractors
Light Industry:	Knitting, footwear, sugar, canned milk, car spares, computer production
Other Commerce:	Mainland technical culture
Agriculture, fisheries and food:	Crop production, livestock, sugar beet
Other information:	Seim River runs through the region.
Useful Websites	http://region.kursk.ru/ (Web pages in Russian) http://en.wikipedia.org/wiki/Kursk_Oblast

LENINGRAD REGION (Including the Federal City of St Petersburg)

Location	Leningrad Region includes the capital of St Petersburg. It borders Finland, the Volga, Neva, Svir and other rivers.
Area KM²	85,900
Population	6,300,000 inc St Petersburg (4.6 m)
Capital City	St Petersburg
Main Airport	St Petersburg-Pulkovo Airport (Pulkova-1 domestic flights and Pulkova-2 international flights)
Principal seaport	Lomonosov Port (St Petersburg)
Natural Resources:	Bauxite, shale, peat, ferrous and non-ferrous metals, timber
Industry:	Defence, technology, ship building, optics, mechanical engineering, metallurgy, chemicals, petrochemicals, petroleum refining, forestry/ agricultural product processing, energy production Ships, atomic and hydro-electric power, heavy engineering, atomic ice breakers, railway rolling stock, pulp and paper, aluminium, plastics, porcelain, silver and gold working, machine building, chemicals
Light Industry:	Breweries, tobacco and automobile assembly, consumer durables, jewellery, watches, computers, scientific and technical equipment
Other Commerce:	Tourism, especially in St Petersburg, fishing
Agriculture, fisheries and food:	Livestock, poultry
Other information:	St Petersburg is the fourth largest city in Europe after London, Paris and Moscow. St Petersburg is classified by UNESCO as a top ten tourist site. It attracts 3.5 million visitors a year. Philip Morris, Kraft, Caterpillar and Ford all have a strong presence The port of St Petersburg is Russia's largest commercial seaport by volume, handling roughly a third of Russia's imports.
Useful Websites	http://eng.lenobl.ru/ www.gov.spb.ru/menu.php http://en.wikipedia.org/wiki/Leningrad_Oblast http://en.wikipedia.org/wiki/Leningrad

LIPETSK REGION

Location	The Lipetsk Region is situated in Western Russia.
Area KM²	24,100
Population	1,247,700
Capital City	Lipetsk
Principal seaport	Landlocked
Natural Resources:	Iron
Industry:	Ferrous metallurgy including steel and rolled metals, machine building, metal-working, metal-cutting machines, tractors, resins, varnishes, nitrogen fertilisers, cement
Light Industry:	Tobacco, food processing, canning, sugar
Other Commerce:	Mineral water treatment
Agriculture, fisheries and food:	Corn, meat and dairy products, rye, buckwheat, sunflowers
Other information:	Forest reserves are in the area.
Useful Websites	www.admlr.lipetsk.ru/eng/title/index.php http://en.wikipedia.org/wiki/Lipetsk_Oblast

MAGADAN REGION

Location	The Magada Oblast lies in Russia's Far East, bordering the Okhotsk Sea.
Area KM²	461,400
Population	251,100
Capital City	Magadan
Principal seaport	Magadan Port
Natural Resources:	Gold, silver, tin, tungsten, coal, mercury, lignite, coal
Industry:	Mining extracts, machine building
Light Industry:	Transport equipment, communications and materials
Other Commerce:	Technical supplies, civil engineering, fishing, seafood, sea mammals, including walrus and whale
Agriculture, fisheries and food:	Deer and cattle ranching, vegetables
Other information:	Large mineral deposits have been discovered off the coast.
Useful Websites	www.magadan.ru/ (Web pages in Russian) http://en.wikipedia.org/wiki/Magadan_Oblast

THE MOSCOW REGION (including The Federal City of Moscow)

Location	This region includes the Federal City of Moscow in which over half its population resides.
Area KM²	47,000
Population	15,753,000 inc Moscow 9.2m
Capital City	Moscow
Main Airport	Sheremetyevo Airport, Domodedovo Airport, Vnukovo Airport
Principal seaport	3 inland river ports with ocean access via canals to the Volga, St Petersburg and the Black Sea
Natural Resources:	Coal, peat, phosphates, limestone, marl and construction materials
Industry:	aviation, space, radio electronics, Mechanical engineering and, in particular, diesel and electric motors and generators, locomotives, buses, mowing machines, sewing machines, ferrous metallurgy, chemical industry, synthetic resins, plastics, sulphuric acid, chemical fibres and threads
Light Industry:	Timber production and by-products including pulp and paper, glass, porcelain and pottery, electronics
Other Commerce:	Tourism, especially in Moscow, Klin and Kolomna, commerce, scientific study
Agriculture, fisheries and food:	grains and flax, market gardening of potatoes and other vegetables, dairy and meat cattle, pigs, poultry
Other information:	The Federal Capital, Moscow, is the largest city in Russia and the third largest city in Europe. The Moscow Customs Department processes one third of Russia's trade turnover.
Credit Rating	**S&P** Foreign currency B+/Stable/-- **Moody's** Issuer Rating: B2
Useful Websites	www.mosreg.ru/ (Web pages in Russian) www.mos.ru/ (Web pages in Russian) www.themoscowtimes.com www.moscow-guide.ru/ www.moscowcity.com/ www.moscowchamber.com/ http://en.wikipedia.org/wiki/Moscow_Oblast http://en.wikipedia.org/wiki/Moscow

MURMANSK REGION

Location	The Murmansk Region is situated in North West Russia on the Baltic Sea and within the Arctic Circle. It also borders Finland.
Area KM²	144,900
Population	892,534
Capital City	Murmansk
Main Airport	Murmansk Airport
Principal seaport	Murmansk Port
Natural Resources:	Bauxite, phosphates, ferrous metal, timber
Industry:	Chemicals, plating, aluminium, machine building, metal-working, ship building and repair, electricity
Light Industry:	Fish processing
Other Commerce:	Fishing, tourism
Agriculture, fisheries and food:	Fishing
Other information:	Sea transport facilities are of the best in Russia. Murmansk itself being the main port.
Useful Websites	www.murman.ru/index-eng.shtml http://en.wikipedia.org/wiki/Murmansk_Oblast

NIZHNY-NOVGOROD REGION

Location	The Nizhny-Novgorod Region is situated North East of Moscow. Over half the population live in its capital, Nizhny-Novgorod, formerly Gorky.
Area KM²	76,900
Population	3,524,028 inc. Nizhni Novgorod 1.3m
Capital City	Nizhny Novgorod
Main Airport	Nizhny-Novgorod
Principal seaport	Landlocked
Natural Resources:	Gypsum, sands, clay, limestone, gravel, dolomite
Industry:	Heavy engineering, automobiles, aircraft, ship building, oil and chemical industry, caustic soda, fertilisers, synthetic resins and plastics
Light Industry:	Consumer and radio electronics, handcrafts and woodworking, washing machines, gas cookers, medical equipment, food processing, leather, knitwear
Other Commerce:	Trade fairs
Agriculture, fisheries and food:	Livestock, grains, hemp, sugar beet, vegetables, flax
Other information:	Considerable British investment has been made in this region. The SOKOL plant produces Russia's MIG aircraft
Credit Rating:	Moody's Bond rating: Caa1
Useful Websites	www.tpp.nnov.ru/ (Web pages in Russian) www.admcity.nnov.ru/english/ http://en.wikipedia.org/wiki/Nizhny_Novgorod_Oblast

NOVGOROD REGION

Location	The Novgorod Oblast borders the Leningrad Region in North West Russia.
Area KM²	55,300
Population	738,500
Capital City	Novgorod
Principal seaport	Novgorod River Port carries out cargo transportation by vessels river-sea from Novgorod Region to Finland, Sweden, Poland, Norway, Germany, the Baltic countries
Natural Resources:	Peat, clay, building materials, minerals, diamonds, timber
Industry:	Chemicals, plastics, fertilisers, synthetic resins, synthetic ammonia.
Light Industry:	Precision engineering, metal-working, electronics, radio engineering, instrument making, televisions, videos, light equipment, glass, porcelain, food processing, woodworking machinery
Other Commerce:	Tourism
Agriculture, fisheries and food:	Livestock, flax, vegetables, fodder, grain
Other information:	Much foreign investment has been placed in this Oblast including Cadbury-Schweppes (UK), Dansk Tyggegummi Fabrik (Denmark), Kymene, Schauman Wood, Raute, Thomesto (Finland), Pfleiderer, Sommer GmBH & Co (Germany), Holzindustrie Preding (Austria), Igienica SA (France), Mo Do Skog (Sweden) and Dresser (U.S.). Simon Baldry, Managing Director of Cadbury Trebor Bassett (UK) stated "We looked at 100 different possible sites in Russia and chose Novgorod the Great. Here we built and opened a greenfield plant in less than a year – faster than we could have done in Western Europe."
Useful Websites	www.adm.nov.ru/web.nsf/pages/englishhome region.adm.nov.ru/web.nsf/eng/home?OpenDocument www.adm.nov.ru/web.nsf/pages/business http://en.wikipedia.org/wiki/Novgorod_Oblast http://en.wikipedia.org/wiki/Novgorod

53

NOVOSIBIRSK REGION

Location	The Novosibirsk Region borders North East Kazakhstan.
Area KM²	178,200
Population	2,504,107 Novosibirsk 1,425,600
Capital City	Novosibirsk
Main Airport	Novosibirsk Tolmachevo Airport
Principal seaport	Landlocked
Natural Resources:	Natural gas, coal, mineral and radon waters, clay
Industry:	Machine building, metal-work, chemicals, aircraft
Light Industry:	Food processing, metallurgy, radio and stereo equipment
Other Commerce:	Business and scientific support, research and development
Agriculture, fisheries and food:	Grain, potatoes and vegetables, dairy and meat products
Other information:	Novosibirsk was an important military and agriculture region in former Soviet times. More recently it has become a leading scientific centre for the Russian Federation. Novosibirsk is Russia's third largest city after Moscow and St Petersburg 62% of industry and 77% of service companies are in private ownership.
Useful Websites	www3.adm.nso.ru/ (Web pages in Russian) http://en.wikipedia.org/wiki/Novosibirsk_Oblast http://en.wikipedia.org/wiki/Novosibirsk

OMSK REGION

Location	The Omsk Oblast is located north of the Kazakhstan border.
Area KM²	139,700
Population	2,174,200 inc Omsk 1,127,300
Capital City	Omsk
Main Airport	Omsk-Fyodorovka airport
Principal seaport	Irtysh River
Natural Resources:	Clay, sands, peat, marl, oil, natural gas, Zirconium, Titanium, Timber
Industry:	Heavy engineering, manufacturing instruments, tractor cultivators, oil processing, petrochemicals, synthetic rubber and tyres, defence equipment, aeroplane engines
Light Industry:	Knitted goods, fur, footwear, food processing including dairy products, canned milk, electrical appliances, machine building, woodworking
Agriculture, fisheries and food:	forestry Sheep breeding, fur breeding, meat and dairy farming, crop cultivation, potatoes and other vegetables
Other information:	Many lakes including ones composed of salt in the south.
Useful Websites	www.omskportal.ru/ (Web pages in Russian) http://en.wikipedia.org/wiki/Omsk_Oblast http://en.wikipedia.org/wiki/Omsk

ORYOL REGION

Location	South of Moscow located in the Middle Russian Hills
Area KM²	24,700
Population	899,000
Capital City	Oryol
Principal seaport	Landlocked
Natural Resources:	Chalk, sand, clays, limestone
Industry:	Engineering, metal-working, chemicals, oil engineering, ferrous and non-ferrous metallurgy
Light Industry:	Textiles and textile machinery, clothing, shoes, hosiery, watches and clocks, canned milk, food processing
Agriculture, fisheries and food:	Livestock, cereals, sugar beet, fodder, fruit and vegetables. dairy and meat cattle, pigs, poultry, horses
Useful Websites	www.adm.orel.ru/ (Web pages in Russian) http://en.wikipedia.org/wiki/Oryol_Oblast

ORENBURG REGION

Location	The Orenburg Region is in the Urals and borders Kazakhstan.
Area KM²	124,000
Population	2,179,551
Capital City	Orenburg
Main Airport	Orenburg
Principal seaport	Landlocked
Natural Resources:	Natural gas, oil, nickel, copper, potassium, coal, precious stones
Industry:	Ferrous metallurgy, steel alloy, big diameter pipes, chemicals, fertilisers, plastics, synthetic resins, road building machinery, forge pressing machinery
Light Industry:	Refrigerators, vacuum cleaners, mohair
Other Commerce:	Salt industry, asbestos
Agriculture, fisheries and food:	Durum wheat, livestock in particular Downy goats
Other information:	There are a wide variety of commercial opportunities in a beautiful setting, 70% of all companies being privatised.
Useful Websites	http://en.wikipedia.org/wiki/Orenburg_Oblast http://en.wikipedia.org/wiki/Orenburg

PENZA REGION

Location	The Penza Region is located in the Volga hills area.
Area KM²	43,200
Population	1,554,700
Capital City	Penza
Principal seaport	Landlocked
Natural Resources:	Coarse-grained moulding sands, marl, chalk, timber
Industry:	Heavy engineering, chemical equipment, polymers, processing equipment, seeding machines, diesel motors, paper, hydro-electricity
Light Industry:	Light woollen cloth, clothing, shoes, meat, butter, whole milk, granulated sugar, pulp and paper, clocks and watches, bicycles, pianos
Agriculture, fisheries and food:	Livestock farming, crop production including sugar beet, wheat, rye, barley, leguminous plants, oats, millet, buckwheat, potatoes and vegetables
Useful Websites	www.penza.ru/root (Web pages in Russian) www.friends-partners.org/oldfriends/mes/centr/penza/ www.penza-gorod.ru/ (Web pages in Russian) http://en.wikipedia.org/wiki/Penza_Oblast http://en.wikipedia.org/wiki/Penza

PSKOV REGION

Location	The Pskov Oblast is situated in North West Russia bordering Estonia and Latvia.
Area KM²	55,300
Population	736,400
Capital City	Pskov
Main Airport	Pskov
Principal seaport	Pskov
Natural Resources:	Peat, limestone, marl, gypsum, clay and sand, timber
Industry:	Engineering, metal-working, peat extraction equipment. electric engines and generators, cables and wiring, electricity
Light Industry:	Flax conversion, knitting and sewing and textiles, food processing, radio electronics, tape recorders, woodworking, clothing and footwear
Agriculture, fisheries and food:	Livestock, flax, potatoes and other vegetables, fodder.
Other Commerce:	Tourism
Other information:	Many joint Ventures have been established in this region.
Useful Websites	www.pskov.ru/en http://en.wikipedia.org/wiki/Pskov_Oblast http://en.wikipedia.org/wiki/Pskov

ROSTOV REGION

Location	The area is also known as the Rostov-on-Don Oblast. It is situated in Western Russia bordering both the Black Sea and the Ukraine.
Area KM²	100,800
Population	4,358,000 inc. Rostov-on-Don 1 m
Capital City	Rostov-on-Don
Main Airport	Rostov International Airport
Principal seaport	AOOT Rostovsky Port – Volga Don Canal connects to Black Sea, Sea of Azov, Baltic Sea, White Sea, Caspian Sea
Natural Resources:	Coal, quartzite, limestone, sands, "black soil"
Industry:	Engineering, metal-working, ferrous and non-ferrous metallurgy, chemical and petrochemicals, coal, steel pipes, electric locomotives, forge pressing machinery, tractors, grain harvester combines, excavators, ceramic tiles, staple yarn, helicopters, ball bearings. Combine harvesters
Light Industry:	Lighting, footwear, vegetable oil, canned fruits and vegetables, wine, watches, clocks, household chemicals, boilers, clothes, shoes, tobacco, televisions and radio receivers, surgical equipment, enamel works, refrigerators, musical instruments, furniture
Agriculture, fisheries and food:	Livestock, sunflowers, wheat, barley, fruit and vegetables
Other Commerce:	Tourism
Other information:	Many Joint Ventures have been set up in this region. The Region is Russia's second largest producer of agricultural products
Useful Websites	www.donland.ru/english/about/ http://en.wikipedia.org/wiki/Rostov_Oblast http://en.wikipedia.org/wiki/Rostov

RYAZAN REGION

Location	The Ryazan Region is based in the Central European area of Western Russia.
Area KM²	39,600
Population	1,284,000
Capital City	Ryazan
Principal seaport	Landlocked
Natural Resources:	Limestone, clays, sands, coal, peat, quartz, phosphorous, natural fertiliser, iron, mineral pigments, timber
Industry:	Engineering and metal-works, machine tool construction, press forging, instrument making, automobile production, tractor and agricultural engineering, metal-cutting and pressing machinery, potato harvester combines, chemical industry, chemical fibres and threads, oil products, lathes, coal and peat extraction, electricity
Light Industry:	Cotton, wool, silk and clothing, food processing, ferrous and non-ferrous metallurgy, fuel, computers, thermal instruments, radio electronics, refrigerators, furniture, footwear
Agriculture, fisheries and food:	Cattle, pigs, poultry, plants, rye, wheat, oats, buckwheat, millet, sugar beet, potatoes and other vegetables and fruits
Other information:	The area is famous for its choirs
Useful Websites	www.ryazanreg.ru/ (Web pages in Russian) http://en.wikipedia.org/wiki/Ryazan_Oblast http://en.wikipedia.org/wiki/Ryazan

SAKHALIN REGION

Location	The Sakhalin Region lies on the Akhotsk Sea and Sea of Japan.
Area KM²	87,100
Population	631,800
Capital City	Yuzhno-Sakhalinsk
Main Airport	Yuzhno-Sakhalinsk Airport
Principal seaport	Aleksandrovsk Sakhalinsky Sea Port, Korsakov Sea Port
Natural Resources:	Offshore gas and oil, coal, timber, natural medicinal resources including more than 100 geothermal springs, mineral springs and curative muds
Industry:	Oil and gas, pulp and paper
Light Industry:	Woodworking
Other Commerce:	Fishing, sea food, tourism, medicinal spas
Agriculture, fisheries and food:	Fodder crops, farming, potato and vegetable growing, dairy cattle and deer breeding, fish
Other information:	1. The Island of Sakhalin is a famous tourist area in the region. 2. Yuzhno-Sakhalinsk has one of the highest foreign populations in Russia
Useful Websites	www.sakhalin.ru/Engl/ http://en.wikipedia.org/wiki/Sakhalin_Oblast http://en.wikipedia.org/wiki/Sakhalin

SAMARA REGION

Location	The Samara Oblast is situated by the River Volga in Western Russia. Its capital, Samara, is east of Moscow.
Area KM²	53,600
Population	3,308,500 inc Samara 1.1m
Capital City	Samara
Principal seaport	Landlocked
Natural Resources:	Oil, natural gas, sulphur, gypsum and limestone
Industry:	Power engineering, chemical engineering, metal-working, oil refining, manufacture of oil extracting equipment, cars, agriculture machine-tool construction, chemical and petro-chemical industries producing nitric and phosphoric fertilisers, chlorine, plastics, synthetic resins, synthetic rubber, synthetic ammonia, gas turbines, metal lathes, ball bearings, aircraft, cables
Light Industry:	Food processing, chocolates, metal working, machine tools
Other Commerce:	Scientific and educational
Agriculture, fisheries and food:	Livestock, poultry, milk farming, rice, wheat, buckwheat, millet, sunflowers, potatoes and vegetables.
Other information:	The region has become of major importance in the export area of the Russian Federation and has established many joint venture operations. Over 60% of Russia's cars are produced in the region and particularly in Togliatti, the home of Lada cars. The local aircraft industry produces the TV154-100.
Credit Rating	Moody's Issuer rating: Ba3 In terms of stability, international rating agencies Standard & Poor's and Moody's have awarded it a rating in the same range as those assigned to Moscow and St Petersburg.
Useful Websites	www.adm.samara.ru/en/ guide.zodchiy.ru/en_invest_guide/ http://en.wikipedia.org/wiki/Samara_Oblast

SARATOV REGION

Location	The Saratov Oblast lies in the Volga Region.
Area KM²	100,200
Population	2,725,800
Capital City	Saratov
Main Airport	Saratov – Tsentralny Airport
Principal seaport	Landlocked
Natural Resources:	Natural gas, oil, shale, construction materials, phosphates, mineral hydrogen sulphate waters, hydro-electric power.
Industry:	Heavy engineering, chemical, petro chemical, construction materials, trolley buses, diesels.
Light Industry:	Lighting, food processing, rayon, synthetic fibres and threads, sulphuric acid, window panes, vegetable oil, refrigerators, aliphatic fat, sewing, fertilisers, rubber, silk, leather goods, domestic appliances.
Agriculture, fisheries and food:	Livestock, cereal and grain production.
Other information:	Many Joint Ventures have been established in this region.
Useful Websites	www.saratov.ru/ (Web pages in Russian) www.geocities.com/WallStreet/7138/text_6.htm http://en.wikipedia.org/wiki/Saratov_Oblast http://en.wikipedia.org/wiki/Saratov

SMOLENSK REGION

Location	Smolensk is situated in the East European Plain.
Area KM²	49,800
Population	1,166,200
Capital City	Smolensk
Principal seaport	Landlocked
Natural Resources:	Coal, peat, limestone, marl, local building materials, phosphates, timber
Industry:	Heavy engineering, metal-working, chemical, petro-chemical, atomic and electric power, peat, coal extraction
Light Industry:	Gem-cutting, food processing, lighting equipment, woodworking, electric machines, computer engineering, soft roofing and insulating materials, linen yarn, knitted wear, canned milk, refrigerators, flour, cereals, cars, nitrogen, computers, thermo-electric power, jewellery, meat
Agriculture, fisheries and food:	Livestock, crop cultivation, horses, cereals, flax, fodder, fruit, vegetables
Other information:	Many Joint Ventures have been set up in this region. 50% of Smolensk Oblast exports are gem diamonds
Useful Websites	http://admin.smolensk.ru/Eng_version/ http://research.rencap.com/eng/government/region_detail0217.asp www.kommersant.com/t-69/r_5/n_413/Smolensk_Region/ http://en.wikipedia.org/wiki/Smolensk_Oblast http://en.wikipedia.org/wiki/Smolensk

SVERDLOVSK REGION

Location	The Sverdlovsk Region is situated in parts of the Urals and into the Siberian Plain. Its capital is Ekaterinburg.
Area KM²	194,800
Population	4,667,800 inc Ekaterinburg 1.4m
Capital City	Ekaterinburg (formerly Sverdlovsk)
Main Airport	Ekaterinburg, Koltsovo International Airport
Principal seaport	Landlocked
Natural Resources:	Iron, titanium, copper, platinum, gold, tungsten, cobalt, nickel, chromium, manganese, coal, asbestos, bauxite, potassium, phosphates, gemstones, building materials, timber
Industry:	Aluminium, chemicals (including radioactive chemicals), shipping, heavy machinery, electrical and chemical equipment, ferrous and non-ferrous metallurgy, turbines, motorbikes, tyres, synthetic rubber, sulphuric acid, fertilisers, cardboard, paper, chipboard, plywood, hardboard, bricks, linoleum
Light Industry:	Food processing, flour milling, footwear, gem cutting, w`oodworking, refrigerators, radio electronics
Agriculture, fisheries and food:	Grain
Other information:	Many British companies are involved in joint ventures in the region and a British Embassy trade office is to be found at Ekaterinburg. The Region is the second largest producer of industrialised output, by volume, in Russia. Ekaterinburg is Russia's fourth largest city VSMPO, the world's second-largest titanium producer is located in the region.
Credit Rating	**S&P** Local currency B-/Positive/-- Foreign Currency B-/Positive/-- **Moody's** Issuer rating: Caa1
Useful Websites	http://en.wikipedia.org/wiki/Sverdlovsk_Oblast http://en.wikipedia.org/wiki/Sverdlovsk

TAMBOV REGION

Location	The Tambov Region is situated in the Central Black Earth Area of Western Russia.
Area KM²	34,300
Population	1,269,000
Capital City	Tambov
Principal seaport	Landlocked
Natural Resources:	Construction materials, phosphates, minerals, peat
Industry:	Heavy engineering, refrigerators, chemical machinery, polymer processing machinery, spare parts
Light Industry:	Wool, woollen yarn, fertilisers, paints and varnishes, sugar, meat, flour, canned goods
Other Commerce:	Annual Rachmaninov festival.
Agriculture, fisheries and food:	Livestock, cereals, sugar beet, sunflowers, fodder, potatoes
Other information:	Many Joint Ventures have been established in the Region. Some 10% of the national wool output is produced in the region.
Useful Websites	www.regadm.tambov.ru/ (Web pages in Russian) http://en.wikipedia.org/wiki/Tambov_Oblast http://en.wikipedia.org/wiki/Tambov

TOMSK REGION

Location	The Tomsk Region is situated in Northern Siberia.
Area KM²	316,900
Population	1,060,800
Capital City	Tomsk
Principal seaport	Landlocked
Natural Resources:	Oil, natural gas, non-ferrous ores, timber (Cedar)
Industry:	Machine building, chemicals, petrochemicals
Light Industry:	Food processing, high technology products
Other Commerce:	Water resources, scientific institutions
Agriculture, fisheries and food:	Dairy and meat cattle, game, vegetables
Other information:	Great marshy territories. Part of the West-Siberian territorial industrial complex.
Useful Websites	http://en.wikipedia.org/wiki/Tomsk_Oblast http://en.wikipedia.org/wiki/Tomsk

TULA REGION

Location	Tula is situated in European Russia.
Area KM²	25,700
Population	1,800,100
Capital City	Tula
Principal seaport	Landlocked
Natural Resources:	Brown coal, iron, limestone, clays and sands
Industry:	Heavy engineering, metal-working, chemicals, petrochemicals, fuel, ferrous metallurgy, construction, fertilisers, synthetic rubber, synthetic ammonia, caustic soda, motorcycles, scooters, household chemicals, cranes, agricultural machinery, nitrogen, sewing items, synthetic resins, brown coal extraction
Light Industry:	Shotguns, food processing, samovars
Agriculture, fisheries and food:	cereals, fodder, potatoes, sugar beet, fruit and vegetables, market gardening, dairy and meat cattle, pigs, poultry, goats
Other information:	Many Joint Ventures have been established in this region. Tula was one of the first Oblasts to commission a fully digitalised telecommunications system
Useful Websites	www.region.tula.ru/ (Web pages in Russian) www.tula.net/ (Web pages in Russian) www.bisnis.doc.gov/bisnis/bulletin/0007bull9.htm www.bisnis.doc.gov/bisnis/bisdoc/000523central-tula-overview.htm http://en.wikipedia.org/wiki/Tula_Oblast

TVER REGION

Location	Tver is situated in North Western Russia, on the River Volga.
Area KM²	84,100
Population	1,642,600
Capital City	Tver
Principal seaport	Landlocked
Natural Resources:	Coal, peat, glass, sands, limestone, dolomites, minerals, timber, fresh water
Industry:	Heavy engineering, metal-work, gifts, road building machines, passenger trains, wagons, cement, bricks, reinforced concrete, plastics, machine building
Light Industry:	Cotton, linen, knitting, footwear, handicrafts, glass, china, fibres and threads, printing and publishing, leather, woodworking.
Other Commerce:	Tourism is also developing
Agriculture, fisheries and food:	Livestock, flax, fodder, grain, vegetables, lumber
Other information:	Many Joint Ventures have been established in this region. Tver is the source of fresh water for Moscow and much of central Russia. 40% of Russia's flax is produced in this region
Useful Websites	www.region.tver.ru/ (Web pages in Russian) www.tver.ru (Web pages in Russian) www.russianamericanchamber.org/regions/tver.html http://en.wikipedia.org/wiki/Tver_Oblast http://en.wikipedia.org/wiki/Tver

TYUMEN REGION

Location	The Tyumen Oblast – Russia's third largest – marks the border between Europe, Siberia and Asia. It is Tundra in the north and Taiga in the south.
Area KM²	1,435,200
Population	3,177,100)
Capital City	Tyumen
Main Airport	Tyumen – Roshchino Airport
Principal seaport	Landlocked
Natural Resources:	Oil, natural gas, (80% of Russia's total), electricity
Industry:	Automobiles, car batteries, petrochemicals, chemicals, plastic material, pharmaceuticals, electricity
Light Industry:	Machine building, metal working
Agriculture, fisheries and food:	Reindeer ranching
Other information:	Considerable foreign investment has taken place in this region. The Oblast produces 7% of Russia's electricity The Oblast produces one third of Russia's car batteries
Useful Websites	http://admtyumen.ru/ (Web pages in Russian) http://en.wikipedia.org/wiki/Tyumen_Oblast http://en.wikipedia.org/wiki/Tyumen

ULYANOVSK REGION

Location	Ulyanovsk Oblast lies in the Volga region.
Area KM²	37,300
Population	1,490,000
Capital City	Ulyanovsk
Main Airport	Ulyanovsk-Vostochny International Airport
Principal seaport	Landlocked
Natural Resources:	Moulding sand, glass quartz and sand
Industry:	Automobiles, aircraft, construction materials, atomic power.
Light Industry:	Woollen yarn, hosiery, tapestry, butter, cheese, dairy products, meat, leather, carpets, light engineering, machine tools, wood processing
Other Commerce:	Wood carving
Agriculture, fisheries and food:	Dairy and meat cattle, pigs, poultry, crop cultivation, potatoes
Other information:	Home of the Ulyanovsk Centre for Aviation Studies
Useful Websites	http://en.wikipedia.org/wiki/Ulyanovsk_Oblast http://en.wikipedia.org/wiki/Ulyanovsk

VLADIMIR REGION

Location	The Vladimir Oblast is situated in Western Russia bordering on Moscow.
Area KM²	29,000
Population	1,636,900
Capital City	Vladimir
Principal seaport	Landlocked
Natural Resources:	Limestone, clays, quartz, sands, building materials, peat
Industry:	Engineering, metal-working, automobiles, tractors, electric power generation, chemicals, non-ferrous metallurgy, pulp and paper, synthetic resins, plastics, magnets
Light Industry:	Cotton fabrics, cotton yarn, linen, artistic glass, crystal glass, food processing, machine building, electrical equipment
Other Commerce:	Tourism
Agriculture, fisheries and food:	Livestock farming, grains, potatoes, berries, fodder, vegetables and fruit
Other information:	Many joint ventures are to be found in the region.
Useful Websites	http://permanent.access.gpo.gov/lps3997/9807vlad.htm www.vladimir-russia.net/ www.bisnis.doc.gov/bisnis/bisdoc/000900central_vladimir.htm http://en.wikipedia.org/wiki/Volgograd_Oblast http://en.wikipedia.org/wiki/Vladimir

VOLGOGRAD REGION

Location	The Volgograd Oblast borders Kazakhstan.
Area KM²	113,900
Population	2,701,600
Capital City	Volgograd
Principal seaport	Landlocked
Natural Resources:	Oil, natural gas, raw cement, table salt, chemicals
Industry:	Ball bearings, tractors, chemicals, petrochemicals, caustic soda, tyres, ferrous metallurgy, fuel, electric power generation, aluminium
Light Industry:	Food processing, soft drinks, beer, ceramics, machine tools, electrical engineering, industrial equipment
Agriculture, fisheries and food:	Crops, livestock, fruit, vegetables, melons, sunflower, mustard seed
Other information:	Many Joint Ventures are currently undertaken in the Region. The largest hydro-electric power station in Europe is based in Volzhakaya.
Useful Websites	www.volgograd.ru (Web pages in Russian) www.bisnis.doc.gov/bisnis/bulletin/2-01bull7.htm http://en.wikipedia.org/wiki/Volgograd_Oblast http://en.wikipedia.org/wiki/Volgograd

VOLOGDA REGION

Location	The Vologda Region borders the Archangelsk and Leningrad Oblasts in North West Russia.
Area KM²	145,700
Population	1,324,000
Capital City	Vologda
Main Airport	Vologda
Principal seaport	Volgo-Balt Canal, to ship goods to ports of the Baltic, White, Caspian, Black and Mediterranean seas.
Natural Resources:	Peat, construction materials, table salt
Industry:	Ferrous metallurgy, timber, pulp and paper, chemical engineering, cast iron, steel, finished rolled non-ferrous metals, coke, fertilisers, synthetic ammonia, sulphuric acid, wood-shaving plates, nitrogen, ball bearings, thermo electric power
Light Industry:	Textiles and in particular lace, food processing, canned milk, butter, woodworking, window panes, machine making, computers
Other Commerce:	Space research, tourism
Agriculture, fisheries and food:	Livestock, crop cultivation, flax, vegetables, dairy cattle, poultry
Other information:	The region is particularly famous for its lace industry.
Credit Rating S+P	Foreign Currency B/Stable/--
Useful Websites	www.vologda-oblast.ru/main.asp?LNG=ENG http://en.wikipedia.org/wiki/Vologda_Oblast http://en.wikipedia.org/wiki/Vologda

VORONEZH REGION

Location	The Voronezh Oblast is situated in the Central Black Earth Region of Western Russia and borders the Ukraine.
Area KM²	52,400
Population	2,495,400
Capital City	Voronezh
Principal seaport	Landlocked
Natural Resources:	Raw cement, fire-clays, sand, construction stone, chalk, minerals
Industry:	Heavy engineering, mining equipment, metal-cutting tools, excavators, chemical industry, food processing, synthetic ammonia, synthetic rubber, aircraft, atomic power
Light Industry:	Electrical equipment, televisions, tape recorders, food processing, sugar, vegetable oil, canned meat, cereals
Other Commerce:	Medicines
Agriculture, fisheries and food:	Livestock, bee-keeping, horse farming, cereals, sugar beet, sunflowers, coriander, potatoes and other vegetables, fodder
Other information:	Large forest reserves
Useful Websites	www.voronezh.ru/ (Web pages in Russian) www.russianamericanchamber.org/regions/voronezh.html http://en.wikipedia.org/wiki/Voronezh_Oblast http://en.wikipedia.org/wiki/Voronezh

YAROSLAVL REGION

Location	The Yaroslavl Region is situated in Western Russia on the River Volga.
Area KM²	36,400
Population	1,442,900
Capital City	Yaroslavl
Main Airport	Tunoshna
Principal seaport	Yaroslavl Port. The Volga-Don River Canal System cargo can travel south to the Black Sea and to the Mediterranean
Natural Resources:	Quartz, sand, gravel, peat, mineral waters, limestone, clay, minerals, oil
Industry:	Engineering and especially diesel engines, metal-work, cables, automobiles, woodworking, pulp and paper, polymers, processing equipment, printing equipment, watches, oil re-processing, machine building, chemicals
Light Industry:	Cotton, flax, wool, clothing, fur, footwear, glass, porcelain, watches, motors, computers
Other Commerce:	Scientific instruments, tourism
Agriculture, fisheries and food:	Livestock, cereals, potatoes, flax, fruit and vegetables
Other information:	There are over 5000 historical and architectural monuments in the region. Many Joint Ventures have taken place in this region.
Useful Websites	www.adm.yar.ru/eng/index.htm (Web pages in Russian) http://en.wikipedia.org/wiki/Yaroslavl_Oblast http://en.wikipedia.org/wiki/Yaroslavl

1 THE REGULATORY BACKGROUND

1.1.   Background

Russia, over the past decade, has transformed itself into a vibrant market economy with a developed economic, commercial, legal, financial, social and political infrastructure. Russia has enjoyed 10 consecutive years of economic growth since the financial crisis of 1998, largely as a result of its huge resources, especially oil and gas. As a consequence of this, as well as high metal prices, Russia continues to enjoy record trade and fiscal surpluses, with reserves currently standing at over $460 billion. To prevent high inflation rates the fund is invested abroad only and has been used to pay off foreign debt. By 1st January 2008 the Fund had accumulated $156.81 billion.

Russia recognises that it needs the support of its trading partners in Europe and the United States as much as they need it to supply resources for much wanted consumer, industrial, technological and other goods and services. Equally, the presidency has been keen to show that Russia is a significant player in the world economy. Membership of the G-8 and other world economic bodies aims to demonstrate that Russia recognises its responsibility to ensure stability in the world economy for the good of all.

The liberalisation of the Russian economy over recent years has encouraged a large number of companies to investigate the Russian marketplace. Encouraged by the significant opportunities, many British companies have established a presence in the country, becoming the biggest investors in the oil and gas sectors and since 2004 and the largest investor overall. In addition, Russia has become a significant customer for British goods and services, with UK exports to Russia worth over £2 billion by the end of 2006. Successive Russian governments have encouraged this transition to a market economy, establishing bodies such as the Foreign Investment Advisory Council, whose aim is to attract foreign investment and to overcome the problems that may deter investors.

While the Russian Federation has made remarkable progress in terms of economic growth, this has not been equally matched by progress in democratic consolidation, the rule of law, and civil society development. Causes for concern include Russia's increasing determination to demonstrate its importance and strength in world economic and political affairs – especially with regard increased State influence including renationalisation, centralisation of power with siloviki (people in authority), and Russia's potential use of its oil and gas supplies as a political weapon. Issues concerning demographic decline; human rights and corruption have not abated, with over 28,000 prosecuted cases in 2006 alone – a third relating to bribery. Successive Russian Governments, particularly under former President Vladimir Putin, have made great strides to overcome these worries. The development of a simple and efficient legal and fiscal framework in which business can operate, low taxation and the encouragement of investment both within and from outside of Russia have made Russia a country of increasing interest to entrepreneurs.

1.2.   Privatisation

Through progressive legislation many former state owned enterprises have been converted into open joint stock companies. The main exceptions to privatisation have been military related enterprises and land ownership. In accordance with the Federal Law Nr. 178-FZ "On privatisation of state and municipal property" (21 December 2001), the Government of Russia adopts Privatisation Programmes annually. By 2004, some 75% of the Russian economy had been fully privatised, with the Government having divested itself of state-held blocks of shares in companies in which it had up to a 50% interest. Both Russians and non-Russians may own equity in companies and participate in local investment. Whilst the privatisation of small businesses, including those in the agricultural sector, has continued there has been a reversal of the trend to privatise natural resources, with the Russian Government taking back into state ownership, both directly and indirectly, much of the gas and oil industry. Rosneft, for example, has scooped up many assets auctioned off by the bankrupt Yukos and TNK-BP and Shell have ceded control of the Kovykta and Sakhalin-2 projects, respectively, to Gazprom.

1.3.   Land ownership

Legislation relating to land ownership has been evolving rapidly since 1990. Article 36 of the Russian Constitution states "citizens and their associations shall have the right to have land in their private ownership." This right is also protected by law (Russian Constitution, Civil Code, Land Code etc.). The Property Law 1990 provided the framework for property ownership in Russia. Under this legislation the Government began to release buildings and other property for private ownership. In addition, the legislation prescribed that Russian and foreign businesses can acquire long-term leases on property for periods of up to 49 years (and for a period of up to 99 years on objects which are most significant for Moscow). These are usually acquired by means of auction.

In December 1991, the Government announced the privatisation of state and collective farms, as well as other land in state and municipal ownership, was announced. Russian citizens are now allowed to own private apartments, small country properties (dachas), small plots of land for private gardens and land in the agricultural sector. The transfer of freehold property was permitted by Presidential Decree on 27 October 1993. Presidential Decree, "On Implementation of Constitutional Rights of Citizens in Land," passed in March 1996 and the Federal Land Code, passed by the Duma in October 2001, extended land ownership further, allowing land plots to be:

- inherited,
- used to start a private farm or as a subsidiary plot,
- sold,
- granted,
- exchanged for property or other land share elsewhere,
- leased out to other farmers and farming businesses (including in an exchange for lifetime support), and
- contributed into a share of a farm.

As a result of these measures some 50% of Russia's 406 million hectares of farmland, and more than 400,000 landholders of commercial and agricultural property, in private ownership.

The Federal Land Code consolidated much of the previous legislation, providing a comprehensive approach to the ownership rights of non-agricultural land and of property. The main thrusts of the legislation are:

- Classification of different forms of land ownership,
- Permitted uses of land,
- Clarification of transfer and registration rights for land ownership, including the purchase of undeveloped land plots,
- Clarification of transfer and registration rights for leases, including the purchase of undeveloped land plots required for construction purposes,

◆ Valuation and taxation of land.

Several provisions of the Federal Land Code which conflict with the Russian Civil Code, sometimes giving rise to confusion. Foreigners are not allowed to own farmland in Russia although long-term leases are permitted. Consequently, for both foreign nationals and Russians alike, the easiest way to obtain use of a site is through a lease agreement. Short-term leases generally range from three to five years and cover the construction period. It is usual to pay the first full year's rent for short leases at the beginning of the agreement. Long-term land lease in Moscow is typically for 49 years although some 25-year terms have been granted.

Decisions concerning the use of land are within the remit of the local authorities, which should be approached at an early stage of the investment process, to ensure adequate title to the land is obtained. All property rights including land leases are subject to state registration.

Despite this, a real estate market for apartment leases is also developing in Russia, and especially in the larger cities. The purchase price for the right to a long-term lease on the primary market in Moscow can be as high as prime sites in London, New York or elsewhere. On average, property in Moscow costs in Moscow were £2,165 a square metre, making a 200 square meter apartment worth more than £420,000. One 2,400 square meter site (a little more than half an acre) on Tverskaya Street in Moscow was actually sold for $US45 million in 2005. The fact that the land tenure was in the form of a 49-year lease, rather than fee simple ownership, did not seem to have much effect on the price. It is possible that the time value of money when used to rent prime site property is practically no different to the economic value of that site if purchased freehold. For prime property in Moscow leasing rates today average $600 with office maintenance costs at $110-$120 per square meter per year.

1.5   The development of commodity, security and financial exchanges

One of the main consequences of the privatisation process was the birth of the Russian securities and financial markets. The Moscow Interbank Currency Exchange (MICEX) is Russia's leading financial and stock exchange Website: www. micex.com). It serves as a base for the nationwide system of trade in the currency, stock and derivatives sectors of the financial market both in Moscow and in Russia's largest financial and industrial centres. Jointly with its partners the MICEX group (the MICEX Stock Exchange, the MICEX Settlement House, the National Depository Centre, regional exchanges and others) provides settlement and clearing facilities as well as depository services for about 1,500 organisations – participants in the stock market. In terms of the total trade turnover (in 2006 — 1,925 billion US Dollars (US$932 billion 2005) with the average daily volume of stock transactions, in 2007, amounted to 3.1 billion US Dollars) the MICEX is the largest exchange in Russia, the CIS and Eastern Europe. Today, under the aegis of the International Association of Exchanges of the CIS Countries, the Commonwealth is developing an integrated orderly stock market, based on the technological resources of the national exchanges of the CIS countries.

The MICEX Stock Exchange is the leading stock floor in Russia and the CIS, where daily trades are held in stocks of over 750 Russian issuing companies. The Real Russia Project (18 May 2007); website: www.russiablog.org/2007/05/russian_ipos_week_18_of_2007_r.php stated: As of early 2007, 586 firms were providing access to trading for 265,000 investors (in 2006 134,000), including over 24,000 legal entities, over 230,000 individual investors, 2,000 non-residents and almost 8,000 institutional investors. In April 2007, the number of participants in trading reached 600 firms which serve over 326,000 clients. Of course, these numbers are still very small compared to the magnitude of the New York or London stock exchanges, but here in Russia, we are learning quickly.

Trades are held electronically, using an up-to-date trading and depositary system, to which regional trading floors and remote terminals are connected. Cash settlements are effected through the MICEX Settlement House, while settlements for securities are effected through the National Depositary Center.

Shares of mutual funds are traded on the MICEX, which promotes the development of the institutions of collective investing. Since 1997, the MICEX has calculated the MICEX Index, which is the leading Russian stock market indicator.

MICEX implements projects for creating and developing commodity exchange markets in close collaboration with the National Mercantile Exchange (NAMEX). NAMEX is mainly engaged in the organization of exchange trading on the cash commodities market and on the market for mercantile instruments and derivatives (futures and options) in Russia via maximum coverage of regional market players. For this purpose NAMEX uses organizational, IT and technical resources of MICEX as well as such resources of regional exchanges, technological partners and commodity traders. NAMEX has concluded collaboration agreements for the development of mercantile trading markets with:

♦ MICEX;
♦ Rostov Currency and Stock Exchange (RCSE);
♦ Nizhegorodskaya Currency and Stock Exchange (NCSEX);
♦ Samara Currency Interbank Exchange (SCIEX);
♦ Urals Regional Currency Exchange (URCEX);
♦ Siberian Interbank Currency Exchange (SICEX);
♦ Saint-Petersburg Currency Exchange (SPCEX);
♦ Asian-Pacific Interbank Currency Exchange.

The RTS Stock Exchange is one of the largest electronic trading floors in Russia. It was established in 1995 by leading professional market participants to consolidate separate regional securities trading floors into a unified regulated Russian securities market. As a non-profit Partnership "The RTS Stock Exchange" commenced operations on 1 January 1997. The creation of the Exchange was the result of a series of initiatives put forward by National Association of Securities Market Participants (NAUFOR) to develop and regulate over-the-counter (OTC) trading.

The highest governing body of the Exchange is the Partnership Council made up of all RTS members that meets annually. In between these meetings the Board of Directors consisting of 17 chief executives of the RTS member firms manages the Exchange. The Partnership Council elects the President of the Partnership who serves as the Chief Executive officer and supervises the Executive Directors of the Partnership.

The RTS Stock Exchange provides a regulated, respected and reliable trading system, with infrastructure that can compete with the leading Western markets. It lists leading Russian securities that are of greatest interest to domestic and foreign portfolio investors, including mutual funds, thus providing the industry with the most important market indicators. The RTS establishes efficient market prices for a wide range of stocks and bonds, and the trading information is distributed worldwide through the largest financial information services companies, such as REUTERS and Bloomberg.

The RTS Index, the official Exchange indicator first calculated on 1 September 1995, has since become the benchmark in Russian securities' industry. The Index is computed on thirty-minute intervals using real-time prices of the most liquid stocks listed on the Exchange and is relayed to the RTS website: www.rts.ru/en/

Shares and bonds in open joint stock companies are tradable both within and outside the Russian Federation, subject to agreement from the Federal Financial Markets Service (FFMS). The Federal Financial Markets Service is the federal executive body, which controls and supervises activity in the financial markets, including the activity of exchanges, and issues the relevant regulations. It also regulates the investment of pension savings. The key objectives of the FFMS are to maintain stability in financial markets, make the markets more efficient and attractive to investors, increase market transparency and reduce investment risks. It achieves these objectives by regulating the activities of financial market participants and by setting out the conditions for securities issuance and trading. For more information about FFMS see website: www.fcsm.ru/eng/

Both institutional and small private investors have shown interest in the Stock Market. The development of internet-trading systems played a major part in this process. The RTS Stock Exchange's aims are:

♦ To encourage close interaction with Russian exchanges in order to build a single trading environment in Russia;

♦ To cooperate with foreign exchanges and other financial institutions to help bring together Russian and foreign market participants and investors working with rouble- and dollar-denominated RTS-listed instruments;

♦ To implement credit settlement mechanisms;

♦ On-going technical innovation, making the Moscow Stock Exchange comparable to Western European stock markets.

♦ To develop corporate governance and protection of investors' rights in the Russian market. An open forum on this has been developed within the framework of the OECD/World Bank – Russian Corporate Governance Roundtable. For more information about OECD roundtable see website: www.corp-gov.org/

The Russian Government, however, is taking a cautious approach to the influx of foreign investment in its capital markets, recognising that the country's infrastructure is not able to handle massive capital flows on a thinly traded market that is heavily dependent upon oil and gas prices.

1.6   The Banking System

Soon after the demise of the Soviet Union, some 3,000 banks were formed in the Russian Federation. Many of these institutions were weak and nearly half this number did not survive the monetary crises of the 1990s, including the crisis of 1998.

Russia, with some 1,350 banks has the third-largest number of banks in the world, behind the United States with 7,475 banks and the running up Germany with 2,400. Five of these account for 64% of all banking assets, with Sberbank accounting for 30%. Some 900 banks have a licence to deal in foreign exchange, including some 270, which have gained full general licences, allowing them to hold hard currency accounts with foreign banks. Foreign banks are not allowed under Russian law to open branches. However, many have been granted licences to operate wholly-owned subsidiaries or offshore branches, serving Russian and foreign customers. Whilst interest in the regions is developing there are few local branches of global banks in operation. Most of the 130 foreign owned banks mostly restrict their activities to Moscow and St Petersburg (See Chapter 15). Conversely, several Russian banks have opened representative offices in London. Asset management, portfolio management and investment advisory services remain underdeveloped. The ECGD (see 16.2) states that further consolidation of the banking sector will need to take place before an effective credit infrastructure, using objective credit profiles on banks and businesses, can be put in place.

Nevertheless, 2005 saw an increasingly controlled and internationally accepted banking system, regulated by the Bank of Russia, also known as the Central Bank. Commercial banks are regulated by the Constitution of the Russian Federation, federal laws, the Civil Code, the Civil Procedural Code, presidential decrees and Central Bank regulations. Federal Law "On Insuring the Deposits of Private Persons in Banks of the Russian Federation," which entered into force on 27 December 2003, offers a measure of Government guarantee of the protection of citizens' deposits in the case of bank failure. Banks receive different types of licences permitting them to carry out a range of banking activities depending on the type of licence held. Furthermore, Federal Law Nr. 218-FZ "On credit histories" (30 December 2004) was enacted and has entered into force.

The banking system is becoming widely accepted, with total banking assets growing to 43% of GDP (up from 30% in July 1998). Banking loans in Russia represent around 19% of GDP (up from 12% in July 1998) – one of the lowest proportions among emerging markets – half of the level of Poland and approximately a quarter of the ratio in the Czech Republic. The loans-to-GDP ratio stands generally at 34% in central Europe and between 12% and 112% in all emerging markets. Russian banking sector remains underdeveloped compared to other emerging markets, which implies substantial room for growth.

The country's largest banks continue to be run by the government or the leading domestic natural-resources companies. Only a few have begun to engage in market-driven deposit taking and corporate and consumer lending. Traditional banking services, such as account maintenance and settlement operations, including trade finance, are widely available. The retail market is beginning to develop and is viewed as one of growth and opportunity with banks now brokering client funds in securities and other investments. Despite the current positive developments and strong economic fundamentals, the Russian banking system is still considered by many as potentially unstable and consequently high risk.

The Bank of Russia publishes materials on the state and functioning of the Russian payment system in the press open for the general public (see Bank of Russia periodicals Dengi i kredit (Money and Credit) and Byulleten bankovskoi statistiki (Bulletin of Banking Statistics) and in publications for office use (the bulletin Obzor platezhnoi sistemy Rossiiskoi Federatsii (Review of the Russian Payment System).

1.6.1 Currency control

On 18 June 2004 the amended version of Federal Law No. 173-FZ "On Currency Regulation and Currency Control" came into force, to some extent softening the currency regime but at the same time introducing new regulatory peculiarities. The amended law stipulated that the foreign exchange transactions could be conducted without any restrictions unless restrictions are introduced by law or the Bank of Russia.

Amendments of the above law introduced the following requirements:
♦ registration requirements;

- requirements to use special accounts in an authorized bank for certain activities;
- deposition requirements.

The Law also stipulated that by 1 January 2007, most of the restrictions on currency transactions would be lifted.

Furthermore, currency control regulations were substantially amended in July 2005. In particular, the list of permitted currency transactions between residents was extended. In addition, the procedure for the import of foreign and Russian currencies in cash as well as traveler's cheques, the documented foreign and domestic securities by individuals into Russia has been changed and a procedure for their export has been established.

Bearing in mind that the Russian legislation on currency regulation and currency control is complex and that violation of it could entail serious legal consequences, it is highly advisable for foreign investors to seek the advice of Russian counsel before making any important business decisions which would involve currency issues.

1.7.1 The Commercial Insurance Market

Russia's insurance regulatory system is governed by

- Federal Law No. 4015-1, "On the Organisation of the Insurance Business in the Russian Federation" (27 November 1992, last amended by Federal Law No. 104-FZ, 21 July 2005) ("1992 Insurance Law");
- Chapter 48 of the Civil Code of the Russian Federation;
- A number of other laws and regulations adopted by the State Duma, the President and the federal government.

There are some one thousand insurance companies operating in the Russian Federation. The largest of these, in terms of regional presence, is Rosgosstrakh, still partially state-owned although a good portion of this company is now privately owned. All remaining companies are fully private and a growing number are foreign–owned or joint ventures.

The industry provides two basic types of insurance: mandatory and non-mandatory. Mandatory insurance is specified in the 1992 Insurance Law and in federal legislation regulating specific types of insurance, and includes domestic, medical, motor vehicle third party liability, civil liability for high-risk activities and industries and personal insurance.

For other risks such as general and professional liability, property and transportation, insurance may be taken out on a voluntary basis provided that general regulatory requirements for insurers and insurable interests are complied with. Commercial insurance is the most developed segment of the Russian insurance market, enjoying growth rates of 25% per annum, which are expected to continue to 2010.

Details of insurance companies operating in Russia may be found on:

www.ins-union.ru

www.allinsurance.ru

1.7.2 Insurance brokers

The 1992 Insurance Law, as amended since 1st July 2007, provides that only Russian organisations and private persons registered permanently in Russia, which have obtained a special licence can act as insurance brokers. Insurance brokers cannot act as intermediaries for insurance companies not registered and licensed to operate in the Russian federation. The three global insurance brokers, AON, Marsh and Willis all have offices in Russia.

1.8   Audit and accounting

In 1998, the Government of the Russian Federation adopted the "Programme for the Reform of Russian Accounting in Accordance with International Accounting Standards." This culminated with the passage in 2001 of the Federal Law ""On Audit Activity," which regulates and defines audit activities and duties.

Despite this aim, Russian accounting practice, except for joint stock companies and other very large companies, continues to differ from International Accounting Standards (IAS) and from General Audit and Accounting Procedures (GAAP). This is often a source of confusion and difficulty to British investors.

The Russian audit is primarily a tax audit and will not, in the case of smaller companies, satisfy international auditing standards. Consolidated financial statements are treated as secondary to the stand-alone statutory financial statements of a company and are often not prepared.

The financial year is the calendar year ending at the 31 December. Where a company begins operations after 1 October, its financial statements will run to 31 December of the following year.

Annual accounts, which in some cases must be validated by a recognised Russian auditing body, must be filed with a local tax authority by 1 April each year (see Section 1.8.1). They must also be submitted to shareholders and the Statistics Authority. Open joint stock companies, banks and other credit institutions, exchanges, investment and other funds (those made up of private, public and state contributions), and insurance companies must publish their statutory financial statements in newspapers and magazines.

Current regulations require that every transaction be written up in an organisation's books and records. To be acceptable, invoices must be drafted in Russian or accompanied by a certified statement (an act). They must also have their value stated in Roubles as at the date of the transaction.

The financial statements presented are unlikely to account for inflation. Fixed assets are often depreciated up to a maximum period of 10 years. Subsidiaries of foreign companies may require an additional audit by an international firm of auditors. A list of these may be obtained from UK Trade & Investment Tel: 020 7215 4891; Website: www.uktradeinvest.gov.uk/ukti/appmanager/ukti/countries?_nfls=false&_nfpb=true&_pageLabel=CountryType1&navigationPageId=/russia

1.8.1 Comparison of accounting and auditing procedures between the UK and Russia

Subject	Russia	UK
Period of accounts	Accounts run to 31st December each year.	Any twelve month period is acceptable but once an accounting d ate is set it must be kept to that date.
Deadline for submitting accounts.	Quarterly accounts must be presented within thirty days of the end of the quarter and the annual accounting statements by 28 March of the following year.	The accounts have to be filed with the Registrar and the deadline is seven months after the year end for a public limited company and ten months after year end for a private limited company.

Subject	Russia	UK
Off Balance Sheet Financing	Shown under section 10 of the accounts, not part of the double entry system.	Must be incorporated in the accounts under double entry to show a true and fair view.
Auditor/Chief Accountant	Chief Accountant who signs the accounts is responsible to the head of a company.	Auditor must be completely independent of the company and qualified under the Companies Act.
Accounts format	In Russia the format is very rigid per the National Chart of Accounts 2000 with stipulated synthetic accounts.	The format is of a very general nature as indicated by Schedule 4 of the Companies Act 1985. These are only general headings, the overwhelming principle being that enough detail must be given to show a true and fair view.
Regulation	State authorities	Independent professional organisations.
Depreciation	Property, plant and equipment are recognised at historic costs with the length of depreciation determined by the company	Fixed depreciation rates and times apply.
Revaluation	Revaluation is based on indexation and market valuation.	Revaluation is based on independently accepted market value.
Required frequency of accounts	Quarterly and annual accounting records are presented to "The Owners", the state taxation inspectorate and the state authorities controlling some aspect of the business activity and enterprise.	The shareholders, the tax authorities, the registrar of companies, these accounts are held there and are available for public examination.
Retention of records	5 years	7 years

1.8.2 Companies subject to statutory audit

In accordance with Russian auditing legislation, commercial non-governmental companies whose annual statutory financial statements are subject to statutory audit include:

1. All open joint-stock companies,
2. Banks and other credit institutions,
3. Insurance companies,
4. Commodity and stock exchanges,
5. Investment funds,
6. Charitable funds,
7. Companies (including state and municipal enterprises set up with the "right of economic authority") with annual sales exceeding 500,000 times the average official minimum monthly wage (these qualifications may be lower for municipal enterprises) for the reporting year,
8. Companies (including state and municipal enterprises set up with the "right of economic authority") with total balance sheet assets exceeding 200,000

times the average official minimum monthly wage (these qualifications may be lower for municipal enterprises) for the reporting year, and

9. Investment or state non-budgetary funds.

1.8.3 Accounting of foreign legal entities, branches and representative offices of foreign companies in Russia

The Law on Accounting is applicable to foreign legal entities, branches and representative offices in Russia, unless otherwise stipulated in international agreements of the Russian Federation. In setting up and maintaining an accounting function, including the preparation of financial statements, foreign legal entities, branches and representative offices in Russia may choose one of the following:

- ♦ Rules existing in the Russian Federation;
- ♦ Rules existing in the country where a foreign legal entity is located provided such rules do not contradict IAS.

1.9   Insolvency and bankruptcy

Federal Law of Russian Federation №127-FZ "On (Insolvency) Bankruptcy" (26 October 2002; the "Law on Bankruptcy") is the governing legislation on insolvency in Russian Federation. If a company with financial difficulties continues to trade, the company and/or its senior management may be liable under civil, administrative or criminal law to the creditors of that company.

At present time a debtor's failure to meet a liability within three months of its falling due is deemed to be a sufficient reason to be start bankruptcy procedures. This ruling is not rigidly applied and creditors can individually negotiate with shareholders for an amicable settlement including a rescue plan or the sale of the company assets to the creditors. The company's management can perform continue to perform its duties unless and until a court decision establishes otherwise.

1.9.1   Rules relating to receivership

Voluntary petitions of the enterprise itself or a procurator's in the event of fraud are acceptable reasons to close the company. Law on Bankruptcy stipulates a number of bankruptcy stages: "observation", "financial rehabilitation", "external management", "bankruptcy proceeding" and "voluntary settlement". Depending on its financial condition, a company may undergo all of these stages or just one or two of them. An application to institute bankruptcy proceedings may be made by any interested party and will be considered by the appropriate Arbitrazh Court of the Russian Federation. The first creditors' meeting is tasked with taking a decision on whether it is feasible to improve the debtor's position through the institution of "financial rehabilitation" or "external management." If improving the debtor's position is not feasible, the creditors' meeting will take the decision to institute "bankruptcy proceedings," which is in fact a liquidation procedure. A liquidated enterprise is subject to sale by auction.

There are strict regulations as to whom may be appointed as an administrator in bankruptcy. Among other requirements, the applicant should possess a higher education, have considerable managerial experience of not less than two years and insure against personal liability. In addition, creditors or a creditors' meeting may require a potential candidate to hold a degree in law or economics. Interested persons, that are among the others creditors of the bankrupt company and members of its management staff, may not be appointed as the administrator in bankruptcy. An additional guarantee of the appropriate activity of the administrators in bankruptcy is the requirement that he/she insures against personal liability with the amount of security depending on the net worth of the company. Prior to the commencement of bankruptcy proceedings (i.e., liquidation procedures), a company may undergo voluntary restructuring by the means of the "financial rehabilitation" procedure. The debtor company, a creditor or in certain cases a third party may propose the initiation of "financial rehabilitation".

In the event the procedure "external management" is instituted and an external manager appointed, the external manager must, within one month of his/her appointment develop and put forward a management plan, which should include, among other provisions the conditions and terms for implementation of the plan,. The "external management" process may last for a period of up to 18 months, and can be extended by the Arbitrazh Court for a period of not more than six months. "Financial rehabilitation" and "external management" procedures should together last no more than two years.

Bankruptcy proceedings under Russian law are generally similar to those prescribed by English law. There exist restrictions related to the debtor's dealing with its estate, appointment of a trustee/liquidator, management of the affairs of the debtor by the trustee, organisation of a creditors' committee, collection of assets and distribution thereof.

After the satisfaction of current payments incurred during the course of the bankruptcy proceedings, there is stipulated the following priorities in paying off the debts:

(a) Persons having a right to demand compensation for the infliction of injury to their health and survival;

(b) Payments to employees of the bankrupt enterprise in terms of their salaries, benefits, copyright and licence fees. This group should include the above said payments to those employees who are shareholders of the company;

(c) Other creditors.

Creditors secured by a pledge enjoy priority before other creditors' claims, except for those indicated in (a) and (b) above and those arising prior to the secured pledges.

Claims which still remain unpaid after the distribution of the entire estate of the debtor are deemed to be discharged.

The Law on Bankruptcy governs bankruptcy proceedings of all forms of enterprises, including joint ventures and enterprises with 100% foreign ownership. Specific rules apply to insurance companies, banks, securities market participants, agricultural, strategic organisations and natural monopolies. Special regulation of bankruptcy proceedings of banks, credit organisation and natural monopolies is governed by the Federal Law №40-FZ of "On Insolvency (Bankruptcy) of credit organisations" (25 February 1999) and Federal Law №122-FZ "On Insolvency (Bankruptcy) of Natural Monopolies in the Fuel and Energy Sector" (24 June 1999; this law is stated to expire on 1 July 2009).

1.10   Dispute resolution

The parties to a contract may handle a contractual dispute in court at their discretion or they may refer the dispute for final settlement to an arbitration tribunal.

Courts of three instances, acting under and regulated by the Arbitrazh Procedural Code of the Russian Federation, settle contractual disputes, grant injunctions, and review court rulings and decisions accordingly to their competent jurisdiction. Finally, a court decision may be reviewed by the Supreme Arbitrazh Court of the Russian Federation as part of supervisory review.

The complexity of procedure and long period of time in state courts as well as little knowledge of legal systems by both Western and Russian companies have led to the development of arbitration as the key means of handling contractual disputes.

Based on the UNCITRAL Model Law on International Commercial Arbitration and UNCITRAL Arbitration Rules (1976), Federal Law "On International Commercial Arbitration" was adopted and came into force in 1993.

The main arbitration tribunals in the Russian Federation (the Arbitrazh Court of the Russian Federal Chamber of Commerce and Industry and Russian Maritime Arbitration Committee) accept disputes for consideration and settlement if an arbitration agreement has been made by the parties, or the jurisdiction of the arbitration tribunal arises from an international agreement.

The enforcement of foreign arbitral awards in Russia, and Russian arbitral awards abroad, is based on the New York Convention on the Recognition and Enforcement of Foreign Arbitral Awards (1958), to which Russia is a party.

1.11 Intellectual property rights

Russia participates in the following international treaties and conventions:
- Convention establishing the World Intellectual Property Organisation
- Berne Convention for the Protection of Literary and Artistic Works
- Rome Convention for the Protection of Performers, Producers of Phonograms and Broadcasting Organisations
- Geneva Convention for the Protection of Producers of Phonograms Against Unauthorised Duplication of Their Phonograms
- World Copyright Treaty
- Nairobi Treaty on the Protection of the Olympic Symbol
- Paris Convention for the Protection of Industrial Property
- Patent Cooperation Treaty
- Eurasian Patent Convention
- Strasbourg Agreement Concerning the International Patent Classification
- Locarno Agreement Establishing an International Classification for Industrial Designs
- Budapest Treaty on the International Recognition of the Deposit of Micro organisms for the Purposes of Patent Procedure
- Madrid Agreement Concerning the International Registration of Trademarks
- Protocol Relating to the Madrid Agreement Concerning the International Registration of Trademarks
- Trademark Law Treaty
- Nice Agreement Concerning the International Classification of Goods and Services for the Purposes of the Registration of Trademarks

The national legislation of the Russian Federation on intellectual property protection is and goes in line with Western standards and reflects Russia's desire to adopt the principles embodied in international intellectual property conventions. Russian laws relating to copyright protection, patents, trademarks, etc. are well drafted and aim to improve the environment for foreign Trade & Investment. Historically, these include, for example, "On Copyright and Neighbouring Rights," "On the Legal Protection of Computer Software and Databases," "On the Legal Protection of Topographies of Integrated Circuits," "Patent Law of the Russian Federation," "On Trademarks, Service Marks, and Appellations of Origin of Goods." English and Russian texts of these documents can be found on website: www.fips.ru/ruptoen/index.htm. On 1 January 2008 the IV Part of the Russian Civil Code came into force, superseding the aforementioned statutes and established a new regime for Intellectual Property law.

The Federal Service for Intellectual Property, Patents and Trademarks (ROSPATENT) is a Federal authority which performs control and supervision in the area of the legal protection and exploitation of intellectual property rights, including patents and trademarks. As its main functions ROSPATENT:

– supervises the examination of applications for intellectual property rights;
– registers intellectual property rights, including rights in inventions, utility models and industrial designs and trademarks;
– registers license agreements and assignment agreements in the sphere of intellectual property;
– registers computer software and databases. Registration of computer software and databases is voluntarily as copyright in these objects originates at the moment of their creation and does not require any formal registration. However, copyright holders may wish to register their software or databases in order to facilitate the evidence and priority dates of their rights in future.
– publishes information on the registered intellectual property rights;
– supervision the procedures for the payment of patent fees and registration charges;
– certifies and registers patent attorneys of the Russian Federation;
– determines the procedure for the collection of state fees including patent annuities and trademark renewal fees.

A list of Intellectual Property agencies is given in Appendix 2

1.11.1 Counterfeit goods

Under the Customs Code, which came into force on 1 January 2004 and was last amended on 18 July 2005, Russian Customs can help owners of trademarks and other registered IP objects to prevent counterfeit goods from being imported into Russia from other countries. The owner who suspects that such importation may file an application with the State Customs Committee requesting assistance in protecting his intellectual property rights.

This will include:

1) details of the IP owner;
2) details of the item of IP in question;
3) details of the goods, which are considered by the IP owner as counterfeit;
4) the term during which the customs authorities are requested to take action in compliance with the Customs Code.

The Federal Customs Service (FCS) will consider the application and decide whether or not to take action. The FTS may refuse in case the information provided by the IP owner is unreliable or the formalities have not been met.

1.12 The Coalition for Intellectual Property Rights (CIPR)

CIPR is a private-public partnership dedicated solely to advancing intellectual property rights protection and reform in the CIS countries and the Baltic States. It works with government and private sector partners to establish transparent IPR regimes that adhere to international standards. The CIPR's corporate members include some of the world's most famous trademark, patent and brand owners. It also receives active support from state Patent and Trademark Offices throughout the region. The CIPR cooperates with the World Intellectual Property Organisation, United Nations Economic Commission for Europe, World Customs Organisation and International Anti-Counterfeiting Coalition, among others. For many of these it acts as their official observer. Through research, education, legislative initiatives, coalition building and legal, a judicial and regulatory reform, CIPR assists governments and businesses in the region to establish transparent and non-discriminatory IPR regimes and to adhere to international IPR standards. The Coalition for Intellectual Property Rights has produced a guide on using Cyrillic trade marks, which can be accessed on website: www.cipr.org./tips/using_cyr_tm.php

Contact:
The Coalition for Intellectual Property Rights
1 Duchess Street
London, UK W1W 6AN
Tel: 0207 580 6367
Fax: 0207 323 9859
Website: www.cipr.org

STEPTOE & JOHNSON

Lawyers to help you grow your business in Russia

We have experience in Russia in the following areas:

- Arbitration

- Corporate & Commercial

- Construction

- Due Diligence

- Energy

- Fraud

- International Trade

- Joint Ventures

- Litigation

- Mergers & Acquisitions

- Projects

- Property

- Technology & Telecommunications

99 GRESHAM STREET, LONDON, EC2V 7NG

TEL: +44(0)20 7367 8000 FAX: +44(0)20 7367 8001

WWW.STEPTOE.COM

LONDON   BRUSSELS   WASHINGTON   NEW YORK   CHICAGO   PHOENIX   LOS ANGELES

STEPTOE & JOHNSON

Lawyers to help you grow your business in Russia

If you would like a free initial consultation please contact any of the following members of our Russian team:

Adam Greaves
+44(0)20 7367 8050
agreaves@steptoe.com

Michael Thompson
+44(0)20 7367 8070
mthompson@steptoe.com

Egishe Dzhazoyan
+44(0)20 7367 8057
edzhazoyan@steptoe.com

99 GRESHAM STREET, LONDON, EC2V 7NG

TEL: +44(0)20 7367 8000   FAX: +44(0)20 7367 8001

WWW.STEPTOE.COM

LONDON   BRUSSELS   WASHINGTON   NEW YORK   CHICAGO   PHOENIX   LOS ANGELES

2. INTRODUCTION

Many forms of business enterprise operate within the Russian Federation. These vary from organisations regarded as a sole corporate to operations regarded as subservient to a legal entity. Setting up a business is becoming easier but considerable bureaucracy is involved in doing so. The Russian Civil Code (Part One) 1994 defines a sole corporate as a legal entity that:

♦ owns, manages or operates separate property,
♦ bears liability for its obligations with this property,
♦ may acquire and exercise property and personal non-property rights and responsibilities in its name, and
♦ may act as a plaintiff or defendant in court.

Foreign ownership and investment is encouraged. The Foreign Investment Law 1999 allows foreign investors to establish business organisations and be involved in joint venture projects.

2.1 Joint ventures

Many organisations investing in Russia do so by means of a joint venture. Whatever the form of the joint venture or corporate structure established, the company will need to be registered with the relevant authorities. A joint venture may be formed either:

♦ by founding a new company or partnership with a Russian legal entity;
♦ by an individual or company acquiring shares in an existing enterprise.

Closed joint stock companies and limited liability companies are the most favoured forms of company structure used by inward investors. Registration remains a complex process and British companies are advised to use the services of specialist organisations, with bilingual facilities, which are experienced in this field of work. Details of these may be obtained from UK Trade & Investment Russia Unit Tel: 020 7215 4891; Website: www.uktradeinvest.gov.uk/ukti/app-manager/ukti/countries?_nfls=false&_nfpb=true&_pageLabel=CountryType1&navigationPageId=/russia

Joint ventures were first permitted by the former Soviet authorities in 1987 as a means of attracting foreign investment into the Soviet economy. Since 1989 foreign companies have been permitted to take an unlimited share (a minimum of 10% is required to take advantage of the profits reinvestment tax privilege) in joint ventures (with several exceptions) and since 1999 have received state guarantees from the future unfavourable changes of the tax regime applied on the date of establishment.

2.1.1. Setting up a joint venture

The term "joint venture" may be interpreted in two ways in Russia. Firstly, it is a joint venture agreement (a.k.a. cooperation agreement) under which the parties undertake to join their contributions in order to achieve certain business goals. That means the parties do not establish a separate company. Secondly, a "joint venture" may refer to any Russian company with foreign investments. Hereafter the second meaning of the term "joint venture" will be used. Federal Law No. 160-FZ "On foreign investments in the Russian Federation" (9 July 1999) provides that companies with foreign investment should be established in the forms provided by Russian Law (e.g. joint stock companies, limited liability companies, etc.).

Joint ventures may be set up between any Russian enterprise and a foreign company. These have mostly been established by investing in privatised companies. The share capital must be denominated in Roubles regardless of the currency contributed.

Like any Russian entities, joint ventures should be registered with the respective local tax authority office. Joint ventures will also need to register their presence with the local tax inspectorate, in non-budgetary funds including the Social Security Fund, Pension Fund and Compulsory Medical Insurance Fund, and with the Statistics Committee.

Local offices (tax inspectorates) of the Moscow Department of the Federal Tax Service of the Russian Federation are in charge of the state registration of companies and some other legal entities, which are located in Moscow.

Contact:

Moscow Department of the Federal Tax Service of the Russian Federation
15 Tulskaya Street; Moscow 115191
Tel: 007 495 957 6410; Fax: 007 495 958 2558; E-mail: u77@r77.nalog.ru
Website: www.mosnalog.ru (This site is in Russian only)

Most companies, however, will want to leave registration to their lawyers or accountants, details of which are available from UK Trade & Investment Russia Unit Tel: 020 7215 4891; Website: www.uktradeinvest.gov.uk/ukti/appmanager/ ukti/countries?_nfls=false&_nfpb=true&_pageLabel=CountryType1&navigation PageId=/russia. Average professional costs for registering a company may range from US$5,000 to $8,000.

The documents required for the registration of a joint venture to be established by means of the foundation are the same as required for any other Russian company, namely:

- An application form, which should be notarized;
- Constitutional documents, or notarised copies thereof;
- A protocol, contract or other document confirming the decision to create the company;
- An extract from the trade register from the state of incorporation of the foreign company or a similar document evidencing the incorporation of a foreign company under the respective foreign law;
- Documents evidencing the payment of state duty.

In accordance with state registration procedures, companies should be registered within five days of the receipt of registration documents, for a fee of 2,000 Roubles.

All documents coming from abroad must be apostilled or legalised in the respective country. If the documents are in English a notarised translation should also be submitted. A document notarised in the UK or anywhere outside of Russia is useless if it has not been legalised.

Russian companies must maintain its books on statutory model forms approved by the Ministry of Finance, have its bookkeeping carried out by the chief accountant and accountants in accordance with Russian accounting standards (governed by Federal law "On accounting and accountancy" and provisions on accounting of fixed assets, cash, intangible assets and other objects of accounting), and file accounting and statistical reports in accordance with established procedure. Russian accounting standards are slowly beginning to follow internationally accepted accounting standards, which means, in the case of Russian companies with foreign investment, keeping only one set of books to satisfy both partners.

Whilst Russian company law stipulates that the provisions of charters or contracts that violate shareholder's rights are void, purchasers of shares in a Russian joint stock company should still carefully scrutinise the foundation documents for details of the shareholders' rights, e.g. voting rights or rights to receive dividends.

2.1.2 Repatriation of profits

The main concern of British partners is the repatriation of profits. Russian resident entities are required to convert 10% of their foreign-currency revenues from exports of goods and services into Roubles. The foreign currency must be sold through an authorised foreign exchange dealer.

With the advent of an alternative form of representation in Russia, there has been a move away from joint ventures by foreign investors as a preferred form of business operation as they are dependent, to a greater or lesser extent, on the commitment and ability of Russian partners, who may not share similar aims and perspectives.

In circumstances where there is little or no interest in management involvement or in long-term earnings, a straightforward contractual arrangement is preferable. These may include (I) licensing agreements involving the transfer of technology in return for defined royalties; (ii) turn key construction involving the provision of engineering and services in return for a fixed fee; (iii) contract manufacturing involving the provision of technology and funding for a negotiated quantity; (iv) straight sales agreements; (v) management contracts; (vi) production sharing agreements; (vii) leasing agreements and (viii) a host of other contractual understandings which may not even have a label, and which are tailored to the specifics of complex transactions. (Joint Ventures in Russia: The ten year lesson- Jeffrey A Burt)

Nevertheless, joint ventures remain a tested and accepted method of investment, particularly for production ventures. Frequently, such projects revolve around the local partner's provision of factory premises and a workforce, with the foreign side investing machinery, capital and know-how. A good joint venture partner can provide not only premises and a skilled workforce but also, often most importantly, local knowledge. The latter may be advantageous if legal and bureaucratic problems arise. In addition, substantial grants and loans may be available to joint ventures through the inward investing partner.

2.2 Open joint stock companies (OAO)

The formation and existence, including corporate governance issues, of an Open Joint Stock Company ("OAO") are governed, like a Closed Joint Stock Company, largely by the Russian Civil Code, Federal Law No. 208-FZ "On joint stock companies" (26 December 1995).

- An OAO is governed by its charters and must be registered;
- The liability of shareholders of an OAO is limited.
- An OAO must be registered.
- Shareholders are free to sell their shares.
- At least 50% of the company shares placed at the time of incorporation should be paid within three months following registration;
- No more than 25% of the shareholding may be preference shares.
- Securities issue tax is payable upon an application to register new shares issues.
- Minority shareholders may have limited control of the operation.
- An OAO must convene a shareholders meeting at least once annually.

- An annual report containing accounts must be published.
- Information in respect of all affiliates must be disclosed to the appropriate registration authorities on a quarterly basis.
- A Board of Directors is mandatory.
- An OAO with more than 1,000 shareholders but less than 10,000, with voting rights, must have at least 7 members of the Board of Directors.
- An OAO with more than 10,000 shareholders, with voting rights, must have at least 9 members of the Board of Directors
- A Management Board is not mandatory.
- The minimum capitalisation required is 1,000 minimum monthly wages.
- Capital contributions may be in cash or in kind, e.g. assets or intellectual property.
- An OAO may be 100% foreign owned, except in certain sectors, for example, defence-related industries where foreign ownership is limited to 25%.
- General Manager (Director) is a mandatory sole executive body, which is generally in charge of running the company and day-to-day operations.
- OAO's must have a reserve fund amounting to at least 5% of Charter Capital.
- Dividends are paid out of profits after taxation and subject to income tax withheld at the source of payment.
- Capital gains are treated as a part of profits for legal entities and as a part of income for individuals.
  An OAO:
- may open and maintain bank accounts in Roubles or hard currency;
- is entitled to enter into contracts with Russian legal entities and individuals;
- may carry forward tax losses for a ten year period, with certain restrictions;
- may import and export goods;
- may issue its own visa invitations;
- must be independently audited.

2.3   Closed joint stock companies (ZAO)

The formation and existence (including corporate governance issues) of Closed Joint Stock Company are governed largely by the Russian Civil Code, Federal Law N 208-FZ "On joint stock companies" (26 December 1995).

- Closed joint stock companies are governed by their charters and must be registered.
- Shareholders (of which there must be at least one but no more than 50) have limited liability.
- Minority shareholders may have a greater control of the business, if permitted in the charter, particularly with regard to the transfer of shares.
- No more than 25% of the shareholding can be preference shares;
- Securities issue tax is payable upon application to register new stock issues;
- Annual meetings are required.
- A Board of Directors is optional.
- A ZAO must have at least one and no more than 50 shareholders.
- A shareholder in closed joint stock company has a pre-emptive right to purchase company shares.
- At least 50% of a company's shares placed at the time of incorporation should be paid within three months of registration.
- Dividends are paid out of profits after taxation and subject to income tax withheld at the source of payment.

- Capital gains are treated as a part of profits for legal entities and as a part of income for individuals.
  The ZAO:
- May be 100% foreign owned;
- Must have a reserve fund amounting to at least 5% of its charter capital;
- May open and maintain bank accounts in Roubles and hard currency in Russia;
- May enter into contracts with Russian legal entities and individuals;
- May carry forward tax losses for a ten year period, with certain restrictions;
- May import and export goods;
- May apply for visa invitations.

2.4   Limited liability companies (OOO)

The formation of a Limited Liability Company ("OOO") is governed largely by the Russian Civil Code and the Federal Law No. 14-F3 "On Limited Companies" (8 February 1998).

- Limited liability companies are governed by their charters and their foundation agreements, except where an OOO has only one shareholder, in which case only a charter is required. The charter is always deemed to be the prevailing document.
- An OOO is not required to issue share capital, but instead has a charter fund.
- The minimum capitalisation required is 100 minimum monthly wages (R100 per person), of which at least 50% should be paid by the date of registration.
- A Board of Directors is not mandatory.
- A Management Board is not mandatory.
- An OOO must have at least one and no more than 50 shareholders.
- An OOO must convene shareholders' meeting at least once annually.
- An OOO may not be a 100% owned subsidiary of a company, which has one shareholder (member).
- Dividends are paid out of profits after taxation and subject to withholding income tax at the source of payment.
- Capital gains are treated as a part of profits for legal entities and as a part of income for individuals.
  Under Article 8 of Federal Law "On State Registration of Entities," state registration must be completed within five working days after the date the application is submitted.

2.5.   Additional liability company

These differ from limited liability companies (see 2.4) only in that members have subsidiary ("appendant") liability together with the company. Within this liability they are jointly and severally liable in proportion to their contributions to the company's charter capital.

2.6. Partnerships

The Civil Code recognises Full Partnerships and Limited Partnerships. These are capitalised by contributions from their participants. In terms of tax and currency regulations, partnerships whose place of business is in the Russian Federation are treated as Russian residents.

2.6.1　Limited partnerships

♦ Limited partnerships are governed by their foundation agreements.
♦ Limited partnerships are deemed as an independent legal entity in Russian Law.
♦ At least two partners (at the moment of foundation) must have unlimited liability in addition to other partners who will have limited liability.
♦ A limited liability partner's obligations are restricted to the partner's charter capital contribution.
♦ As shares are not issued they are usually not subject to securities legislation, unless such companies issue bonds.

2.6.2　Full partnerships

♦ A full partnership is an independent legal entity under Russian Law.
♦ All partners bear joint and several responsibilities for the obligations of a full partnership.
♦ Liability is unlimited.
♦ Any commercial organisations and individual entrepreneurs may become partners in the partnership.
♦ The profits and losses of a general partnership are shared between the partners and are commensurate with each partner's respective share in the charter capital, unless otherwise stipulated.

2.7　100% Foreign-owned subsidiaries

Overseas companies are permitted to own fully owned subsidiaries in most industries (except for defence-related enterprises, aviation, several types of activities in mass media business etc.). The establishment of a fully owned subsidiary is becoming the favoured route taken by retailers owing to the control it offers them over the running of their operation in Russia. 100% foreign-owned subsidiaries should be established in the forms provided by Russian law (e.g. joint stock companies, limited liability companies etc.).

♦ Foreign-owned subsidiaries require a charter and/or other foundation documents, provided by Russian laws.
♦ Share participation in any enterprises established jointly with Russian legal entities is permitted.
♦ The right to trade within Russia independent of the parent company is established.
♦ There is no liability of the subsidiary for the debts of the parent company. A parent company that has the right (including on the basis of a contract) to give its subsidiary company instructions, which are mandatory, shall be jointly liable with the subsidiary for transactions made by the latter in the performance of such instructions.
♦ Subsidiaries can issue their own visa support.
♦ Russian taxation applies.
♦ Establishment of an accredited representative office is not a legal requirement.

2.7.1　Registration procedures of 100% foreign-owned subsidiaries

Registration of an organisation can only be obtained through the respective tax office. Registration requires the submission of:

♦ Application form;

- Constitutional documents, or notarised copies thereof;
- A protocol, contact or other document confirming the decision to create the company;
- Extract from the trade register from the state of incorporation of the foreign company;
- Documents evidencing the payment of state duty.

The respective tax authority office should issue a certificate of registration within five working days of the application.

2.8.   Branches of a foreign company

- Branches of a foreign company in Russia must be accredited.
- Branches can be accredited for a maximum term of five years, after which accreditation must be renewed.
- Branches are not independent legal entities under Russian law.
- The parent company has unlimited liability for the activities of a branch office.
- Branches operate under a parent company's power of attorney. This must be stated expressly in the foreign company's charter.
- For the purposes of currency regulation branches are considered to be non-residents.
- Branches are allowed to carry out commercial activity in Russia. The proceeds from such activity are subject to the same corporate taxation rules as applied to other Russian companies.

2.9.   Representative offices of foreign companies

Representative offices are not independent legal entities under Russian law. Other rules relating to representative offices include:

- A representative office may be accredited for up to three years.
- After accreditation, a representative office must be registered with the State Registration Chamber.
- The parent company is liable for any obligations arising out of the activities of the representative office.
- A representative office may open and maintain bank accounts in Roubles and hard currency.
- A representative office is entitled to enter into contracts with Russian legal entities and individuals on behalf of the head office and on the basis of a power-of-attorney.
- A representative office may register automobiles.
- A representative office participating in commercial activities of foreign companies in Russia are considered to comprise a taxable permanent establishment and proceeds (including deemed proceeds) from such activities are subject to the same corporate taxation as is applied to Russian companies.

2.9.1 Registration/accreditation procedures for a representative office

The below text is taken from the website of the State Registration Chamber of the Ministry of Justice. The link below is in the Russian language only.

www.palata.ru/cgi-bin/get_page.cgi?pid=60

To accredit a representative office of a foreign company at the State Registration Chamber the following documents should be submitted:

- Written application indicating the name of the company, the date of its establishment, location, core business activities, purpose of the representative office, proposed period of operation of the representative office, information about the company's business ties with Russian partners and prospects for the development of cooperation;
- Extract from the Trade Register or other official document confirming the fact of registration of the foreign company in accordance with the requirements of the country where the company was registered;
- By-laws or statute of the company (or another adequate document replacing the said documents or an official confirmation that these documents are not required for the certain company) in accordance with the requirements of the country where the company was registered;
- Document confirming the decision of the company to open a representative office on the territory of the Russian Federation;
- Statute of the representative office (original and a notarized copy);
- Bank certificate or another document containing information that evidences the firm's solvency;
- Reference letters from Russian business partners (at least two);
- A notarized copy of the general power of attorney issued to the head of the representative office;
- A notarized power of attorney to a representative of the company empowering him/her to represent the company before the State Registration Chamber and to take all necessary actions for the opening of a representative office;
- Document confirming the address of the representative office in the Russian Federation (e.g. a guarantee letter or a lease agreement including confirmation of the landlord's title to the premises);
- Document confirming the consent of local authorities of the Russian Federation to the opening of the representative office (in case the representative office is located outside Moscow or St Petersburg);
- Questionnaire in respect of the representative office.

Documents issued abroad must be legalized or apostilled. In addition, these documents should be translated into Russian and a notary must certify the translation.

2.10. Franchises

Franchises are becoming more common in the Russian Federation, particularly in Moscow and St Petersburg. The operation of a structured franchise provides some protection to the principal and may free it of many of the day to day worries concerned with running a business.

2.11 Production cooperatives

These are voluntary associations organised for the purpose of joint production or other business activities of individuals who contribute their personal labour and who pool together property contributions. These organisations are rare and are largely limited to the agricultural sector.

2.12 Consumer cooperatives

Consumer co-operatives are non-commercial associations that supply goods and services to their members. Members undertake to pay membership dues.

2.13　Individual entrepreneurs

Individuals may register in their own right to undertake business activities in the Russian Federation. Generally individual entrepreneurs are subject to a simplified system of taxation (individual entrepreneurs are entitled to elect either 6% of the gross proceeds or 15% of the net proceeds). For certain types of activities as determined by the regional authorities, imputed income tax may be applied calculated on the basis of the potential profitability of that particular type of activity.

2.14　Non-governmental organisations (NGOs) and charities

Today in Russia there are approximately 300,000 NGOs, all of which are trying to improve the conditions and lives of the Russian people.

The Charities Aid Foundation – CAF Russia, since 1993, has helped hundreds of charitable and non-profit organisations in Russia, awarding them over $6,000,000 in grants.

CAF Russia's activities include:

NGO services:

◆ Free consultations on legal and financial problems, fundraising and the development of civil society.

◆ An NGO School. (See website: www.ngoschool.org/)

◆ Monthly meetings of the Lawyers and Accountants clubs for NGOs.

Donor services:

◆ Collecting and disseminating information about Russian non-profit organisations.

◆ Assisting in the development and management of philanthropic programmes. Grant making programmes:

◆ Distributing grants for international charity foundations, government agencies and companies.

Developing new ways of bringing funds to the non-profit sector:

◆ Setting up community foundations and local charitable organisations to distribute funds at a local level.

◆ Managing programmes to encourage funding from Russian émigrés who wish to support their country of birth.

Information services:

◆ CAF Russia Library, which houses over 6,000 publications related to philanthropy in the third sector.

◆ Magazine 'Money and Charity'.

◆ Websites in English and Russian.

Contact: CAF Russia, 24/2 Tverskaya Street, Build. 1, Entrance 3, 5th floor, 125009 Moscow

Tel: 007 495 792 5929; Fax: 007 495 792 5986; E-mail: cafrussia@cafrussia.ru

Website: www.cafrussia.ru

Moscow · London · Nicosia

10 services you need
to start up your
business in Russia

01. Legal Advice

02. Tax Planning

03. Rent Assistance

04. Market Research

05. Staff Recruitment

06. Accounting Support

07. Company Formation

08. Document Translation

09. Work Permits and Visas

10. IT Installation & Support

www.go2russia.org   www.gsl.co.uk

Moscow · London · Nicosia

Services you need
to start up your
business in Russia

Tax Planning

Corporate Tax Structuring · Payroll Services · Indirect Tax and Customs · International Taxation "Transfer Pricing · Personal Income Tax · Utilization of Regional Tax Concessions · VAT and Customs Duties Exemptions · Preferential Tax Treatment Offshore Solutions · Cross-Border Structuring · Inheritance and Estate Planning

Accounting and Audit

Russian Statutory Audit & Accounting · International Financial Reporting Standards · Russian Accounting Procedures Bookkeeping · Accounting Advisory · Preparation and Filing of Tax Returns · Corporate Reporting Improvement · Financial Statement Audit · Assistance in Negotiations with the Tax Authorities · Compliance & Due Dilligence · Internal Audit

Legal Services

Corporate Law and Securities Regulations · M&A and Capital Raising · Company Formation · Litigation Services · Tax and Other Dispute Resolutions with Official Authorities in Courts and Out of Court · Migration Services and Work Permits · Legal Support of Transactions · Real Estate and Land Law.

3. TAXATION AND FISCAL POLICY

3   TAXATION AND FISCAL POLICY

3.1   The Russian tax system

The tax and fiscal system in Russia has developed rapidly over the past 15 years, culminating in the Tax Code, 1999. Since 1991, the number of taxes and duties and registration fees that an average business taxpayer has to consider has reduced from 64 to fewer than 20. Cumulatively, this is not very different to the number of taxes paid, in one form or another, by companies in the United Kingdom. Whilst the evolutionary process is far from complete, principle forms of taxation have been established and accepted.

The structure of the Russian tax system provides revenues for three budgetary tiers: federal, regional and local. All taxes are legislated at the federal level, although regional and local governments have the power to set tax rates in respect of taxes given to their competence.

Part 1 of the present Russian Tax Code, dealing with administrative matters, came into force on 1 January 1999. The first four chapters of Part 2 deal with VAT (Chapter 21), excise duties tax (Chapter 22), individual income tax (Chapter 23) and Unified Social Tax (Chapter 24) entered into force on 1 January 2001, while Chapter 25, on profits tax, became effective on 1 January 2002. Further the Tax Code was added with Chapters on business property and transport taxes (which are regional taxes), land tax (local), taxes on extraction and use of natural resources, special tax regimes for small and specific businesses (e.g. gambling), Chapter on stamp duties.

The Tax Code made significant and welcome improvements in the regime, including a flat rate income tax rate of 13%, and a company tax rate of 24%, low rates international and historical standards. As is usual with tax laws, "the devil is in the detail" and this Chapter flags some of the warnings. Many of these problems are being discussed at official level, and may in due course be overcome. With these caveats, taxation is no longer a serious obstacle to investing in Russia.

The headline rates are misleading. Employment income is also subject to the unified social tax (up to 26%) and so called workplace accident insurance (rates from 0.2 to 8.5% depending on the risk). Dividends received by Russian resident companies are taxed at 9%, but because there is no credit for the underlying company tax, the effective tax burden on distributed profits is 30.84%. Therefore virtually the only categories of income taxed at the 13% rate are some (by no means all) types of interest and gains from realising securities and other property ("capital gains").

VAT was first introduced in Russia in 1992, replacing turnover tax and sales tax. The law on VAT was replaced in 2001 by the VAT chapter of the tax code. In principle, it follows the European Union model, with a general rate of 18%, and a reduced rate of 10% on certain basic food products and goods for children. Some goods and services are subject to VAT at a zero rate (VAT incurred on inputs may still be reclaimed). Exports are also zero rated. As in the EU, financial services are exempt which means that input VAT cannot be recovered. Unlike EU practice, certain professional services are similarly treated, creating some surprising problems.

There are still many serious complaints about the way in which the tax system is administered. There are many instances where the local inspector is less familiar than one might have hoped to expect with the current legal provisions, the appeal procedures are not satisfactory and the system of penalties even for honest mistakes can be arbitrary and severe.

The legal system in Russia is based on civil law and lower courts are not formally bound to follow precedents or judgments issued by superior courts except for the Higher Arbitration Court and the Constitutional Court. To enforce the payment of taxation, tax collectors have salaries tied to the amount of fines levied. Owing to ambiguity in legislation, taxes levied and fines imposed are often challenged. Evasion and a high level of tax arrears still present a problem.

3.2 Corporate Profits Tax

The tax code corporate profits tax chapter, effective 1 January 2002, reduced the maximum rate of profit tax from 35% to 24%. Since 1 January 2005 6.5% of this sum goes to the Federal government, 17.5% to the Regional governments. Regional legislative authorities are allowed to reduce (for certain categories of taxpayers) the tax payable to their respective budgets by maximum four percentage points, thus in some regions of Russia the regional portion of profits tax may amount to 13.5%.

Dividends paid to another Russian entity which is a resident of the Russian Federation are subject to a 9% withholding tax (Article 275(2).

Dividends received from a foreign company are subject to 9% tax, payable by the Russian company recipient (Article 284(3(2)). Russian domestic law imposes a 15% withholding tax (Article 284(3(3)) on dividends payable to foreign corporate shareholders.

Some organisations believe, or have found, that where dividends are paid from one Russian company to another, the "9%" rate is applied with no credit for underlying tax. This is not necessarily the case. Since 2008, dividends received this way can in fact be treated as "franked" and paid on up the chain with no further charges.

Foreign companies having no taxable presence in Russia are also taxed on
• Gains from the distribution of property, including liquidation payments (20%),
• Gains from sale of shares and derivatives based on such shares in a qualified company (24% of net profit or 20% of total takings if expenditure evidence is not available). A company will be qualified if its assets are comprised of immovable property located in the Russian Federation and the share of such property exceeds 50% of total assets.
• Leasing payments (10%-20%)
• Royalties (20%)
• Interest (20%)
• Other "similar" income (20%) as explained in the recommendations of the Ministry of Taxes published in May 2003.

Foreign legal entities working through a Russian permanent establishment can rely on Articles 306-308 where the definition of such activity and rules of taxation are contained.

It is also provided that several Russian branches of the company carrying on business activities as a part of one technological process or with a special permission of the Ministry of Finance, can calculate their tax liability for the whole legal entity and not separately for each branch as normally required

3.2.1 Deductible expenses

Formally deductible expenses cover all major types of expenditure including:
♦ most insurance premiums;

- entertainment expenses up to a limit expressed as a percentage of payroll;
- certain types of advertising up to a limit expressed as a percentage of turn-over;
- interest on loans with application of the thin capitalization rules;
- business trips, again within the allowed limits.

Strict documentation requirements apply.

Deductibility of expenses remains one of the most controversial areas as it is conditional on two subjectively treated criteria – "economically justifiable expenses" and "expenses borne for the purposes of activity carried on to earn profit".

3.2.2 Treatment of losses

The treatment of carry forward losses is ill-defined, and great care needs to be taken, particularly when new businesses are likely to incur start-up costs in Russia, as such costs incurred before an entity is registered are non-deductible. Generally losses can be carried forward for 10 years and there are certain further restrictions. Carry-back is not available.

3.2.3 Filing and payment procedures

(i) An annual declaration must be filed by March 28 of the year following the end of the reporting year. Interim declarations (quarterly or monthly) must be filed within 28 days following the end of a reporting period. Profits tax is payable by the 28th day of the chosen period.

(ii) For small businesses, tax may be computed on either an accruals or on a cash basis. A small business for the purposes of this article is defined as an organisation having no more than 4 million rubles turnover within preceding 4 quarters.

(iii) Late payment interest is 1/300 of the official Refinancing rate (currently 10%) per day. Fixed late filing and late payment (non-payment) penalties also apply.

3.2.4 Arms length rules

Basic transfer pricing rules are stipulated in Article 40 of the Tax Code. Prices may be questioned by the tax authorities not only in related party transactions, but also in any international operation or in cases where the actual price deviates more than 20 % from the «price level used by the taxpayer on the same or identical goods and services within a short period of time». Generally the transfer pricing legislation is known to be vague and unsatisfactory and is going to be completely replaced from 2009.

A key anti-avoidance provision for international business is Art 269 of the Russian Tax Code, which deals with non-arms length loans.

Debt interest may be charged at a rate which does not deviate more than 20% from "the average level of interest calculated on similar liabilities issued in the same quarter on comparable terms" At the tax-payer's option debt interest may be charged at 1.1 times the re-financing rate of the Central Bank of Russia (for loans in Roubles) or 15% for debt liabilities in foreign currency.

The above restrictions apply to both domestic and international transactions but the thin capitalisation provisions apply only where there is a debt due to a foreign organisation (or its Russian affiliate), which directly or indirectly owns more than 20% of the capital of the Russian organisation. This debt is known as a controlled debt. To prevent the avoidance of tax by stripping out profits as tax deductible interest instead of as dividends paid out of after-tax profits, part of interest on any debt in excess of a debt equity ratio of 3:1) is disallowed as a deduction, and treated as a dividend taxed under Item 3 of Art 284. The exact amount of disallowable interest is calculated under a special formula.

3.3 Employment income

Employment income of tax residents is subject to income tax and also to unified social tax and workplace accident insurance, which now replace contributions to the four Russian social funds. The unified social tax and the insurance are the employer's liability.

3.3.1 Income Tax

Income tax is levied at 13% from income of tax residents and 30% from income of tax non-residents.

3.3.1.1 Tax residence and tax compliance

Income tax is payable by all residents. If an individual, irrespectively of citizenship, is physically present in Russia for 183 days or more in a calendar year, he is considered permanently resident in Russia for tax purposes, and will be subject to tax on worldwide income for that year. If an individual is physically present in Russia for less than 183 days, he is considered to be non-resident, and is subject to tax only on income (benefits-in-kind) received for work in Russia (irrespectively of the place or entity of payment) or from sources in Russia. In case no payment (recharge of expenses) is made from (to) a Russia based entity, most of double tax treaties protect non-residents from Russian tax.

Individuals having Russian tax underpaid liabilities are obliged to submit a declaration before 30 April of each subsequent year. Tax due under the declaration should be paid before 15 July.

In case an individual leaves Russia before the year end the tax return should be submitted one month prior to departure from Russia. A formal exit permit is not required.

3.3.1.2 Allowances, deductions and exemptions

State social benefits, including maternity pay, severance payments and reimbursement of business expenses, up to a statutory limit, are exempt (Article 217). Other allowances, deductions and exemptions include:

- Personal allowance of Roubles 400 a month. Children allowance of Roubles 600 a month per child.
- Gifts and inherited property between close relatives. Employer reimbursement of medical service expenses.
- A one-off amount spent on the purchase or construction of a residence within the limit of Roubles 1,000,000.
- Interest from deposits in Russian banks within 9% annual rate in foreign currencies and within Centrobank Rate of Refinancing in Roubles (currently 10%).
- Mortgage interest on residential housing.
- Charitable donations within certain limits.
- Education and medical costs up to Roubles 100,000 a year.
- Disability and war injury allowances.
- Proceeds from sale of a real estate property within the limit of Roubles 1 million if it was owned by the taxpayer for less than three years; total proceeds are exempt if property was owned for more that 3 years.

◆ Proceeds from the sale of other property (with certain exceptions for securities and shares in companies) within a limit of Roubles 125,000 if it was owned by the taxpayer for less than three years and full exemption if owned for 3 years or more.

3.3.2 Unified Social Tax (UST)

The UST has three elements: federal budget, social insurance and medical insurance. The unified social tax is levied on employers on all payments to individuals under employment agreements, civil-legal contracts of a service nature, and on copyright agreements (Article 236), including certain benefits in kind (Article 237). Since 1st January 2003 the UST has been applied to expatriates as well as Russian citizens. Tax residence status does not influence the UST liability.

3.3.2.1 UST liability

Tax is calculated separately for each employee based on the cumulative annual income at regressive rates as follows: (Article 241).

From 0 up to Roubles 280,000 26%

From Roubles 280,001 to Roubles 600,000 Roubles 72,800 + 10% of the amount exceeding Roubles 280,001;

More than Roubles 600,000 Roubles 104,800 + 2% of the amount exceeding Roubles 600,000.

These turning points are adjusted for inflation. In addition to UST employers must pay "workplace accident insurance" The rate depends on the degree of risk, varying from 0.2% to 8.5% of payroll.

3.3.3 Pensions

There are both compulsory (part of UST) and voluntary pension arrangements in Russia. Recent reforms are unclear, complex and changing. In addition, there are useful, but not yet wholly satisfactory, provisions for voluntary private pensions and a new regime by which some part of the compulsory pensions can, at the option of the pensioner be transferred to a private fund manager.

3.4 Individual income taxation of interest, dividends and other non-employment income.

Non-employment income is generally taxable at 13% or 30% tax rates depending on tax residence. There are however some exceptions. Dividends of tax residents are taxable at 9% and 35% tax is established for residents' excessive bank interest, insurance payments and material gain arising from interest free or low interest loans from non-banking institutions unrelated to purchase of accommodation.

3.4.1 Tax withholding

Income paid to an individual by a Russian organization or from the Russian permanent establishment of a foreign company is subject to income tax withheld at source. Where an individual receives income subject to Russian tax but where the tax was not withheld at source, a taxpayer has an obligation to submit a Russian tax return. Article 218 imposes an obligation on Russian companies, permanent establishments of foreign companies and individual entrepreneurs to act as tax agents, while other articles list specific payments which have to be taxed at source. There is no further guidance (apart from the above obligation to pay) on how to tax Russian non-residents receiving untaxed income. Enforcement is difficult, with the unified computerized system for circulating and processing documents not yet in place, the process is still bureaucratic and cumbersome.

Any income payable to a non-resident is subject to withholding tax at 30%, unless reduced by a treaty provision (Article 224(3)). The simple Russian definition does not deal with the various forms of financial instruments used in company finance, and since a dividend is defined by exclusion in Russian tax law, all relevant payments not explicitly dealt with appear to be taxed as a dividend income.

3.4.2   Sale of securities and other property

Russian tax law does not recognize a separate tax on capital gains. All gains realized by a resident individual are taxed under the provision of Chapter 23 of the Tax Code. Non-residents are taxed only on
* Russian immovable property,
* Securities in the Russian Federation
* Other types of property in Russia belonging to a taxpayer.

It provides that gains from alienation of property are taxed as ordinary income of an individual, adding such income to the income from other sources. The rates of tax are 13% for residents and 30% for non-residents (Article 224). The taxable amount is calculated as the difference between sale proceeds and historical cost or application of a statutory exemption. The statutory exemption is provided for all property sold by tax residents during a calendar year and is limited to Roubles 1 million in the case of real estate and Roubles 125,000 for other property. Proceeds received from the sale of property are fully excluded from taxation if the property is owned for three years or more.

3.5   Value Added Tax

VAT was first introduced in Russia in 1992. The present law is based on the new Tax Code (Part 2, Chapter 21) effective 1 January 2001.

Russian VAT is based on the EU "credit invoice" model. Registered businesses add VAT to the price of assets, goods and services supplied ("output tax") and at the end of each month pay over the total of the output tax so charged, less the "input tax" borne on goods and services supplied to them.

Whilst VAT is generally levied at a rate of 18%, there is a reduced rate of 10% on certain basic food products, drugs and medical goods, printed materials and goods for children.

Some goods and services are subject to VAT at a zero rate, e.g., medical services and transportation of export cargo. Exports are also zero rated.

VAT incurred on inputs used for the zero rated operations may be reclaimed. (Article 164, 165), though in practice reclaim may often be seriously delayed or even refused

Starting 2006 constructors may heave a sigh of relief, because finally they may claim input VAT monthly before completion of a construction.

Generally, registered traders are required to file VAT returns and pay VAT due for each quarter by the 20th of the following month.

A small trader has the right to operate without VAT if his turnover from sale of goods or services during a period of three preceding months falls below Roubles 2,000,000 (Article 145).

3.5.1   Coverage and exemption

Article 146 gives a list of taxable events for VAT purposes, and expressly excludes:

- Currency transactions (including both Russian and foreign currency) (Article 39(3(1)))
- Various company property transactions (Article 39(3(2-6))
- Article 149 gives a list of transaction not subject to VAT, i.e. exempt without the right to reclaim input tax. As in the EU, these include a wide range of financial services including basic banking and insurance services, educational services by certified establishments, sale of certain vitally important medical equipment, passenger transportation, and certain other socially important services.
- Leasing of buildings to foreign companies and individuals, provided that there is an analogous regime in place for a Russian taxpayer in a home country of a foreign taxpayer (Article 149(1)) (This is a very odd provision, which could inhibit a valuable source of funding for Russian SMEs.)
- Services supplied outside Russia do not fall in the scope of Russian VAT. Consequently, tax credits are not available for input tax. Services are deemed to be provided in Russia if they are performed by an enterprise that conducts economic activity in Russia. However, there is an important exception to this rule. The transfer of intangible property and the provision of consulting, legal, accounting, advertising, engineering, leasing of any movable property (with an exception of road vehicles) and certain similar services are deemed to be rendered in the country where the buyer of such services conducts its activities (Article 148(1(4))).

This means that professional firms based in Russia and having foreign customers can in practice only recover part of their input tax, which is a serious distortion of the principles of VAT.

3.5.2   Registration for foreigners

There's no separate VAT registration procedure or VAT number – all the taxpayers which have been allocated a general Taxpayer Identity Number (TIN) are automatically within the VAT scope and use their TIN for VAT filing.

Registered Russian and foreign businesses are obliged to withhold VAT upon payment for VATable transactions to non-registered foreign partners. This obligation became generally unavoidable due to recently banks have become required to refuse payment transfer if VAT is not simultaneously withheld and paid to the budget, i.e. their clients have to prove that VAT is not due. VAT withheld can be deducted in a regular way as the company's input VAT.

This provision places a considerable additional compliance cost on Russian businesses: they must review all inputs to determine that no withholding must be applied (including satisfying themselves that all exempt items have been correctly classified and are not in fact items to which a withholding tax should be applied.).

3.5.3 VAT on exports

Under the EU system, a registered trader whose input tax exceeds output tax (typically because the trader is exporting or making other zero rated supplies, or because there has been a substantial purchase of capital assets) will receive a prompt cash refund. In Russia the reclaiming procedure still involves a lot of bureaucracy and is made by the tax authorities with significant delays. Delays can seriously inhibit business. International businesses operating in Russia complain of serious bureaucratic delays, while senior government officials complain of a substantial leakage of revenue as some traders (using methods not adopted by the international community) succeed in recovering VAT fraudulently. The government and courts have made already some serious attacks on such taxpayers, bringing more transparency and efficiency into the system.

3.5.4 VAT on imports

Technological equipment, their components, and spare parts imported as contributions to the charter capital of enterprises, humanitarian aid and goods designated for diplomatic corps are exempt from import VAT.

3.6 Regional taxes

3.6.1 Corporate property tax

The corporate property tax is levied on the worldwide property qualifying as fixed assets of resident legal entities, including banks, insurance companies and non-profit organizations as well as on fixed assets of non-resident companies carrying on a business through a permanent establishment or owning immovable property located in Russia.

The corporate property tax is a regional tax, which is regulated at the federal level. The maximum rate is determined by federal law (currently 2.2%), but the actual rates may vary from region to region.

The corporate property tax is imposed on the average aggregate annual depreciated value of fixed assets as reported on the balance sheet of a company or permanent establishment. If a non-resident company does not have a permanent establishment with a separate balance sheet in a region, it is taxable on any immovable property located in that region.

The tax is payable in quarterly instalments. The terms for the advance payments and for the final tax liability are established by the regions.

3.6.2 Transport tax

The transport tax is a regional tax and is payable by Russian registered legal entities, foreign legal entities, other institutions, organizations and individuals who own vehicles registered in Russia. The tax is levied on cars, motorcycles, buses and other means of transport, including air and water transport. The taxable base is the engine power (horse power) or, for certain water transport, the tonnage. Some means of transport are, however, taxed per item. The tax year is the calendar year.

The tax rates vary broadly depending on the engine power and type of vehicle.

3.6.3 Land tax

Land tax is a municipal tax payable by all companies and individuals who own plots of land or possess them on the basis of certain in-rem titles. Religious organizations, scientific institutions and certain other organizations are exempt from this tax for the land that they use for their statutory purposes.

The taxable base is the value of the land as stated in the state land register on 1 January of the relevant tax year. The tax rate varies depending on the purpose for which the land is used. At the federal level, the maximum rates are established at (i) 0.3% for agricultural land and land used for housing purposes, and (ii) 1.5% for other types of land. At the municipal level, the actual rates are set by the relevant municipality. The tax liability is calculated by self-assessment. Advance payment of tax is due in four equal instalments.

3.7 Double tax agreements

The Russian Federation has honoured and maintained treaties signed by the former USSR until new tax treaties were renegotiated. These treaties tend to follow the guidelines of the tax convention model of the Organisation for Economic Cooperation and Development (OECD), although the UN Model Convention for developing countries has had an influence as well. The treaty with the UK was updated in January 1998.

Agreements typically provide for reduced withholding taxes on interest and dividends and (particularly important) remove the liability to certain capital gains tax that would otherwise apply on the disposal of Russian assets by a foreign entity. They also affect the function of `permanent establishment' and the period of time which volunteers notably including technical specialists can work in Russia without becoming involved with Russian taxation.

3.8 Inward investment

Portfolio investment by foreigners into the Russian market is inhibited by foreign exchange control and other obstacles. In practice, much of this investment is undertaken by institutions, including specialist offshore funds.

Direct investment is more straightforward. It is prudent to route investments through a country that has a double tax agreement with Russia. This may be the parent company in the case of a British or American firm but in other cases the Netherlands or Cyprus may be used as an intermediary.

3.9 Financial instruments

Russian legislation covering the tax treatment of interest, foreign exchange and derivative transactions has been substantially rationalised by the new Tax Code but is still far from comprehensive or satisfactory. In contrast, both the U.S. and the U.K. now have hundreds of pages of regulations without getting it quite right! It cannot be assumed that a transaction which would be regarded in the UK or the United States as a `hedge' will be so treated in Russia: the profitable side of the transaction may well be taxed without corresponding relief for the matching loss. There are also tax, exchange control and other restrictions which make it virtually impossible for a Russian entity to raise money on international markets directly and intermediate jurisdictions have to be used.

3.10 Other taxes

These include a range of duties and tariffs on imported goods and services (see Chapter 5), excise taxes, tax on gambling business, natural resources usage and extraction taxes.

Besides there are special beneficial tax regimes for small and medium businesses or engaged in retail through small shops, restaurant business, consumer services. There may also be registration, license fees and stamp duties. Detailed advice should be sought from your advisers.

4   Trading in Russia

4.1 Trading with Russia

The methods and scope for conducting business in Russia are as varied as anywhere else in the world. Western manufacturing investment in Russia is growing substantially, not only due to the improved climate for investment but also due to the vision that Russia, and especially its Regions, offer a great investment potential. By 2007, foreign investment had reached $67,887 million. In 2006, the UK ranked second amongst major investors in Russia. This sum was exceeded only by Cyprus with an investment total of $9.6. It should be noted, however, that much of the money invested from Cyprus is Russian capital, re-routed in and out of Cyprus for tax and other purposes. The $7billion invested currently by British companies each year represents some 12.7% of all foreign investment. These investments have been made in all sectors of the economy including service, financial, retail and manufacturing industries. UK companies have established a large number of joint ventures and in many sectors, the UK ranks among the largest investors.

4.2   Approaching the Russian market

Governmental and trade sources are now making great efforts to help British manufacturers and service companies harness the potential of the Russian Federation. It often surprises Russians that the British have not made as great an attempt to enter the market as other European or American companies. However, while it is true that Great Britain's potential is greater, there is more British activity than may appear at first sight.

Although the Government and trade associations can be of help, it is ultimately up to companies themselves to judge whether to enter the market. Market entry has to be carefully planned and budgeted. If British companies approach the Russian market in the right way, they will be successful.

While any market entry entails certain risk, the dynamic and constantly changing nature of the Russian market makes this stage particularly complex, and consequently, particular attention must be paid to all aspects of the business. Russia is not the market for the 'fast buck', but is certainly the market for the big buck. Companies that are willing to persevere, to be flexible in their approach, and to commit to the long term, will build up a long-standing and lucrative business. Paradoxically, while some parts of the present market do not seem to be geared to western practice, and are subject to rapid legislative change, it is precisely the ability to think quickly, and react to these changing situations that represent the key to successful business.

Attitudes are also important. The key concern should be how to trade successfully in an evolving and unpredictable market. Companies that are organised, assess the potential and risk, research thoroughly, and have drive and resilience are likely to succeed.

Developing permanent and consistent business in Russia, or with Russians, can take time. This process involves much legwork, time and research. Businessmen who have succeeded in the Russian market believe that their success is largely due to their being methodical, persistent and open minded in their approach to the market. They have also, invariably, been the ones to use senior management to keep the business venture on course.

4.2.1   The approach

Up until the collapse of the command economy, the former Soviet Union was one of the most reliable payers in the world. A contract, once signed, would be honoured. The trading contracts, usually signed with centralised, state trading houses, would usually be on the basis of open terms, Cash Against Documents. Following the turmoil that ensued as plans were altered, and budgets dried up, there were payment defaults, not because the Russians were prone to not paying, but because a system was winding down. For this reason both buyers and sellers changed to the option of 100% advance payment and for two or three years much business could be done this way. Now, however, the situation has changed again. Legislation has appeared in Russia, which tightens up on such payment mechanisms, in order to halt capital flight. Internationally recognised payment systems, based on Incoterms (See 5.3) are accepted. An established Russian company will be happy to work with you if you offer credit, and will invariably pay you on demand and on time. After all, they can build up a lucrative long-term business in this way.

As in any trading situation care is needed. Increasingly, credit ratings and credit insurance are obtainable on all but the newest companies in Russia. The growing reputation of Russia as a trading nation means that Russian businesses can be selective on whom they deal with. If you do not offer more flexible payment terms, then the chances are that your competitor will.

4.2.2   Finding a Russian partner

Finding a local partner may be advisable. As in any business situation, caution should be taken before investing heavily in any venture where your money is at risk. There are several organisations that will help you find or check any potential partner. Such investigations should also examine the business as well as the individual. It is vital to work with partners to develop an understanding based upon experience, trust and confidence. Once this has been done your relationship should be set out in a binding agreement.

Trading with Russia can take many forms. How exactly you structure your business is one of the most crucial decisions you will make. The preferred way for most regular traders, and particularly manufacturers who are small to medium sized enterprises, is to find a business partner in Russia to undertake the sale and distribution of their products. A company can also establish a representative office or branch office. Both are subject to Russian taxation

Besides conducting ad hoc or regular trade deals, an organisation may wish to establish a permanent presence. This can be done effectively by setting up a warehouse in order to provide a short delivery period. If you, as the seller, do not wish to become involved with issues such as inventory, security, stock handling, etc., then this is best done through a distributor with the appropriate controls. He should have the necessary infrastructure to handle these issues, and, of increasing importance, to set up a nationwide distribution network. For fast moving consumer goods issues such as quality control, packaging and after-sales service, if appropriate, may be more important than price. Again, support systems in Russia will be invaluable. It will also give you the ability to sell products for Roubles, while still receiving payment in hard currency.

4.2.3   The Russian businessman

Foreign business success stories share a common ingredient – the willingness to learn about the Russian way and adapt parts of their operation to it.

Russians, perhaps more than Western Europeans, place a great emphasis on intuition. Business with Russians is a "people" business and your attitude, demeanour and commitment may be as important as your company's history and track record. Character is all-important. A smart appearance and formality are the norm during a business meeting. You should always address people, in letters, in the formal mode. Use of Christian names initially is not a polite form of address.

Unlike Western Europe and the USA it is not unusual to get through to senior decision makers. Often, and especially if they like you, you will be given their mobile number.

Specific information is extremely difficult and sometimes frustrating, to obtain. Extreme patience is often required when trying to elicit information, even if you speak the language fluently.

4.2.4 Business meetings

Business is rarely conducted over the phone. Where meetings are arranged confirm them in writing if possible.

Appointments may be cancelled at little or no notice. Often, meetings will begin 30-40 minutes later than the appointed time. This should not be taken as a sign of disinterest, and is not considered to be as rude as it might be in the UK. Equally, if you are late for a meeting, you should not "over-apologise". Always be sure to greet everyone personally and do so again when saying goodbye.

Do not feign interest in something, or give the impression that something can be done, if you know it cannot. Do not promise to "get back to them on that", and do not give the impression that you are not the decision-maker. Do not make promises that you cannot keep.

Generally, when in a formal meeting room, you are expected to sit on the opposite side of the table to your Russian partner. The beginning and end of the meeting may start with a formal handshake, and the most senior member of each group will normally shake hands with his counterpart first. Similarly, meetings are "led" by the senior member of the group, in a way that is no longer the case in the UK. A Russian is usually very direct, and expects you to be too. This applies to all aspects of the meeting too, including the discussion of discounts!

Always ensure that a senior person is sent to discuss business with a senior Russian counterpart. To do less is regarded as a breach of protocol. Remember that business meetings will also take longer if an interpreter is needed. Do not watch the clock. This will be seen as a sign that you are not interested in the company.

Small talk is customary prior to discussing business. Russians are likely to hold a number of meetings to establish a business relationship. And do not be surprised if the most important business is discussed last. It may even be the concluding matter raised on a trip that has lasted several days.

After a meeting, it is customary to give small gifts, e.g., pens, or something from your country, to say "hello" or offer a small gift by way of thanks for assistance. Gifts must be appropriate for the time, place and extent of help. One common custom is not to shake hands over a doorstep (See 4.2.5)

Russians being meticulous, warm and generous hosts are likely to invite you to restaurants. This may involve vodka, which is drunk only when a toast is proposed (starting with the senior person from the Russian side). The next to make a toast should be the senior person on your team, and so on until the ceiling appears to move slightly. Refusing to drink vodka on certain occasions or to a certain toast may sometimes be considered rude. Your glass should not touch the table from the time a toast is proposed to the time you drink. Your glass should remain on the table when it is being refilled. Time is usually taken over a lunch or dinner with frequent toasts made. It is also considered bad form to drink alcohol, including beer, without eating something.

Russians when drinking usually do so over a meal, and tend to be surprised (as most Europeans) at the British ability to go to a pub and quaff several pints of beer with only a pork scratching for sustenance. Sipping a toast is unusual, but acceptable if you are not a drinker. The interpreter is expected to join in the toasting, but rarely has a chance to eat because he is busy interpreting. A guide to how much has been drunk is usually to look at the angle of the interpreter to the table and how many hands he is using to retain that position. They sometimes have to be carried out.

"If your contacts invite you to the banya or to their homes, it is a sure sign that the meeting has been successful and they want to develop the relationship further. The banya is the traditional Russian sauna and it is often the custom for those who have developed a good business relationship to continue discussions there." UK Trade & Investment

You should never go to someone else's house empty handed. Alcoholic beverages and/or desserts are common gifts to bring when invited to someone's home. It is usual to remove the shoes in somebody's house

UK Trade & Investment warns "Be wary of companies who invite you to 'do business Russian style' – in other words, bend the rules." It also stresses the importance of a contract, stating "Seek good quality legal advice and get the details right."

4.2.5   Dos and Donts

Whilst superstition is getting less common, certain customs should be remembered. Reference has been made to not shaking hands over a doorstep (See 4.2.4). Other considerations include:

- ◆ Men in Russia will always shake hands (or at least offer a wrist if a hand is dirty, wet or otherwise unavailable) when they greet for the first time during the day. It is taboo to shake hands with your gloves on. A glove must be removed, no matter how cold it may be. Russia is one of the many countries where this handshake tradition is rigorously upheld.
- ◆ As well as shaking hands, giving presents across the threshold of a house is taboo. Usually a guest will come inside before shaking a host's hand when arriving and shake it before leaving the threshold when leaving. Sometimes people will even avoid saying "hello" and "goodbye" across the threshold.
- ◆ A purse (or any other money holder) as a gift requires a little money inside. Given empty it causes bad financial luck.
- ◆ Before leaving on a long journey, travellers, (and those seeing them off), sit for a moment in silence before leaving the house. It is often a useful time to sit and think of anything you may have forgotten!
- ◆ After someone has left the house on a long journey, their room and/or their things should not be cleaned up until they have arrived back. This explains some hotel bathrooms.
- ◆ Returning home for forgotten things is a bad omen. It is better to leave it behind, but if returning is necessary, one should look in the mirror before leaving again.
- ◆ It is traditional in Russia for men to give flowers to women on nearly every occasion, but only an odd number can be given. Giving an even number of flowers is taboo, because even numbers are brought to funerals.

- Traditional Russian cheek kissing is done using three kisses.
- Unmarried people should not sit at the corner of the table. Otherwise they will not marry. This mostly applies to girls, and often only young girls. Sometimes it is said that you will not marry for 7 years, making it alright for young children to sit there.
- It is impolite to point with your finger. But if you must point, it's better to use your entire hand instead of your finger.
- It is considered bad luck to put keys on a kitchen table.
- When someone sneezes you say Bud'te zdorovy, "Be Healthy" or bless you.
- Knocking on wood is practiced in Russia as in other countries. However Russians tend to add a symbolic three spits over the left shoulder (or simply with the head turned to the left), and Russians will often knock three times as well. Traditionally one was spitting on the devil (who is always on the left).
- If you accidentally step on somebody's foot, it is common for the person who was stepped on to lightly step on the foot of the person who stepped first, so allegedly avoiding future conflict. This does not work in the UK, where it guarantees immediate conflict.
- Whistling indoors is taboo. Russians sometimes say superstitiously that you will "whistle away your money". The origins of this are in superstition, as it used to be considered a sin: it was believed that when you whistled you were entertaining the devil.

Russia lacks some of the superstitions that the British find commonplace. Most Russians are not particularly concerned with the number 13, opening umbrellas indoors or walking under ladders.

4.2.6   Business cards and company literature

Business cards and company literature should, as a courtesy, be in Russian or in Russian and English. Any price lists should be in Euros if possible. It is prudent to take a company stamp and a blue ink blotter with you. All official documents require stamps. Without these, many Russians will not regard a document as meaningful

There are several considerations when it comes to providing Russian language literature all of which point to the sense in using a specialist provider:

- Translation. You may well have a Russian partner. Chances are you might ask him/her to translate your existing literature into Cyrillic. The good news is that they'll probably be cheap. However, always remember that if you spent time, effort and money to ensure your English marketing message was nicely honed with just the right nuances, you will definitely have lost that perfection in Cyrillic if you go this route. It always pays to have a specialist localise your translated text and then typeset the job properly in Cyrillic.
- Artwork. Bear in mind also that Cyrillic usually makes 25% more than English. If using an existing design this may mean your specialist will have to adapt the design, if possible or edit the copy. Bear in mind also that it is rare for Russians to use acronyms quite like we do in English – this doesn't help your 25% problem!
- Schedule. Allow plenty of time. Translating and then localising plus proper checking prior to producing artwork, then checking again before to going to print all takes time if you are to avoid mistakes. Often several people are involved in different locations. It all takes longer than you might think.
- Where to print? This will depend upon the quality you want, how many units you need printed and your budget. Undoubtedly you'll get a cheaper print

quote around Moscow than UK and the quality can be very reasonable. It'll be even cheaper outside Moscow, If you are producing a high quality job, say a report & accounts or a glossy high value corporate brochure with a relatively low quantity it may be better to print in UK and ship. The same goes for digital print (which will be short runs anyway) – for the moment at least. Equipment is improving all the time.

The bottom line then is, if you cared about how your marketing message was portrayed in UK, you should spend a little time and effort in ensuring it is shown off to its best to your Russian customers. It will reap dividends in the long run.

4.3   Russians visiting the UK

Increasingly Russian buyers will visit the UK, particularly when visiting trade fairs, etc. When invited it is usual for Russian buyers to pay for their own flights. The British company pays for accommodation and expenses. When Russian buyers do visit the UK they prefer to stay in good quality hotels, as near their point of destination as possible. You would be expected to treat the Russian visitor as generously and warmly as he would treat you in his country.

A Russian citizen's entry into Britain is not completely straightforward. Advice from the British Embassy or a good travel agent should be sought. Formal, written invitations must be issued to partners well before they plan to come to the UK otherwise visas may not be issued in time.

For longer visits, or where salaries are involved, or an individual is handling issues, which might be normally dealt with by a native of the country, a work permit may be needed. For further information see www.workingintheuk.gov.uk/working_in_the_uk/en/homepage/work_permits0.html

4.4   Market entry

Very few businesses have ever done well, especially long-term, in the Russian market by just dipping their toe into the water. However, if the businessman takes a long-term view, and perseveres, the rewards for properly planned ventures can be enormous. Providing you plan your campaign and determine the resources you are prepared to commit to it, you are likely to succeed. This does not mean you should not initially attempt market entry through a low budget, small project, providing the basis for future expansion in the market.

You will no doubt have a business plan for guiding your market entry. However, a word of warning: a business plan should be exactly that: a plan for structuring your business. No business plan should be treated as a set of rules from which deviation is impermissible. On the contrary, in a market as exciting and as dynamic as Russia, the business plan is only a useful document if it can constantly be amended and updated. Things change. Structures are modified, and what made perfect sense yesterday is irrelevant. A business plan should therefore be flexible. It should be regarded as a guide, a discipline, but not rulebook.

4.5   The Distribution System

A number of distribution networks are in use. Few are able or would claim to offer a countrywide service. The vast proportion of goods arriving into the Russian Federation are shipped through importers with their own distribution network. Most are based in European Russia and especially Moscow and St Petersburg. The former, being the capital and still very much the centre in terms of wealth and influence. It is prudent to ask about the links that any Moscow-based representative may have with the regions and in the long-term how they will represent you on a regional basis. Companies engaged in the distribution system include:

♦ Trading houses: Such firms comprise the majority of importers of goods into the country. Selling goods directly to the ultimate customer, especially in hard currency, may be fraught with difficulties. As a result, the trading house will generally purchase goods from the manufacturer and then sell them on to Russian customers, in Roubles, in its own name.

♦ Agents: Agents provide indirect access to the market. Their key function is to establish business relationships between a buyer and a seller. In almost all cases agents work on a commission only basis. Relatively few British trading companies act as agents. Some of the larger agents may purchase goods for onward sale through their own private network or sales force.

♦ Manufacturer's representatives: Manufacturer's Representatives act directly on behalf of the producer and are paid by them, usually on a salary/commission basis. Some companies may use their representatives as agents for others wishing to enter the marketplace.

♦ Importers: Importers range from large organisations acting independently in overseas markets to limited companies operating fully or partially under the control of the Ministry of Foreign Economic Relations. Joint ventures account for about 30% of the market with independent companies comprising some 50%.

♦ Wholesalers: Wholesalers are organisations who, in the Russian context, have direct access to production of raw materials and goods. Both private and state companies operate in the wholesale side of business. Increasingly they are using agents and manufacturer's representatives to assist them in the sales process.

4.6   Financing business operations in Russia

Careful consideration must be given to financing an operation in Russia. Capital available from Russian banks is limited. Whilst the Russian Government encourages investment it should be noted that capital movement requires a Central Bank licence. Long-term loans from abroad are subject to licensing requirements, and any transfer of funds may, without careful structuring, be subject to VAT.

4.7   Repatriation of profits

Under the Foreign Investment Law, 1999 foreign investors are guaranteed unrestricted use of after-tax income, both within Russia and abroad. This could include, for example, the transfer of foreign currency to currency accounts at authorised banks opened in the name of non-residents, as payment for imported goods, work or services.

4.8   Payment Mechanisms

Outside up front payments, the typical method of trade settlement is by direct bank transfer, i.e. from a Russian bank to a UK bank on a Letter of Credit.

Full or partial advance payment, against pro-forma invoices is often not possible, especially for the supply of services. Where an advance payment has been allowed, the goods must be imported within six months of that payment.

Russian banks can issue letters of credit on their clients' instruction, and advise the beneficiary through a bank in the UK in the normal way. Russian banks will only do this where a customer can deposit the requisite funds in its account ahead of time. UK banks, including foreign banks with UK operations, which have relationships with Russian banks, are able to add confirmation to letters of credit issued by a short list of acceptable Russian banks. This list changes frequently. Exporters should find out which bank or banks are currently acceptable to your own bank and whether their buyers intend to use them. Even so, the routing of the credit and its advice remains at the Russian bank's discretion.

4.8.1 Open account

Open account terms are based on trust, with the seller issuing an invoice directly to the buyer for goods and services provided. It is prudent to state clearly the terms of the contact, including the payment due date and currency accepted, when dealing on an open account basis. Credit insurance should always be sought. This method of dealing is becoming more common but caution, as in any country, with any customer, is required.

4.8.2 Factoring

Within Russia, factoring started in 1999. Factoring is a mechanism used by vendors to obtain immediate payment for of up to 90% of the invoice value of a valid debt, immediately following shipment of goods, with the balance either on receipt of the buyer's payment or on an agreed date. Factoring consequently avoids the problem of waiting for payment, which on normal trade terms can vary between 90 and 120 days.Factoring often releases the seller from all responsibilities for obtaining payment from the buyer, with the factor taking over the exporter's sales ledger and credit management functions. The seller's costs of internal administration are thus minimal. Agreement can be reached with the factor on markets, the amount and level of business with customers and which customers to factor. Factoring may be "Non-recourse", meaning that the factoring company takes the bad debt risk, or "Recourse", which absolves the factor from this risk. If the customer defaults, the seller would then need to refund the factor the amount advanced. Factors are remunerated by interest, at "Russian Commercial rates", typically 12% – 18% for Rouble and 12% for "hard currency", such as US$; charged on the sum advanced on a daily basis. This is paid either after a fixed interval or when payment is received from the customer. Factors will also charge an administration fee, which varies according to sector and size of "factored sales" but is normally between 0.5% and 3.0% of "factored" turnover. Whilst there are about 70 banks offering "factoring" services, there are only six "true" factoring businesses. The remainder are departments of banks and treat factoring like bank loans/credit and may require collateral. For International Factoring in Russia and elswhere, contact one of the two main Factoring Associations (Chains), listed below, where a list of members may be obtained. For Russian domestic factoring, contact Barry R Rogers whose details are below. Factoring is experiencing huge growth in Russia (largest growth in World) and is highly competitive so "shop around" to get the best deal.

For International Factoring, including Russia, there are two Worldwide Factoring "Chains" who, between them, have six members in Russia. These are:

1. International Factors Group (IFG) Tel: 00 332 2772 6969; Website: www. ifgroup.com/ifg-presentation.asp

IFG members in Russia are:

♦ National Factoring Company (Joint-Stock Company) Tel: 007 495 705 9039; Website: www.factoring.ru

♦ Eurokommerz Tel: 007 495 502 9904; Website: www.eurokommerz.ru/page/ home/2.aspx

♦ Interregional Factoring Company Trust

- Banque Societe Generale Vostok
- International Factors Group (IFG) Tel: 00 332 2772 6969
  2.Factors Chain International (FCI) Tel: 003 312 0627 0306;
Website: www.factors-chain.com/members/RUS
  FCI members in Russia are:
- Promsvyazbank (a Joint-Stock Commercial Bank)
- National Factoring Company (Joint-Stock Company)
- Joint-Stock Bank of Gas Industry "Gazprombank"

The Asset Based Finance Association (ABFD) can provide advice and guidance on factoring and invoice discounting. A full list of its members in the UK, can be obtained by contacting Tel: 0208 332 9955; Website: www.abfa.org.uk

For independent advice on every aspects of domestic and international factoring, invoice discounting and banking involving Russia and UK one may contact:

Barry Rogers MICM, Dip ABFA,
Dom 32, KB 46
Dmitry Ul'yanova Ul
Moscow, 117036
Tel: 007 917 598 5162
E-mail: info@abacusfactoringconsultants.com
Website: www.abacusfactoringconsultants.com

4.8.3 Invoice discounting

A substantial exporter, with a good credit management record, might not wish the involvement of a factor to be known to his buyers. In such cases, the vendor could sell his invoices to the discounter at an agreed discount for immediate settlement, usually up to 85%, of the invoice value. The buyer will, on settlement of his invoice, repay the exporter the amount advanced. Contact: FDA Tel: 020 8332 9955; website: www.factors.org.uk

4.8.4 Merchant finance

Through Merchant finance, goods are technically sold to a merchant financier, who is invoiced directly. The merchant financier then invoices your customer, with the manufacturer acting as their sales agent. Merchant finance may be offered against individual customers or orders, rather than on a global basis. Once confirmation of the acceptance of goods has been received, the merchant financier will transfer up to 85% of the sales invoice value to you, with the balance, less commission being released when they are paid. Contact merchant banks.

4.8.5 Forfaiting

Through forfaiting the exporter's bank, acting as a forfaiter, will purchase the entirety of his customer's debt, for an agreed discount rate, in exchange for instant payment or payments on due date. The key to the procedure is the purchase by one bank of another banks irrevocable unconditional guarantee on its customers debt (avalisation) stated on a bill of exchange, promissory note or other instruments. The exporter is thereby effectively removed from any further involvement with the financial aspects of the transaction. Forfaiting is suitable where the value of goods, a transaction or series of transactions, is in the region of $250,000 or more, lasting from about 30 days to three years.

The forfaiting market has traditionally been one of the major sources of finance for exporters selling to Russia. Several Russian banks are considered acceptable for forfaiting for periods of up to 3 years. Other banks are not generally acceptable and sellers should use confirmed letters of credit.

A guide to costs of forfaiting is available on the internet through Mezra Finance Limited (Tel: 0208 290 4110; website: www.mezra.com/). Assistance on forfaiting may also be obtained from London Forfaiting Company plc (Tel: 0207 481 3410; website: www.londonforfaiting.com), TFI FX (Tel: 00 357 22 817 469; website: www.tfifx.com/) and many commercial banks.

4.8.6 International leasing

Liquidity problems in the Russian economy have given rise to alternative methods of paying for high value capital equipment, for example, aircraft. Leasing is also widely available for most capital goods including trucks, motor cars and most equipment. Russian Leasing regulations offer the same tax advantages as mainland Europe. Currently, some 5% of imported equipment is leased.

4.8.7 Offshore accounts

Russia has very strict exchange control regulations deterring the use of offshore companies while doing business in Russia. Permission may, however, be obtained subject to written permission from the Central Bank. In practice this is extremely difficult to get.

Establishing an "accumulating" or escrow account is one method used by some companies to mitigate the effects of currency exchange costs that could be payable. The escrow account would be the recipient of money from:
- the sale of products;
- the re-conversion, in accordance with Russian legislation, of Roubles into hard currency to meet hard currency loans and operating costs;
- any proceeds from insurance claims.

Re-conversion of Roubles into hard currency is allowed under Russian legislation if it can be demonstrated that the money is required to cover a deficiency in meeting hard currency operating costs and repayments of interest and principal and hard currency loans. These receipts will immediately be transferred to a trust account at a third party bank. The trust account would preferably be structured under English law with a clear legal obligation that funds would be separate from those of the bank in which the escrow account is held.

For the Central Bank of Russia, the escrow structure solves several problems at once. For them it is a form of exchange control since they can audit payments whilst at the same time account for export receipts remitted to the Russian Federation.

It is acceptable to declare dividends in respect of any profits obtained, and to distribute (post-tax) profits accordingly. However, it is also important to bear in mind that such profits, especially in the early years of the business, may also be required for reinvestment.

Extreme caution should be taken when receiving money from Russian citizens from offshore accounts. There is a risk that the funds may be held illegally and this failure to comply with the law may rebound on the exporter.

4.9   Free Economic Zones (FEZ)

To encourage development of the regions, the Regional Government may establish Free Economic Zones. Incentives available vary from FEZ to FEZ, Currently, only Kaliningrad offers a FEZ. The following benefits apply:
- Goods produced for export generally attract exemption from licences and quotas;

♦ Goods imported into and re-exported from FEZs are not exempt from customs duty, except in Kaliningrad;
♦ Compulsory sales of hard-currency earnings are lower than elsewhere in Russia and range from 10% to 20%;
♦ Profit tax rates for foreign investment are up to 50% lower than those existing elsewhere in the Russian Federation, for the first five years or if profit used for re-investment;
♦ Up to 50% reduction on VAT on goods sold in Russia
♦ Reductions in water and land use payments;
♦ Tax holidays may be applicable;
♦ Long-term land leases may be granted for up to 70 years, with rights to sub-lease.

Other regions do offer specific initiatives, including special economic or incentive zones and corridors.

4.10   Customs Zones and Free Customs Warehouses

Free customs zones and free customs warehouses are located in customs areas such as airports, seaports, railway and truck terminals. In these areas:
♦ Customs duties do not apply in free customs zones and free warehouses.
♦ Production and commercial transactions can take place within these zones, but not retail sales.
♦ Unlimited storage periods apply

4.11   Currency exchange and profitability

For the last 7 years, Russia's monetary system has been relatively stable. Exchange restrictions and controls do apply, although there are moves to liberalise them. It should be noted that:

(i) The Rouble is not an internationally traded currency although it is now convertible on the internal market. There is a shortage of Roubles and hard currency with which to exchange them;
(ii) The Russian Central Bank requires a licence for foreign currency capital movement and a separate licence to trade in hard currency;
(iii) There are extremely high interest rates for both Dollars and Roubles.
(iv) The internal financial markets are unsophisticated and therefore local assistance is difficult to obtain.

Invoicing within the Russian Federation for foreign currency is restricted under Currency Regulations. The Russian Central Bank is only prepared to issue new licences to invoice in hard currency in exceptional circumstances.

All Russian legal entities, including those with foreign investments, are subject to the compulsory purchase of Roubles for 25% of their foreign currency receipts. Enterprises are, however, able to obtain foreign currency in exchange for Roubles through their banks, provided that they have foreign currency invoices to settle or to repatriate profits.

4.12.1 Currency control

Since 1994, the use of foreign currency for cash transactions has been illegal. Non-residents should be aware of this, especially in the medium-term, if they plan to create subsidiary companies or joint ventures in Russia. Non-residents can bring to Russia unlimited amounts of hard currency. This may be repatriated at a later date subject to currency regulations and taxation.

Non-cash transactions, e.g., credit card, debit card and check transactions are not affected by the 1994 regulations. Consequently, establishments such as international hotels in Moscow, which previously accepted payment via credit cards continue to do so.

Corporations may withdraw foreign cash from their bank accounts for business trips of their employees abroad. After the employee returns, any remaining cash must be repaid into the employer's bank account.

4.12.2 Currency regulations

Since 18 June 2004 currency transactions may be freely conducted between resident and non-resident individuals with the exception of:

1. long term loans, i.e., loans over 180 days
2. foreign currency loans
3. the settlement of share holdings or other securities

Currency transactions between residents in the Russian Federation in foreign currency or with foreign securities are generally prohibited

Non-resident individuals may hold foreign cash and monetary instruments, which may be purchased and sold, through licensed exchange offices operated by the banks. The customer must prove his identity but need not confirm the origin of the cash deposited. Individuals must declare the import and export of foreign cash to the Russian customs authorities. Since March 2003:

♦ Up to $10,000 may be imported into the country without being declared. For sums greater than this, a TC-28 certificate needs to be completed.

♦ Up to $3,000 may be taken out of the country without being declared

♦ If you are taking out over $3,000, but less than $10,000, you must declare this on departure. Form No 0406007 should be completed in this respect.

♦ If you take out over $10,000 you must have declared it on arrival, or be able to provide documentary proof of the transfer, remittance or purchase of the amount while in Russia. Again, Form No 0406007 should be completed

♦ These rules are subject to change and should be checked.
(See also Section 7.8)

5 FREIGHT AND CUSTOMS

5.1.   Freight

Transportation of goods poses few problems in Moscow or St Petersburg other than congestion at the port of entry. Both these cities are catered for with doorstep delivery and collection being available. However, transport becomes increasingly difficult in more distant regions, cities or towns. Some large companies, most of which are trading companies or regional wholesalers, are establishing their own collection and distribution system serviced by their own warehouses and fleets of vehicles.

When dealing with any Russian buyer you should always ask whether they will be able to deliver onwards. If they are unable to do this, you could use independent freight companies but should be aware of the costs.

5.2.1   Types of freight

A range of air, sea, river and canal, rail and road options are available to transport goods to and within the Russian Federation. The most common routes are by road or rail overland across Western Europe, or by ship via Finland to Moscow or by sea direct to the port of St Petersburg. The port of St Petersburg, which is steadily growing in size and in efficiency, has become the natural gateway for container traffic between the UK and Russia.

Within Russia most industrial goods and raw materials such as coal, coke, ores, ferrous metals, chemical and mineral fertilisers and grain are transported by rail.

Urgent consignment and small goods may be sent by airfreight. The postal service is improving but may still be unreliable, especially outside of Moscow and St Petersburg.

Examples of freight forwarders include:

Sea: Containerships Group Tel: 0207 495 1316; website: www.container-shipsgroup.com

Air: O'Grady Air Services Tel: 01753 680 580; website: www.ogradyair.com/uk/about.asp

Road: Allways International Freight Forwarding Limited Tel: 01708 227711; website: www.allwaysinternational.co.uk

5.2.2   BIFA

Details of companies that can help with freighting operations, freight forwarding and Customs clearances can be obtained from The British International Freight Association Tel: 020 8844 2266; website: www.bifa.org/

The British International Freight Association's (BIFA) New Importer / Exporter Initiative aims to provide specialist help and assistance to companies who are new to exporting. This service, available through selected BIFA registered members, offers up to one day's free consultancy to advise companies on such matters as modes of transport, distribution methods, costing, documentation and payment terms.

5.3   Documentation

Usually, freight companies experienced in doing business with Russia are well versed in the procedures necessary to safeguard and facilitate shipment of goods to or from that country. Most transactions for goods are undertaken ex works or on an FCA basis.

For every transaction you will need:

- A sales contract. This should be written in English and Russian. Standard forms of contract are developing. This will include delivery terms. Most Russian importers will use either the International Chamber of Commerce IN-COTERMS2000, which define terms used commonly for export transactions, e.g., CIF, FOB, ex factory, etc. For further information See Chamber of Commerce website: www.iccwbo.org/index_incoterms.asp
- A pro-forma or normal customs invoice must be issued. This will state payment terms. The contract or a codicil attached to it must also include a packing list giving the description of goods grouped in TNVED Codes (Commodity Codes). Often six copies are required. For each group should be given its Code, Gross weight, quantity and value. The invoice should also state the country of origin of the goods supplied;
- Shipping documentation, including the Customs invoice, will be required. All documentation would normally be prepared by the freight forwarder. The freight forwarder would also prepare an international Customs form for shipping use.
- Prikaz GTK 217 dated 25 May 1994 & Government Postanovlenie 287 dated 29 April 2002 stipulates that imported goods have to be certified and identifies the type of certification needed. This may include a GOST R certificate, (see 5.11). The Law on Protection of Consumer Rights of February 1992 delegates certification authority to the Russian Standards Committee, Rostekhregulirovanie (see 5.9).
- An "import passport" must be issued by the importer's bank to allow payment against the import contract. Where goods cannot be supplied in 90 days, the importer must obtain special permission from Central Bank.

Examples of customs documents used currently may be found at www.vch.ru/index_eng.html or www.tks.ru/ (Russian only).

The Association of European Businesses, which is in regular contact with the Russian State Customs Committee, and their Transport & Customs Committee, can give practical advice on various customs issues.

Contact: Association of European Businesses, Bolshaya Ordynka Ulitsa. 40, bldg. 2, Moscow 119017 Tel: 007 495 721 1760; E-mail: info@aebrus.ru; Website: www.aebrus.ru/

5.4   The Sales contract

A contract should be scrutinised carefully to eliminate ambiguity. As in any country, contracts are written and signed with the underlying premise that they will not be broken. Often there will be an unwritten premise that if there is a minor infringement, the contract will not be subject to legal action. Russian law backs contracts, but enforcement tends to be difficult and the process of resolving disputes is highly complex. As the legal system is only evolving, sound legal advice should be sought Details of British law firms operating in Russia may be obtained from UK Trade & Investment Russia Unit Tel: 020 7215 4891; Website: www.uk-tradeinvest.gov.uk/ukti/appmanager/ukti/countries?_nfls=false&_nfpb=true&_pageLabel=CountryType1&navigationPageId=/russia. Much emphasis will be placed on the oral promises of the parties to an agreement, with face-to-face meetings and close relationships holding great importance.

A basic contract will be expected with each sale or transaction. Such transactions are governed by the second part of the Civil Code of the Russian Federation, enacted in 1996. An example of a standard sales contract may be found in Appendix 1. Also included, is an example of an agreement granting rights to sell specific products in specific regions.

It should be noted that a contract is associated with several other documents issued against it. The main document is called the "passport of transaction". This determines the currency of the contract, payment terms, value of the contract, the seller, the buyer, etc. If the parties to the transaction wish to change the contract in any way, it will be necessary to reissue the Passport and all other documentation anew.

5.5   Trade agreements

The Russian Federation has few free trade arrangements, other than a Customs Union with members of the Commonwealth of Independent States. It also has an association agreement with the European Union, with whom free trade treaties exist on steel and textiles. Russia has commenced accession procedures into the World Trade Organisation (WTO), currently holding observer status. Russia is also negotiating a free trade association with North America. Under the terms of the May 2004 agreement, Russia in return for higher gas and petroleum prices will lower tariff levels on industrial goods, fishery products agricultural goods, fresh and frozen meat and poultry.

5.6   Licensing and quotas

Since 13 October 1995 quotas on many imports have been reintroduced. These measures are largely aimed at reducing the imbalance of trade in certain products with the European Union and the United States and to establish its own manufacturing capacity in certain industries. Meat and poultry are particular areas where quotas apply. Restrictions equally apply to the import of weapons, narcotics, precious metals and stones. Details of goods that are restricted may be obtained from the Russian Ministry for Economic Development and Trade Licensing.

The Bill also stipulates the right of the government to introduce export quotas "in order to avert a reduced critical shortage of commodities on the domestic market".

Licensing is not always a one way measure. The British Government also controls the sale of certain products to Russia, and many other countries, for example armaments. Certificates are required from the Department for the Environment, Food and Rural Affairs (DEFRA) or Ministry of Health for exports of plants, animals, birds, raw products of origin (including raw wool) and animal fodder. For circumscribed goods exported to Russia, Customs Pre-Entry is necessary for goods exported under Licence (other than Open General Licence), or otherwise under Customs control.

For licensing information contact: Department for Business Enterprise and Regulatory Reform, Export Control Organisation, 3rd Floor, Kingsgate House, 66-74 Victoria Street, London SW1E 6SW. E-mail: eco.help@dti.gsi.gov.uk; Website: www.berr.gov.uk/europeandtrade/strategic-export-control/index.html

5.6.1. Selling to the Russian Government

The Law on Federal Procurement, 1999, allows foreign firms to participate in public tenders if the product or service is not available from domestic producers or if Russian production is not considered economical.

5.7   Customs clearance

As a general rule Customs clearance will take place at the Customs Office designated as the registered address of the importing company. Customs require that a recognised form of guarantee is in place whilst goods are moving from border crossing or port of arrival to the clearance point. Specific procedures cover the entry and transit of excisable goods, and exporters should contact their forwarders for advice before arranging shipment. In October 2003 "a green corridor" was opened on the Russia-Finland border. Russian importers may use this, after complying with agreed procedures, to let goods cross the national borders without any checking.

It should be noted that many UK insurance underwriters will wish to approve the choice of carrier for high-risk cargoes. Since 01 January 2004, Customs officers have been given a maximum of three days to complete clearance formalities. If goods are not cleared by that time, they must be returned to their country of origin.

5.8. Customs regulations

Since 01 July 1994 all Customs documentation must be drafted in Russian. Customs duty rates are based on a Presidential Decree of June 1995.

Import duties and Customs processing fees are normally paid by bank transfer. This can take up to two days. Regular importers often pay large advance sums to Customs to utilise as a rolling balance. This speeds up the import procedure. In most instances, there will also be processing fees for Customs clearance of 0.1% of the contract value, payable in Roubles, plus 0.05% payable in the hard currency of the contract. These payments can be made in advance to the Russian State Customs Committee. It is legal for third parties to pay import duties on behalf of the importer. In general, Customs brokers and forwarders are not keen to pay large duty payments on behalf of their clients. Customs may require invoices to be translated. Contracts must always be translated into Russian.

Transport of uncleared goods within Russia by road can only be done under TIR Carnet or by Customs Licensed Carriers. Exporters should check that their chosen carrier can deliver to a point suitable to the Russian importer for clearance purposes.

For excisable goods destined for the Russian Federation all payments must be made to Customs prior to the arrival of the goods at the entry border. Russian Customs are very sensitive to attempts artificially to under-declare value of cargo in order to pay less duty. Goods will only be released into the country after confirmation of receipt of payment to Customs Accounts. It should be noted that goods carried by rail are presently exempt from these regulations.

An accepted way to overcome customs and import regulations is to set up a strategic partnership with an existing European Union trading company with a permanent presence in Russia. This would largely overcome the difficulties of establishing your own company in the Russian Federation.

5.9   Quality control

Many products exported to Russia require a GOST R Certificate of Conformity (CoC), confirming that they satisfy Russian quality and safety requirements, set by Rostekhregulirovanie (formerly Gosstandart). See website www.gost.ru. UK exporters are advised to use the services of a reputable independent inspection and testing company.

To reduce risks as much as possible, the UK exporter should discuss their product requirements and certification procedures, including the possible need for CoCs with SGS United Kingdom Ltd, an independent inspection, certification and testing company accredited by Rostekhregulirovanie to conduct certification throughout the world. SGS is accredited to issue Certificates of conformity for a wide range of goods, including electrical items, industrial equipment, food, clothing, toys, cosmetics and toiletries. They can issue certificates for single shipments or for serial production.

SGS can find out the certification required for your product and assist in obtaining it. For further information on certification see section 5.11.

Contact:

SGS United Kingdom Ltd,

GOST Department,

SGS House,

217-221 London Road,

Camberley

Surrey

GU15 3EY

Tel: 01276 697 890; Fax: 01276 697 888

E-mail: UKGost@sgs.com

Website: www.gost.sgs.com

Another organisations offering testing and quality control services is

Rostest (Russian Testing & Certification Centre)

31 Nakhimovsky Prospekt

Moscow 117418

Tel: 007 495 129 8625

Fax: 007 495 124 9996

E-mail: info@rostest.ru

Website: www.rostest.ru/content/ru/section-eng.htmlcontent/ru/section-about.html?sNewLang=en

5.10   Tariff classification

Since 01 January 1997, and subsequently the Customs Code 01 January 2004, Russia has been party to the Convention on a Harmonised System of the Description and Encoding of Goods, which brings Russian Customs in line with international norms. This is also known as Harmonised System or HS codes. The Revenue and Customs Classification Helpline (Tel: 01702 366 077) can provide advice on tariff classification numbers. The Helpline is open from 08.30-17.00, and a voice E-mail service is available outside these hours.

Once an HS code for the item you wish to export has been obtained you may then access the European Commission's Market Access Database's Applied Tariff Database section which will give you the tariff rate for the goods to be supplied (See website: http://mkaccdb.eu.int). This database also has a section on Import Formalities for exporters, which offers an overview of import procedures to a country, as well as any general and specific requirements for the product concerned.

5.11   Certification

The consignee normally arranges import clearance. For goods entering the Russian Federation, Customs require recognised Certificates of Origin for goods produced in countries without favoured nation status agreements. Some kinds of goods require more than one type of certification, such as:

◆ GOST R

◆ Sanitary – Epidemiological Conclusion

- Rostekhnadzor permit
- Certificate for explosion-proof equipment
- Pattern Approval Certificate
- Fire Certificate
- Telecom permit

The above certificates may be required at Russian customs and for products to be marketed, sold or used in Russia. Shipments must usually be accompanied by GOST R certificates. Failure to produce this may result in Customs stopping the shipment and placing of the goods in a bonded warehouse until certificates are produced.

In addition, importers are usually required to provide original contracts of purchase and company registration documents to Customs before clearance can take place.

The type of certification required depends upon the tariff code, the product and its application/where it will be used. Therefore, it is possible to have two similar products being used in different applications but they could attract different certification. There are other factors that may determine certification requirements for products and the UK exporter should always check the certification requirements as there are many subtle variations that could influence the final requirements.

One misconception from UK exporters is that their product is "simple" and will probably not require certification, but the Russian Authorities, who determine certification requirements, often have a different view and you can find that very simple, low value products can attract numerous certificates.

Once the certification requirements have been identified, SGS will advise on the procedures in order to obtain the certificates. Again, it will depend upon the tariff code, product and application/where it will be used as to the documentation required, if testing is needed and the requirements for an audit. This can also be influenced by the length of the certification. A consignment certificate will not attract an audit, but a serial certificate (lasting for 1-3 years) could require audit and testing.

Over the years the amount of Russian documentation required to obtain the certification has increased dramatically. The GOST R certificate, issued by SGS, will need some documentation in Russian and this may vary depending upon the product. If additional certification is required, Sanitary – Epidemiological Conclusion for a food product for example, most, if not all documentation will need to be in Russian. The reason for this is that the certification may be issued by the Russian Authorities such as Rospotrebnadzor, and they demand documentation in Russian. SGS can assist in obtaining these certificates from the relevant authority.

One of the most common questions is "why do we need Russian certification, our product meets British/European/international standards?" The Russian authorities do not recognise international certification schemes, but having international certificates might help to speed up the process. Should they not meet Russian standards, you will be advised if additional requirements must be met. At present the Russian Authorities are bringing a number of their standards into line with European standards. Whilst this may provide better read across between Russian and European standards, Russian certification is still required.

The table below provides an indication of the certification that product can attract.

Issuing Department	Certificate	For product type
Rostekhregulirovanie	GOST R Certificate of Conformity	For industrial equipment, electrical equipment, food, toys, cosmetics and toiletries, clothes, furniture.
Rostekhregulirovanie	Pattern Approval (Metrological) Certificate	for measuring devices
Rospotrebnadzor (formerly Sanepidemnadzor, SAN)	Hygienic Conclusion	for products such as toys, food, cosmetics, clothing, textiles, furniture, some industrial/ mechanical equipment
Ministry of Health	Product Registration	for medical equipment, medical devices including diagnostic products, drugs, biologically active supplements
Rostekhnadzor (formerly Gosgortekhnadzor GGTN)	Permit, Licenses and Technical Passports	for industrial equipment used in oil and gas, petro-chemical and mining industries, and also for certain equipment such as lifting equipment, pressure vessels, gas burners, etc.
Ministry of Emergencies	Pozhtest Certificate	fire safety certification for certain products
Ministry of Construction	Gosstroy Licenses	for engineering and construction projects
Ministry of Communications	Telecom Permit and Licenses	for telecommunication equipment

* Adapted from Doing Business in Russia – UK Trade & Investment

5.11.1 Investment projects

Goods imported into Russia from foreign companies as part of founding investment to Russian registered companies are subject to specific import regulations designed to encourage such investment. They also require a certified statement (akt) if they are to be used for Russian accounts purposes. This is also known as a Chartered Capital Agreement.

5.12 Labelling

The following regulations should be complied with:
- all products are to be labelled in Russian;
- where appropriate, product contents should appear on packaging;
- consumer warnings related to use and to storage should be visible;
- products should be marked with a safety symbol confirming compliance with Russian standards;
- packaging should be appropriate for the purpose required;
- Warning labels on any product that could be dangerous to the consumer;
- A GOST certification mark including certification number should also be printed on the label.

121

◆ Exporters of food products to the Russian Federation must ensure that they comply with regulations on the labelling of foodstuffs. The following information should be included on the container or label of the products:
  – product name,
  – country of origin,
  – name of the manufacturer,
  – the weight and volume of the product,
  – names of the main ingredients in the product (including food additives),
  – nutritional information (e.g. vitamins),
  – storage conditions,
  – date of production and use-by date,
  – cooking instructions (for half-finished products and baby food), recommendations for use (for biologically active food additives),
  – conditions of use.

In addition, all goods for retail sale in Moscow must bear a bar code conforming to EAN.UCC (European Article Numbering – Uniform Code Council) standards. (See 5.10) These provide unique keys to fixed or variable information characterising an item using a standard format.

The Moscow City and Regional Government has also made a decision restricting the retail sale of alcoholic products to those products that have been quality tested and that bear a regional bar code. There are currently insufficient local testing facilities to implement this decision.

5.13 Packaging

Packaging requirements are specified usually in individual contracts.

Care should always be taken with the above as failure to comply with such conditions could be a let-out clause for both customers and for insurers in the event of a claim.

Exporters of delicate or fragile goods are also advised to protect their products against adverse weather, poor roads and transport and long-term storage conditions. Consumer warnings relating to use and storage should be visible.

5.14 Export Tariffs

Export tariffs are established on natural resources, produce, agricultural products and armaments. Two tariff rates are set. The first is the basic level of tariffs and varies depending on the item in question. The second is the level for goods that do not fall under the terms of mandatory currency sales. These include:

1. barter operations or non-currency operations;
2. goods produced by wholly-owned subsidiaries of foreign firms or joint ventures with at least 30% foreign ownership that are not subject to mandatory currency sales.

The tariff on this second level is 50% above the basic level.

5.15   Import Tariffs

Presidential Decree 340/1994 and the joint instruction by the State Customs Committee and the State Revenue Service on the "Procedure of VAT and Excise Tax calculation and the payment of goods imported and exported through the Russian Federation" define the regulation of Russian import taxes. Under this legislation, and Resolution 886, effective from 01 January 2001, imports are subject to three taxes:

a) import duty, generally calculated as a percentage of the customs value of the goods;

b) excise duty, also calculated as a percentage of the customs value; and

c) Value added tax, calculated as a percentage of the customs value, transport costs, import and excise duties.

In general, all enterprises are liable for the payment of import duties, which are ad valorem and based on the CIF value of the goods. Exemptions can only be granted by the Russian Government and come into effect only when confirmed by the State Customs Committee. The following are eligible for exemption:

◆ Goods imported into Free Economic Zones (see 4.9);

◆ Goods for re-export;

◆ Goods placed in bonded warehouses;

◆ Goods in transit.

Equipment imports into Russia for periods of up to 2 years are charged Customs Duty at 3% plus VAT per month, up to the customs limit for that equipment. Other import tariffs vary generally from 5% to 30% on the value of the goods. Lower tariff rates apply to goods imported from developing countries. Higher tariff rates apply mainly to excised items like alcohol (150%), cigarettes (100%) and cars (35–70%). The tariff is doubled for goods originating in countries with which Russia does not have most favoured nation status. Classification of customs codes follows the worldwide harmonised system of tariff headings. Details on import duties may be found on website: http://vch.ru/index_eng.html

Tariffs are denominated in Euros and payable in Roubles at the current rate of exchange.

Only companies registered to take part in international trade can import goods. Customs will require company registration documents from the importer and bank reference letters. In general, Customs will only allow clearance of goods once funds have been cleared into Customs Accounts. Furthermore, a recent Joint Instruction (No 30) of the Central Bank and the State Customs Committee has introduced the requirement of an import transaction passport for contracts involving the sale of goods. The Instruction prohibits banks from making payments abroad in the following circumstances:

◆ information in the passport differs from that on the contract;

◆ the contract fails to provide precise delivery terms or provide terms for refund of prepayments in the event of non-delivery;

◆ the contract provides for payment by a party other than the importer.

Payments in excess of the contract value of imported goods are also effectively prohibited as a result of the Instruction.

5.16   Samples and temporary imports

Commercial samples can be imported into the Russian Federation in specified limited quantities. There are strict rules regarding value and quantity. Individuals or companies not legally registered in the Russian Federation cannot import goods into Russia.

Temporary importation of goods into Russia is allowed provided that the goods are consigned to a Russian registered company or an accredited representative office of a foreign company. The importer will be required to pay a percentage of the normal duty for every full month the goods remain in the country. This percentage will not be returned on export. This charge does not apply to goods sent to international trade fairs and exhibitions. Specific regulations apply for these.

◆ Failure to comply with the rules may result in goods being seized and, in more serious cases, penalty fines also being levied.

◆ Russia is a member of the ATA (Admission Temporaire/Temporary Admission) Convention, established by the World Customs Organisation (see website: www.wcoomd.org). Under this procedure the temporary importer, usually an exhibitor, will have completed HM Revenue and Customs form C&E1246 and a detailed list of items on headed paper (four copies if flying direct to Russia) showing:

  – the details of travel within Russia (e.g. location of the goods),
  – period within the country,
  – a description of the goods including serial numbers and identifying marks (if possible),
  – The value of the goods and the purpose for the visit.

A manager or director within the exporting company should sign the document

In practice, only a handful of Customs posts in Russia are able to handle goods brought into the country under this system. Consequently, a system known as the Duplicate List system is still in use. Under this system the exhibitor will present HM Revenue and Customs with form C&E1246 and a copy of the list of items to be taken into Russia at the port/airport of departure prior to entering passport control. Customs will endorse both forms, certifying that the goods were removed from the UK. The applicant should retain copies of both forms. On arrival in Russia the goods and two copies of the duplicate list should be presented to Russian Customs. They will also endorse the lists and retain one copy for their records. Russian Customs may require an amount of money (bond) to secure the potential duty and tax liability on the goods whilst they are within Russia. The amount demanded should be based on the value of the goods, the period within Russia and the information provided in the duplicate list. Whatever amount is paid as a deposit, a receipt will be issued and should be kept safely, as it will be required to reclaim the money. On departure from Russia, the list, receipt and the goods should be presented to Russian Customs. An inspection may be carried out to ensure that all the goods are present. Providing this is the case the list will be stamped (and a copy retained by Russian Customs) and the deposit repaid.

On arrival back in the UK, the goods and the C&E1246 (with list) should be presented to HM Revenue and Customs to allow re-entry into the UK. (If arriving by air, then enter the Red Channel to report to Customs

5.17   The British Standards Institution (BSI) Business Information Consultancy Services

The British Standards Institution publishes and sells British, European and international standards to which importers must adhere in order to meet British and EU requirements for product certification. Business Information of BSI can investigate and report on legislation & regulations, standards, testing & certification as well as environmental, packaging, labelling, documentation and language issues. You will be well informed of your trade obligations, thus gain confidence when exporting or importing.

The above services are delivered by research reports, in-house or onsite consultancy or training programmes or written guides.

BSI BICS also offers services including:

(a) enquiry service to help identify standards;

(b) a consultancy service to advise on how to apply standards;

(c) research service to identify technical barriers to trade;

(d) publications for importers and exporters for particular industrial sectors;

(e) a library of over 500,000 foreign standards and regulations for many countries; and

(f) A foreign standards section that can obtain any standard worldwide for you and which has over 13,000 English translations of foreign documents available for sale.

Contact:

BSI Business Information Consultancy Services 389 Chiswick High Road, London W4 4AL. Tel: 020 8996 9001; Fax: 020 8996 7001; E-mail: cservices@bsi-global.com; Website: www.bsi-global.com/

5.18   SITPRO Limited

SITPRO Limited, formerly the Simpler Trade Procedures Board, was set up in 1970 as the UK's trade facilitation agency. Reconstituted as a company limited by guarantee in April 2001, SITPRO is one of the Non-Departmental Public Bodies for which the Department Business, Enterprise and Regulatory Reform has responsibility and is funded by a grant-in-aid from the Department. SITPRO is dedicated to encouraging and helping business trade more effectively and to simplify the international trading process. Its focus is the procedures and documentation associated with international trade.

SITPRO's mission is to use its unique status to improve the competitive position of UK traders by facilitating change through:

♦ identification and removal of barriers in the international trading process;

♦ identification and promotion of best trading practices;

♦ delivery of practical, value for money electronic commerce and associated trading solutions; and

♦ influencing future trade policies.

SITPRO offers a wide range of services including a trade procedures helpline. Its website (www.sitpro.org.uk) includes briefings and checklists covering international trading practices, answers to frequently asked questions and information about SITPRO's policy work. It also publishes a bi-monthly newsletter, SITPRO News.

SITPRO also manages the UK Aligned System of Export Documents, based upon the United Nations Layout Key, and licenses the printers and software suppliers who sell the forms and export document software. Details of these suppliers are available on the SITPRO website.

Contact:

SITPRO Ltd. 7th Floor, Kingsgate House, 66-74 Victoria Street, London SW1E 6SW. Tel: 0)20 7215 8150; Fax: 020 7215 4242; E-mail: infor@sitpro.org.uk; Website: www.sitpro.org.uk

6   SETTING UP IN THE UK AND IMPORTING FROM RUSSIA

6   SETTING UP IN THE UK AND IMPORTING FROM RUSSIA

6.1   What Russia has to offer

Russia is a country rich in resources, with a highly educated population, willing and able to produce goods of the standard, quantity and quality required by its export markets. Whilst not renowned for consumer goods, this situation is changing. Imports to the UK alone were £5,820 million (2006), which not only represented an 11% increase on 2005 but was also nearly three times greater than the imports it purchased from the UK.

Whilst import / export regulations echo each other in many ways, certain organisations emphasise the opportunities for British companies and businessmen to buy production, goods and resources for the domestic market.

Finance available from Russian investors should also not be under-estimated. Whilst the CIS, Eastern Europe and Africa are regarded as the preferred choices for investment, Russian businessmen have been active in Western Europe and the UK too. In 2006, Russian businesses and individuals invested US$2,006 million in the UK. Russian involvement in English football clubs and in the UK property market is well-known. There has also been activity in other areas. Gazprom, for example, has been purchasing heavily in the UK energy market.

The UK is also seen as a key source of finance for major Russian enterprises, with London the financial centre of choice. To date 24 Russian and Commonwealth of Independent State companies are listed on the London Stock Exchange, with Gazprom, Rosneft, Sistema, Comstar and Vneshtorgbank being the most prominent.

6.2   The "FinLab" project

The Financial Laboratory (FinLab) of the London Stock Exchange was launched in October 2004. It is a joint project between London Stock Exchange and Advantix Ltd (Business Communications with Russia and CIS) Finlab's main purpose is to inform and educate Russian and CIS companies on how to raise capital in the London financial markets.

It also organizes events, private consultations and publications and advises Russian companies on a range of other issues including good corporate governance, management structures, .corporate restructuring and cultivating investor relationships in the global and regional markets,

Contact
Advantix Ltd (Business Communications with Russia and CIS)
7-10 Adam Street, The Strand, London, WC2N 6AA
Tel: 0207 520 9341, Fax: 0207 520 9342
E-mail: advantix@advantix.co.uk, Website: www.finlab.co.uk/en/

6.3   Russian Venture Capital Association (RVCA)

The Russian Venture Capital Association was created in 1997 by venture capital funds. It now comprises 28 full members and 28 associated members.

Its objectives are:

◆ to create a positive political and entrepreneurial environment for investment activities;
◆ To represent the RVCA members interests at the government level, in press, in financial and industrial markets within the country and abroad;

127

- To provide information, advice and support to Russian venture market participants;
- To develop qualified professionals who will work in venture capital companies.

Contact

Russian Venture Capital Association

Tel: 007 812 326 6180, Fax: 007 812 326 6180

E-Mail: rvca@rvca.ru, Website: www.rvca.ru/eng/

6.4   UK Trade and Investment, Investment Services

UK Trade & Investment, Investment Services aims to help businesses locate in the UK. Investment Officers across its global network, who are usually based at the UK Embassy or Consulate, help firms, discover the potential for global growth from a UK base. The section works closely with all other government departments and agencies, to help smooth the path for investment. It will also act as a conduit to potential grant support.

UK Trade & Investment

Kingsgate House, 66-74 Victoria Street,

London SW1E 6SW, United Kingdom

Tel: 020 7215 8000, Fax: 020 7828 1281

Website: www.ukinvest.gov.uk/index.html

6.5   HM Revenue & Customs (HMRC) Inward Investment Information Unit.

Most investors into the UK will receive advice from international legal and accountancy firms both in Russia and the UK.

Advice and guidance is also available from the HM Revenue & Customs (HMRC), formed on the 18 April 2005, following the merger of Inland Revenue and HM Customs and Excise Departments. One section, The HMRC Inward Investment Information Unit offers investors who do not have a UK tax presence but want to set up business in the UK. Investors who already have a UK tax presence and would like advice in connection with an expansion of their activities may contact the Inspector of Taxes currently dealing with their tax affairs. The inspector will have a direct link with the Inward Investment Information Unit.

The Unit is able to provide investors with general advice about tax issues including:

- Capital allowances
- Enterprise zones
- Research & development tax credits
- Taxation of employees
- Residence
- Loan relationships
- Funding
- Treaty Claims
- Transfer Pricing
- Leasing

HMRC also publishes a wide range of import and export publications, information sheets and business briefings, mostly obtainable on-line.

Key sections of interest to any importer of goods and services from the Russian Federation are:

128

- Introduction to Import & Export – See Website: http://customs.hmrc.gov.uk/channelsPortalWebApp/channelsPortalWebApp.portal?_nfpb=true&_pageLabel=pageImport_InfoGuides&columns=1&id=INTRODUCTION_TO_IMPEXP
- Classifying your goods – See Website: http://customs.hmrc.gov.uk/channelsPortalWebApp/channelsPortalWebApp.portal?_nfpb=true&_pageLabel=pageImport_InfoGuides&columns=1&id=IMPEXP_CLASS-GOODS
- Reliefs and exemptions – See Website: http://customs.hmrc.gov.uk/channelsPortalWebApp/channelsPortalWebApp.portal?_nfpb=true&_pageLabel=pageImport_InfoGuides&columns=1&id=RELIEF_EXEMP
- The Tariff – See website: http://customs.hmrc.gov.uk/channelsPortalWebApp/channelsPortalWebApp.portal?_nfpb=true&_pageLabel=pageImport_InfoGuides&columns=1&id=TARIFFS
- Reporting and documentary requirements – See website: http://customs.hmrc.gov.uk/channelsPortalWebApp/channelsPortalWebApp.portal?_nfpb=true&_pageLabel=pageImport_InfoGuides&columns=1&id=REPDOC_REQS
- Procedures and electronic systems – See website: http://customs.hmrc.gov.uk/channelsPortalWebApp/channelsPortalWebApp.portal?_nfpb=true&_pageLabel=pageImport_InfoGuides&columns=1&id=IMPEX_PROCANDSYS
  Contact:
  Inward Investment Information Unit International CT
  HM Revenue & Customs
  100 Parliament Street, London SW1A 2BQ
  Tel: 020 7147 2704, Tel: (International) 00 44 20 7147 2704
  Website: www.hmrc.gov.uk/international/inward.htm or,
  HMRC Enquiry Centres – For nearest office see website: www.hmrc.gov.uk/enq/index.htm
  Tel: 0845 010 9000 or 00 44 2920 501 261 if outside UK

6.6   Embassy of the Russian Federation

In addition to its consular role, the Embassy of the Russian Federation provides advice, support and guidance to Russian businessmen wishing to invest in the UK and to British businesses wishing invest in Russia or sell goods and services to it. Commercial and trade advice is most usually routed through The Trade Delegation of the Russian Federation in the UK (see below).

Contact:
Embassy of the Russian Federation
13 Kensington Palace Gardens, London W8 4QX
Tel: 020 7229 2666/3628/6412, Fax: 020 7727 8625
E-mail: office@rusemblon.org, Website: www.great-britain.mid.ru

6.7   The Trade Delegation of the Russian Federation in the UK

The Trade Delegation of the Russian Federation promotes and facilitates, on behalf of the Russian Government, the development of trade and economic relations in the United Kingdom.

On the basis of Agreements signed by the Government of the Russian Federation and the Government of the United Kingdom, the Trade Delegation is responsible for monitoring and co-ordinating, in the UK, the commercial activities of all

Russian foreign trade organisations, joint stock companies and industrial enterprises. The Russian Trade Delegation provides to Russian and British businesses

♦ Information on economic and social development in Russia and in the UK as well as on activities of the official bodies and companies of the two countries;

♦ Consultancy on the legislation in the field of investments and trade both in Russia and the UK including the establishment of representative offices, on the setting up branches of British companies in Russia and on the implementation of joint projects;

♦ Assistance in finding of potential partners for co-operation in various areas of activity, including the export and import of goods, services and investments.

Members of the Russian Trade Delegation can offer representatives of the British business community practical advice on Russian foreign trade, specific opportunities in various regions of the Russian Federation, Regional Development Programmes, etc.

Contact: The Trade Delegation of the Russian Federation in the UK, 33 Highgate West Hill, London N6 6NL. Tel: 020 8340 1907; Fax: 020 8348 0112; E-mail: info@rustradeuk.org; Website: www.rustradeuk.org

6.8   The Russian Chamber of Commerce and Industry

The Russian Chamber of Commerce and Industry, with formal origins dating to 1813, undertakes a number of roles to promote Russian business in the international arena. The Chamber comprises 156 regional chambers of commerce and industry, some 100 federal associations, 16 foreign representative offices, 6 mixed chambers established in cooperation with other countries. It has some 20,000 members throughout Russia.

Contact
The Russian Chamber of Commerce and Industry
6 Ilynka Street, Moscow 103684.
Tel: 007 495 929 0334, Fax: 007 495 925 0360
E-mail: tpprf@rbcnet.ru, Website: http://eng.tpprf.ru/
A Chamber of Commerce is also at St Petersburg:
Contact
St Petersburg Chamber of Commerce and Industry
Ulitsa Chaikovskogo 46-48, St Petersburg 191123
Tel: 00 7 812 273 4896, Fax: 00 7 812 272 6406/8612
E-mail: info@spcci.ru

6.9   Importing goods and services from Russia

Any business that brings goods or services into the UK from another Russia should consider carefully practicalities such as how to get goods out of Russia, how to get goods into the UK and all related legal and regulatory requirements. Much of the information on exporting goods from Russia is given in Chapter 5. As with exporting, it is often preferable to use the services of a freight forwarder to handle all imports on your behalf.

Imports from the Russian Federation will require an import declaration, known as a Single Administrative Document (SAD), which is also known as form C88. Authorised users, such as freight forwarders, usually make this declaration electronically. The declaration will require:

a) the correct customs classification or commodity code, which is obtainable from Her Majesty's Revenue and customs (HMCR) and
b) a customs procedure code explaining what is being done with the goods, e.g. import to free circulation or use of one of the customs procedures such as temporary import. Together they determine what rate or type of import duty is to be charged and how the goods are to be treated.

You generally have to pay import duty and import VAT, although use of some customs procedures may suspend or relieve you from these taxes. Your goods might also be subject to import quotas or liable to additional duties such as anti-dumping duties. Certain goods attract a zero rate of import duty. Goods imported from Russia will not normally be released by HMRC until all charges raised have been met.

VAT is charged on goods imported from outside the European Union at the same rate as if you bought the goods in the UK. VAT-registered businesses can reclaim the VAT as input tax in the same way as VAT is paid on UK purchases. Instead of paying VAT to the supplier, you pay the VAT directly to HMRC. You will have to fill out HMRC's C79 form, showing the VAT paid. You can use this as evidence of the VAT paid, as you would on a normal VAT invoice. Authorised traders may also be able to use the deferred accounting scheme to pay VAT.

Goods such as tobacco and alcohol products are subject to excise duty.

Special rules apply to goods imported for re-export and the re-import of previously exported goods.

6.10   Import Licensing

The majority of goods can be imported into the United Kingdom without the need to apply for an import licence. However, there are a number of Government departments who operate import restrictions amongst which are:

6.11.1 Department for Business, Enterprise and Regulatory Reform (BERR)

Import licensing arrangements apply to certain iron and steel products originating in Russia. These arrangements may be prior surveillance or quantitative restrictions (quotas) depending on the products.

For reasons of domestic legislation, an import licence will also be needed for the importation of firearms and ammunition.

As a result of international obligations there is prohibition on the import of anti-personnel mines and torture equipment.

Department for Business
Enterprise & Regulatory Reform
Import Licensing Branch, Queensway House
West Precinct, Billingham TS23 2NF
Tel: 01642 364318, Fax: 01642 364203
E-mail: enquiries.ilb@berr.gsi.gov.uk
Website: www.berr.gov.uk/europeandtrade/importing-into-uk/import-licensing/notices-to-importers/page22864.html

6.11.2 Rural Payments Agency (RPA)

The Rural Payments Agency (RPA) is a governmental agency under the auspices of DEFRA (The Department for Environment, Food and Rural Affairs). The RPA issues import licences for agricultural, horticultural products and certain items of

131

food and drink. All imported food must obey certain rules to ensure that it is safe to eat. Further information on this can be found on the Food Standards Agency (FSA), see website www.food.gov.uk/foodindustry/imports/. There may be other import restrictions and it is the responsibility of importers to ensure that they are aware of them.

Contacts for imported food enquiries:

An A to Z of imported food and some health related topics with contact details for enquiries may be found on website: www.food.gov.uk/foodindustry/imports/contacts/importcontactus/

A full list of import restrictions and prohibitions is listed in volume 1 part 3 of HM Revenue and Customs Integrated Tariff available from TSO.

6.12   Countertrade

Russia over the past two decades has undergone major political, social and economic changes. Financial stability during the 1990's was fraught; reaching a crisis point in 1998. To enable international trade to continue unabated creative ways of trading were developed and refined. Amongst them was countertrade.

Countertrade is an umbrella term for a variety of reciprocal trading mechanisms that decrease or negate the need for the exchange of convertible currency for goods or services. Countertrade transactions are often arranged by third party specialists. All companies are strongly advised to seek up-to-date legal advice before signing contracts.

Legislation banning the export of joint ventures' goods other than their own products means that the countertrade option is now possible only where the product has been partly processed by the joint venture.

Forms of countertrade include:

a) Offset: In direct offset deals the supply of goods raised includes materials, components or sub-assemblies, which are obtained from the importing country. This method has often been used in defence contracts but is becoming more common in other sectors, especially where the importing country is seeking to develop its own individual capabilities.

b) Counter Purchase: Through counter purchase the exporter undertakes to purchase goods and services from the importing country, as a condition of securing the sales order. The value of the counter purchase undertaken may vary from between 10% and 100%, or more, of the original export order. This is the most common form of countertrade.

c) Barter: the direct exchange of goods for goods. This form of countertrade is rarely used.

d) Advance Purchase: a variation of counter-purchase with the aim of obtaining payment in advance for the exporter's goods. This form of countertrade is increasingly used in deals with heavily indebted countries.

e) Buy-back: an agreement for full or part payment in the form of goods produced from a production co-operation.

f) Bilateral clearing agreements: government-to-government trade agreements established for reciprocal trade flows in designated product/industry lines, measured by bilateral clearing accounts evidencing two-way trade flows in clearing currencies. With the emergence of radical political and economic changes in the former Soviet Union many bilateral agreements have been allowed to expire.

g) Tolling: One method favoured as a payment mechanism is tolling. Tolling occurs where manufacturers chosen have no money, and therefore cannot commence production. In a tolling deal, the customer provides the raw material and hires the capacity of a factory to turn his raw material into a final product. As a result, the supplier becomes an outside contractor to the purchaser. Finished goods are then supplied to the customer who pays in cash. Throughout the process the customer retains ownership of the raw material.

6.12.1 The structuring of a countertrade deal

The structuring of a countertrade deal can take an inordinate amount of time to complete. There is a very low success rate involved, and only a small percentage of deals actually come to fruition. More often than not this is due to the unavailability of export goods, of acceptable prices and/or marketable quality, suitable for linkage. Many of the deals that do occur relate to the countertrade of raw materials and commodities where market values are known and can be equated to goods or services supplied in exchange. It should be noted that such deals, as they are priced and sold in US dollars, may negate the need for countertrade.

7 SETTING UP IN RUSSIA

ANTAL INTERNATIONAL

Executive Recruitment

Sales · Marketing · Accountancy · Finance · Banking · HR · Legal · Engineering · Manufacturing · Logistics · IT

'A Global Recruitment Solution Applied Locally'

Continuous presence since 1994 in Russia

Leader in «Rising Star» Recruitment

Over 100 consultants in Russia, focusing on skill discipline as well as industry sector – expanding office network

Highly international business. We can do business in Russian, German, French, Italian, Spanish, Japanese, Korean, Portuguese and others

Great Britain
China Switzerland **Italy**
Hungary **Germany** UAE/Dubai
Russia Bulgaria Malta
Spain Belgium **India**
Netherlands Turkey Peru
France Croatia **Luxemburg**
Baltic Romania **Poland**
South African Republic

Moscow
+7 (495) 935-86-06
Moscow@antal.com

Ekaterinburg
+7 (343) 216-51-30
Ekaterinburg@antal.com

www.antal.com.ru

ANTAL INTERNATIONAL
Executive Recruitment

'A Global Recruitment Solution Applied Locally'

7.1   Travel arrangements

You are advised to arrange your travel through a specialised travel agent, who has the experience in the Market and preferably an office in Moscow.

7.1.1   Regular flights

7.1.1.1 bmi (British Midland International)

bmi operates three flights a day between Heathrow and Moscow Domodedovo Airport. The service includes a bilateral interline agreement with Transaero (See 7.1.1.2) through which the two operators jointly offer flights between the two cities as well as.sell and accept each other's tickets.

See website: www.flybmi.com

7.1.1.2 Transaero UK

Transaero UK offers scheduled services from London Heathrow to Moscow Domodedovo (DME), with connections to other parts of Russia and the CIS. Bookings may be made through your specialist travel agent or via bmi. See website: www.transaero.com

7.1.1.3 British Airways

British Airways operates three daily flights between Moscow (Domodedovo International Airport) and London-Heathrow (BA872-BA873, London – Moscow, 08:55 –15.50, Moscow – London, 17:10 – 18.20 and BA874-BA875, London – Moscow, 13:05 –20.00, Moscow – London, 21.20 – 22.15)

London – Moscow, 22.00 – 04.55 next day, Moscow – London 05.50 – 06.55 BA 880 – BA 881 .

Since 2003, British Airways has had a self-service Check-in Kiosk in Domodedovo airport. It also has an exclusive Lounge in Domodedovo for Club Europe passengers (business class) and Executive Club members (frequent flyer programme).

From St Petersburg British Airways operates daily to London-Heathrow (BA878-BA879, London – St Petersburg, 09:55 – 16:10, St Petersburg – London, 17:05 – 17:35).

British Airways, through bmi (see 7.1.1.1) also operates direct flights to Ekaterinburg, Monday, Thursday and Saturday 14.30 – 00.50 BA7585 and return Tuesday Friday and Sunday 13.10 – 14.00 BA 7586.

Tel: Reservations & All Other Enquiries: 0870 850 9850; Website: www.britishairways.com/travel/home/public/en_gb

You may also telephone your specialist travel agent who has access to promotional fares

British Airways office in Moscow is located in: 1st Tverskaya-Yamskaya, 23
Tel: 007 495 363 2525
Fax: 007 495 363 2503

7.1.1.4 Aeroflot

Aeroflot, the national airline, operates 8 flights a week out of Heathrow to Moscow. A daily service. London-Moscow flight time is usually around three hours, 40 minutes.

Aeroflot does not fly to St Petersburg (Pulkovo II), this is now handled by Rossiya-Russian Airlines

Do not buy non-refundable air tickets unless your visa arrangements have been settled.

Contact:

Aeroflot Russian International Airlines, Reservations Bookings and Reservations, 70, Piccadilly, London W1J 7NJ Tel: 020 7355 2233

Aeroflot, Leningradsky Prospekt 37 build 9, Moscow

Tel: 007 495 753 5555; website: www.aeroflot.ru/eng

Or your specialist travel agent

7.1.1.5 Other flights to Russia

It may be best to book flight arrangements that do not have immediate ticket issue restrictions, but still represent considerable savings over scheduled fares. The Russia House has such arrangements with Aeroflot, SAS, Austrian, Lufthansa, Czech, British Airways and Transaero.

Contact:

The Russia House Ltd

London Tel: 0207 403 9922; Fax: 0207 403 9933; E-mail: russiahouse@btinternet.com

Moscow Tel: 007 495 911 2609; Fax: 007 495 911 9232; E-mail: bmterra@co.ru

7.1.2. Regional flight information – arrival at Moscow.

If you have an onward journey your baggage must be custom cleared at Moscow.

Domestic flights operate from Sheremetyevo I (Website: www.sheremetyevo-airport.ru/?act=part&pid=512), Domodedovo (Website: www.domodedovo.ru/en), Vnukovo (Website: www.vnukovo.ru/eng/index.wbp) and Bukovo Airports.

A two hour thirty minute gap in flight schedules is generally required for connections to be made from Sheremetyevo terminal II to Sheremetyevo terminal I and vice versa. Similarly, allow for a longer gap in flight schedules between Domodedovo and other airports. For other airports it is prudent to allow a five hour gap. When transferring to a Russian domestic flight you and your luggage must clear Customs and immigration on arrival at Sheremetyevo's terminal II. Once completed you can transfer to terminal I and check in for your continuing flight. If you're connecting onto another CIS country your bags will usually be checked through to your final destination and you will remain in transit through the airport.

Domodedovo airport has only one terminal building and onward connections can usually be guaranteed provided you allow at least one hour 35 minutes between your arrival and your onward departure.

Meet and greet services and chaperoning services between airports is advisable for new visitors, and should be arranged, in advance. Help with this may be provided by any good, specialist travel agent.

7.1.3. Internal flights

There are over 100 regional airlines, euphemistically as "babyflots", in Russia. Internal flights within the Russian Federation from Moscow, St Petersburg and other cities can be arranged by most business travel agents in this country.

Transaero (see 7.1.1.2) has regular flights to most principal Russian cities. Flights on Transaero may also be booked with most business travel agents in this country.

Transaero agency
Sheremetyevo-I Airport City Terminal, ticket window N 46, 47,
Central Air Terminal, 37, Leningradsky prosp
RESERVATION IN MOSCOW
Tel: 007 495 241 4800 / 7676 (24 hours)

In addition, the larger domestic airlines – Sibir, Pulkovo, Kras Air and UT Air all have regular flights to most principal Russian cities from both Moscow & St Petersburg.

7.1.4. Charter flights

Chartering aircraft is now becoming common within the Former Soviet Union, with aircraft such as the YAK 40 and Tupolev 134 being refitted and offering executive class travel for 19 or 30 passengers respectively. For international routes corporate jets such as the Challenger 604, Gulfstream V or the Falcon 900 are also now available. Chartering aircraft for exclusive use provides flexibility, security and safety for the business traveller, enabling him to travel to specific destinations at a time convenient for him, and not for the scheduled timetable. This could be particularly important when travelling to remote regions where flights are infrequent, or where security is an issue. Where used by several highly paid staff, the saving on executive time and salary often outweighs the cost of chartering.

One of the most experienced companies in the corporate charter business is Clintondale Aviation, which can be contacted via their website: www.clintondale.com or in Russia Tel: 007 501 258 0651; UK Tel: 0117 929 7739; USA Tel: 001 845 8835277

7.1.5 Rail travel

Rail travel is cheap and reliable, although often slow and impractical in view of the sheer size of the country. Rail travel is popular with foreigners shuttling between Moscow and St Petersburg. There are several railway terminals in Moscow and St Petersburg, depending upon your destination.

In theory, foreigners are required to buy train tickets at a Central Railway Agency ticket window specifically designated for foreigners. Two of the most convenient are located at the Belorussky Station and the Leningrasky Station in Moscow. You can book tickets at stations or online via the state railway (tel: 007 495 262 9901; website: www.eng.rzd.ru). Children under five years of age travel free. Children aged five to nine pay half fares. It is possible to buy train tickets through agencies at a slightly higher price.

Most long distance trains have two different classes: coupe and "soft class" or SV. SV, the preferred option for most foreigners, is a private cabin with two beds, one on each side of a small table. Coupe has two sets of bunk beds. For overnight journeys, your travel agent should book SV.

Barry Martin, of The Russia House states: "If you are travelling alone and book one berth your travelling companion could be a coal miner or a glamorous model – Russian Rail carriers do not differentiate between the sexes. Play safe and book soft class 2-berth compartment for sole use."

You could request that your travel agent book these in advance – it will be more expensive than station prices, but for a westerner to buy a ticket at the station could be an impossible task. Imagine a non-English speaking Russian trying to book a ticket to Edinburgh at British Rail at Kings Cross – it would be worse!

There is a luxury overnight train service, called the Grand Express, which operates between Moscow and St Petersburg. It is a luxury service offering "hotel on rails" compartments complete with plush furniture and furnishings, showers, toilets and air conditioning. It also offers TV, DVD and internet access.

The Trans-Siberian Express is the world's longest continuous train journey, crossing seven time zones and 9,745km (5,778 miles) from Europe to the Pacific, with 91 stops from Vladivostok to Moscow. It runs from Moscow to the Pacific coast of Siberia and then on to Yokohama, Japan. There is a daily service. The through journey from Moscow to Yokohama takes 10 days. The Trans-Manchuri-an Express follows the same route, before heading southeast into China and down to Beijing.

Reservations on the Grand Express, Trans-Siberian Express or the Trans-Manchurian Express may be made through The Russia House Tel: 0207 403 9922

When travelling by rail certain precautions should be taken. Where possible, do not travel alone. Store valuables in the compartment under the bed/seat. Do not leave the compartment empty. You may ask for a locking device, which fits the door-handle internally, or use a belt to ensure that no one may gain access whilst you are asleep.

7.2   Visa requirements

All visitors to Russia must be in possession of a valid passport and visa. Travellers who arrive without a passport or entry visa may be subject to large fines, days of processing requirements imposed by Russian officials, and/or immediate departure by route of entry, at the traveller's expense.

Most airlines will refuse boarding to passengers with no visa and there will be no ticket refund.

7.2.1   Types of visa

Visas take three forms:
- business
- visitor / tourist
- homestay

7.2.2.1   Obtaining a visa

Visas may be obtained from:

Russian Embassy, Visa Section, 5 Kensington Palace Gardens, London W8 4QS. Tel: 020 7229 8027; Fax: 020 7229 3215; Website: www.rusemblon.org

Mon – Fri 9.00 a.m. to 12 noon (last admission 11.30am).

Consulate General of the Russian Federation in Edinburgh, 58 Melville Street, Edinburgh EH3 7HL. Tel: 0131 225 7098; Fax: 0131 225 9587; E-mail: edconsul.co.uk

Monday to Friday 9.00 a.m. to 12.30 p.m., 2.00 p.m. to 5.00 p.m.

Be prepared to queue up early in order to gain entry by 11.30. If you are late and the queue is long you may be turned away for another day. In the busy Easter and summer weeks the couriers are in the queue at 5.00 in the morning. Postal applications are not recommended.

Alternatively, and in many ways preferably, you should use the services of a specialist travel agent who will have couriers who visit the Consulate on a daily basis. They charge fees from £25 – £79 per application in addition to the Consulate charge.

7.2.2.2 Procedure for obtaining a visa

There are two stages to obtaining a visa
1.   Support/invitation from Russian Ministry of Internal or External Affairs
2.   Endorsement of the visa into the passport by the Russian Consulate, London

7.2.2.3 Endorsement of the visa into the passport

To endorse your visa into your passport, you or your travel agent will need:
◆ Your passport
◆ A completed visa form
◆ A passport photograph
◆ A visa support document or reference number

The Consulate should issue your visa on the same afternoon for a premium rate or in

seven working days at the most economical rate. The time keeping and control on cost is uncertain and a good travel agent should be used.

7.2.3   Business visa

There are five types of business visas:
◆ Single Entry 1 Month
◆ Double Entry 1 Month
◆ Single Entry 3 Month
◆ Double Entry 3 Months
◆ Multiple Entry 1 Year

To obtain a business visa support an invitation has to come from a Russian organisation that is accredited with the Ministry of Foreign or Internal Affairs. You will need to send a letter addressed to the Russian Consulate requesting the type/dates and purpose of the visa.

This can be faxed with an enlarged and light copy of the information page of your passport. It should be noted that some Russian firms do not have the contacts to invite or support you.

To do this
1) Fax over an enlarged (170%) and lightened photostat copy of the special-ised information page of your passport.
2) Fax over a 4 paragraph letter addressed to the Russian Consulate in London containing the following information:

Para. 1 Name the applicant and request the visa type and duration.

Para. 2 Confirm applicant has return air ticket and ample sojourn funds

Para. 3 Confirm that data on the visa form is true and correct

Para. 4 State nature of business and with whom and add ….. on a business programme organised by (name of business contact)

3) Send by Special delivery post or courier
a.   Passport
b.   Form completed
c.   Photograph
d.   Original letter

The support takes 5-7 days for a single or double entry visa. Cost from £98 to £177 according to type of visa and speed of request.

A multiple entry support takes 21 days. Cost from £259.00 Businessmen could also consider hotel supported tourist visas.

Alternatively, you may find it easier for your travel agent to supply your support through their Russian contact. The Russia House Ltd, for example, has been accredited with the Ministry of Foreign Affairs since 1980 and can support your visit and supply the necessary invitation.

7.2.4.1 Tourist Visa

Tourist visas are relatively simple to obtain. They are valid only for the dates that the hotel has been confirmed . Tourist support has to come from a Russian travel agency that is accredited with the Ministry of Foreign or Internal Affairs, or directly from the hotel. The cost of tourist support varies from hotel to agency used.

The hotel/tourist package booked for you should supply all of the necessary documents to support your visa. The hotel must be prepaid for the full period of stay. It is preferable to book your hotel through the specialised travel agent, as this enables them to control the situation and possibly obtain discounts for you.

7.2.4.2 Action to be taken for a tourist visa

1) Fax over an enlarged (170%) and lightened Photostat copy of the information page of your passport.
2) Fax over instructions to book hotel for the whole period of intended stay
3) Send by Special delivery post or courier
a.   Passport
b.   Form completed
c.   Photograph

7.2.5. Businessmen Travelling on Tourist Visitors/ Tourist Visa

Business travel on a tourist visa has been accepted since 1993. You should, however, be aware that the visa is only valid for the dates and number of days that you have booked hotels for. Should your Russian customer suddenly decide he cannot see you on the days you have booked (a regular occurrence) then that visa and cost is wasted and you have to start all over again. A business visa can be valid for 1 month starting from your first intended date of travel, thus giving you some flexibility in amended travel arrangements.

7.2.6.1 Homestay Visa

This type of visa is intended for persons staying with friends and relatives in flats in the cities of Moscow and St Petersburg only. Basically the home is used as a 'hotel address' with invitation provided by the hosts. You need to supply name, address and telephone number and the support invitation can be organised within a few hours. The cost of making these arrangements is included in the visa package offered by your travel agent.

Alternatively, you may apply through their relatives/friends for a visitor's visa with support from the local PVU (visa and registration department) office. The PVU's central office is located at Chernishevskaya Ulitsa 12, Moscow. Tel: 007 495 207 0113

This process can take 1 to 2 months to complete. In addition, many Russians are not keen to bring their attention to the PVU office. Homestay visas are valid for up to one month only.

7.2.6.2 Action to be taken for a homestay visa

1.   Fax over an enlarged (170%) and lightened photostat copy of the information page of your passport,

2.   Advise your travel agent of your host's details i.e. full name, address, telephone number in central Moscow or St Petersburg

3.   Send by Special delivery post or courier

a.   Passport

b.   Form completed

c.   Photograph

7.2.7   Transit visas

Transit visas are only issued to those stopping in Moscow en route to a third country. They are valid for a maximum of 72 hours in Russia.

7.2.8   Migration cards

Since 10 February 2003, all foreign nationals entering Russia must fill in a Migration card.

You must complete a new migration card each time you enter Russia, even if you have a multiple entry visa.

7.2.9.1   Employment Permits, Work Permits and Work Visas

On July 25, 2002, the President of Russia approved Federal Law # 115, "On the Legal Status of Foreign Citizens in the Russian Federation." This law came into force on the 29th of October 2002. The law defines the legal position of foreign citizens in the Russian Federation; it covers entry, exit, stay, and employment of foreign citizens in Russia.

Preferential procedures for obtaining work permits for highly qualified specialists to fill such positions as directors, their deputies, or directors of subdivisions by companies with foreign investments were abolished. In addition, preferential procedures for the employment of foreign employees by accredited representative offices and branches of foreign companies were also abolished.

Since June 9, 2003 every foreign employee working in a Russian legal entity or representative office or branch of a foreign company has had to obtain a work permit. On the basis of the work permit they will also need to obtain a work visa (Federal law "On legal status of foreign citizens in the Russian Federation" and Decree # 355). These must state the name of the foreign employee and the employee's company. Adherence to this provision is essential The Migration Service conducts outer checks of all the legal entities, representative offices, and branches that employ foreign citizens to verify the existence of work permits and work visas. Failure to have these will result in a fine and possible deportation. (See 7.2.9.4 and 7.2.9.5).

Once an employment permit is obtained, foreign employees must obtain personal Work permits. This is required even if the employees have accreditation cards from the Representative office. In addition to the work permit, a foreign employee must obtain a work invitation, which allows him to obtain multiple entry work visa for a year.

7.2.9.2 Stages of obtaining employment permit and work permits.

The following stages must be adhered to employment permits and work permits

1. Obtaining Approval to employ foreign employees at Territorial Employment Service.

2. Obtaining Approval to employ foreign employees at Moscow Department of Federal Employment Service.

3. Obtaining Employment Permit at Federal Migration Service.

4. Obtaining Work Permit at Migration Service

Visa support for representative offices and branches of foreign companies is conducted through the body that accredited them, for example,

◆ the State Registration Chamber (Russian abbreviation – GRP),
◆ the Chamber of Trade and Commerce (Russian abbreviation – TPP),
◆ the Ministry of Science, Industry and Technology

It is essential for a foreign employee to have the name of his company stated on both his work permit and his visa, except in the cases of representative offices and branches. These obtain visas through the body that has accredited them, such as the State Registration Chamber, the Chamber of Trade and Commerce, etc.

Resident business representatives will also need to register their passports and visas with the PVU office (see 7.2.6.1)

7.2.9.3 Visa support for foreign employees working at Russian legal entities

Company work permits are required of any Russian-based [domestic or foreign owned] businesses wishing to hire foreign nationals. To do this, the business must be registered with the PVU office. In addition, extensive documentation is required for initial application to the Department of Employment, Ministry of Interior. Further documentation may be required on an ad hoc basis. Once the application is submitted, the process time is normally four to eight weeks. The company work permit will be valid for one year and it can cover more than one employee. The permit must state the job titles and nationalities of each employee, but not their name—take advantage of this flexibility. Once this process is completed, the business organisation may then provide visa support for their foreign staff members by applying for the following types of invitations and visas:

– Work visas – for foreign employees working at Russian legal entities
– private visas – for family members
– business visas – for business trips of foreign staff members

This requirement is not necessary for representative offices or branches of foreign companies.

7.2.9.4 Penalties

According to Article 18.10 of the Administrative Code of the Russian Federation, a breach of the rules of employment by the employer, such as failure to obtain employment permits for foreign citizens, incurs a fine in the amount of 1000 to 2000 Roubles US$30-$60 USD.

If a foreign citizen breaches the rules of employment, for example by failing to obtain a work permit and work visa, he is subject to a fine in the amount of 500 to 1000 Roubles US$15-$30 USD, and a repeated breach results in deportation.

7.2.9.5 Necessity for personal registration

Foreign citizens who have entered the Russian Federation are obliged to register within three working days from the day of their arrival in Russia. If the foreign citizen changes the place of his stay in the Russian Federation, he must register at the new place of stay within three working days of arrival there. Registration of children under 18 is conducted at the same time as the registration of their parents. Registration is undertaken by the PVU office (see 7.2.6.1)

If a foreign citizen has lost the documents on the basis of which he entered the country, he cannot be registered. This foreign citizen will have to leave the Russian Federation not later than ten days after obtaining, upon his written request, a document proving that he lost the documents.

A breach of the above stated order of registration by a foreign citizen incurs a fine of 500 to 1000 Roubles (US$15-$30). A repeated breach of the order of registration may result in deportation (Article 18.10 of the Administrative Code of the Russian Federation).

7.2.9.6 Exemptions

Federal Law #115 stipulates some exceptions regarding the necessity of obtaining work permits for the following categories of foreign citizens:
- those who permanently reside in the Russian Federation
- those who temporarily reside in the Russian Federation
- employees of diplomatic representations; for example, workers at consular institutions of foreign states in the Russian Federation
- employees hired to assemble and maintain equipment imported into Russia by their companies
- journalists who are accredited in the Russian Federation
- students studying in Russia and working in their spare time
- lecturers and teachers

Obtaining Employment and a personal Work permits requires the approval of the Federal Migration Service and the Migration Service respectively.

7.2.10. Temporary residence permits

A temporary residence permit is a document proving the right of a foreigner to reside in Russia before obtaining a permanent residence permit. This should be issued within six months from the date of application. A temporary residence permit is issued for three years.

A temporary residence permit may be issued to a foreign citizen from within the quota established by the federal government or to any person:

1.Who was born in USSR and was a citizen of the USSR, or a person that was born in the Russian Federation

2. Declared disabled, who has a son or a daughter who is a Russian citizen

3. Who has at least one disabled parent who is a Russian citizen

4. Married to a citizen of Russia, who resides in Russia

5. Investing in Russia

7.2.10.1 Procedures for obtaining a temporary residence permit

1. The foreign citizen applies for a visa as a temporary resident (four-month single entry visa).

2. The foreign citizen applies for a temporary residence permit.

3. After obtaining a temporary residence permit, the visa of the temporary resident is prolonged.

4. If a foreign citizen wants to exit Russia he should apply for an exit/entrance visa.

7.2.10.2 Rights and obligations of a temporarily residing foreign citizen

1. A temporarily residing foreign citizen cannot, at his own discretion, change his place of residence within the territory of the region where he obtained the temporary residence permit, or reside outside the region where he obtained the temporary residence permit.

2. A temporarily residing foreign citizen cannot work outside the region where he obtained the temporary residence permit.

7.2.11 Residence permits

After obtaining a temporary residence permit, and residing in Russia no less than one year on this basis, a foreign citizen may apply for a permanent residence permit. A residence permit is issued to a foreigner for five years and can be prolonged for another five years. The residence permit enables a foreign citizen to travel in and out of Russia without a visa.

7.2.12 Exit visa

All foreigners must have an exit visa to depart. For short stays, the exit visa is issued along with the entry visa. For longer stays, the sponsor must obtain the exit visa after the traveller's arrival. Visitors who overstay their visa's validity, even for one day, or neglect to register their visa, may be prevented from leaving at the required time and risk future visa refusal.

7.3   Arrival and Customs Control

Most business visitors arrive at Sheremetyevo II or Domodedovo Airport in Moscow. Particularly at the former, the process of passport control, baggage collection and Customs is slow and can be frustrating. Sheremetyevo, with years more experience, is more adept at causing unnecessary discomfort and delay.

When you arrive in Russia you will be obliged to fill in a Customs declaration form, and retain a second identical form for presentation when you leave the country. These are usually handed out on the aircraft. If they are not, they should be obtained and completed in the arrivals hall.

If you are arriving in Russia with less than $10,000 or departing with less than $3,000 you do not need to complete Customs declaration forms and you can pass through the green gate (See 4.12.2).

If you do not declare an item on entry, especially large sums of currency, and you have it with you when you leave, it may be confiscated. The rule, therefore, is to write down everything of value (e.g. watch, wedding ring, camera) and insist a Customs officer verifying and stamps your Customs declaration and ensure it is given back to you. You should keep your Customs declaration in a safe place, as you will need to show it when you leave the country. If declaring large sums of money, ensure that you are met immediately you leave the Customs post.

Lost or stolen Customs forms should be reported to the Russian police, and a police report (spravka) should be obtained to present to Customs officials upon departure.

7.4   Gratuities and tipping

Taxi drivers, who pre-arrange the fare with you, do not expect gratuities and tipping. Small tips should be given to porters. Tipping is increasingly expected at restaurants, with a tip of 10-15%, rounded up to the next round figure, being the norm. Where help has been pre-arranged by a business associate, for example, arranging a chaperone, a small gift such as chocolates is appreciated.

7.5.   Transportation

7.5.1. From the airport

Transfer services from the airport to the hotel are recommended. This can be arranged, in advance, through the company that sponsored your visit, good travel agents and some hotels. Visitors may also hire a car without a driver (see 7.5.4).

Taxis may be hired from booths available at the airport. With taxi fares, much will depend upon your level of Russian, familiarity with the city, general ability to haggle with the driver. Note that taxis may not always be clean, comfortable or safe. It is inadvisable to flag down cars on the street.

7.5.1.1 From the airport (Moscow)

Sheremetyevo Airport is 30km (18.5 miles) north of Moscow. Minibuses go to the airport from metro station Rechnoy Vokzal (journey time – 20 minutes). Taxis are also available to the city. Taxis are not usually metered and businessmen will be charged a fare of 2,000 Roubles (about US$70) to get to central Moscow.

Domodedovo is 48km (25 miles) southeast of Moscow. An Aeroexpress train runs from the domestic arrivals lounge to Paveletsky station in the centre of Moscow. Journey time is 40 to 50 minutes and a single ticket costs 75 Roubles (approximately US$2.5). Express buses and a 24-hour shuttle service are also available. Two official taxi firms operate at the airport. From Domodedovo, the price should be 800 Roubles (about US$30).

Prior to taking any taxi ensure that you get the name of the individual you are booking from, the name of the driver and registration number of the car.

Journey times from the city to the airport can take up to 2 hours depending on traffic conditions, particularly on Friday afternoons and Sunday evenings.

7.5.1.2 From the airport (St Petersburg)

The airport in St Petersburg, Pulkovo, is located 17km south of the city. International flights arrive at Pulkovo-2, while internal flights arrive at Pulkovo-1.

There is a bus service (route N13) from the airport to the nearest Metro station (Moskovskaya). A mini bus called "route taxi" serves the same route.

Travel from the airport to the city centre usually takes an hour by public transport and half an hour by taxi. The cost by taxi will be about 1,400 Roubles (about US$50).

7.5.1.3 From the airport (Ekaterinburg)

International flights to Ekaterinburg arrive at Koltsovo airport. The taxi from the airport to the city centre should cost no more 800 Roubles (about US$30).

7.5.2.1. Public transport (Moscow)

Getting around Moscow is relatively easy – especially if you can speak Russian. Moscow has an extensive bus, trolley-bus and tram system. Buses operate 0500-0000. It is recommended that you only use these if you are familiar with Moscow or speak Russian. Tickets are purchased inside the station or on board from the drivers or bus conductors (look for the red armband) directly.

The famous Moscow Metro is clean, inexpensive and aesthetically pleasing but also very crowded. The fee for one trip by Metro is fixed irrespective of the length of your route. Entrance is by way of a travel card, which may be purchased in the Metro entrance halls. Alternatively, for more than one journey, you may purchase a magnetic card. Prices for magnetic cards are:

1 journey – 13 Roubles
2 journeys – 26 Roubles (valid three calendar days)
5 journeys – 65 Roubles (valid thirty days from first entry)
10 journeys – 105 Roubles (valid thirty days from first entry)
20 journeys – 195 Roubles (valid thirty days from first entry)
60 journeys – 375 Roubles (valid thirty days from first entry)
Monthly card (maximum 70 journeys) – 385 Roubles

A monthly card for the Metro and other means of public transport costs 770 Roubles.

If you purchase a monthly pass or season ticket simply show it to a ticket collector.

Tickets must be punched in the machine provided on the bus.

7.5.2.2. Public transport (St Petersburg)

St Petersburg has a well-developed system of public transport, which includes a metro, buses, trams, trolley-buses, commuter trains. A trip on the metro is 5 Roubles.

7.5.3 Taxi services

Taxis, too, are plentiful. They are either the distinctive yellow volgas or simply private cars prepared to run you to your official destination for a small fee. You should note that drivers of private cars might not have adequate third-party insurance. Private cars are an alternative worth considering, but use common sense, and exercise extreme caution. There have been occasions when foreigners have been robbed. As in other countries, check the rate prior to entering a taxi or private car and agree the price first. The average price for a journey within the centre of Moscow is approximately 90 – 180 Roubles. As taxis are still relatively cheap, it is recommended that, if you have several places to visit, you hire a car for the day or even the week. You should only pay fares in Roubles.

7.5.4 Car hire

Western cars and minibuses can be hired from main hotels or the airport. Car rental is also available from Avis, Budget, Europcar and Hertz and other local car hire firms. Chauffeured cars are available in major cities. Credit card payments are accepted by nearly all car hire firms.

7.5.5 Use of own car

Visitors travelling in their own cars must possess the following documents at all times:
- passport and visa,
- international driving licence (The AA – see website www.theaa.com/getaway/idp/ – can provide details on how to obtain one),
- national licence with authorised translations,
- itinerary card bearing visitor's name and citizenship,
- car registration number,

♦ full details of itinerary presented upon entry to the Russian Federation relating to the route and the date and place of stopovers,

♦ insurance documentation (See 9.4.3)

♦ The form issued to all tourists entering Russia by car guaranteeing that the vehicle will be taken out of the Russian Federation on their departure. This obligation also applies to vehicles, which may have been damaged during your travels. Road tax is payable upon entry to the country.

The European part of the Russian Federation depends heavily on its road network. Generally, the few roads in Siberia and further east are impassable during the winter. It is not recommended to drive in Russia as harassment from traffic police is endless. If you do decide to drive, it is advisable to pre-plan the itinerary and accommodation requirements. On the majority of tourist routes, signposts are also written in the Latin alphabet. Sample distances: Moscow to St Petersburg: 692km (432 miles); Moscow to Minsk: 690km (429 miles); Moscow to Rostov-on-Don: 1,198km (744 miles); Moscow to Odessa: 1,347km (837 miles).

Motorists should avoid driving at night if possible.

7.5.5.1 Speed limits

Traffic drives on the right. The standard speed limit for built-up areas is 37mph (60 kph), outside built-up areas is 55 mph (90 kph) and 68 mph (110 kph) on motorways (Brest-Moscow). Visiting motorists who have held a driving licence for less than two years must not exceed 43 mph (70 kph).

7.5.5.2 Other driving regulations

♦ Hooting the horn is forbidden except when to do so might prevent an accident;

♦ Children under twelve cannot travel as front seat passenger unless using restraint system appropriate to size;

♦ Every car must display registration plates and stickers denoting the country of registration and be fitted with seat belts, a first-aid kit, a fire extinguisher and an emergency sign (triangle) or red light;

♦ It is compulsory for front / rear seat occupants to wear seat belts, if fitted as standard to the car;

♦ There is zero tolerance for driving under the influence of alcohol or drugs;

♦ It is against the law to drive a dirty car.

7.6   Inter-city bus travel

Long-distance coach services are "slow, uncomfortable and only marginally cheaper than train travel with none of the romance." World Travel Guide: Website: www.worldtravelguide.net/country/236/internal_travel/Europe/Russian-Federation.html

7.7   Walking

Normal care should be taken when walking in Moscow, St Petersburg or any other city. Place names and local road signs are in Cyrillic and few Russians will be able to direct you to where you want to go (see 7.13).

7.8   Obtaining currency

Russia is still largely a cash economy. Legislation stipulates the sole recognised currency in the Russian Federation is the Rouble. Nowadays, therefore, all payments should be made in Roubles, and the Rouble is now freely convertible within

Russia. Businessmen can convert currency in their hotel, banks and many shops. Businessmen are advised not to exchange money at unregistered kiosks, which are illegal and may be dangerous.

Generally, the US dollar or the Euro is more familiar as an exchange currency. It is recommended that travellers take these in small denominations (ideally nothing higher than US$20 or €20). The notes should be relatively new issues, if possible. ATMs are becoming more widespread in Moscow, St Petersburg and Ekaterinburg. Nearly all major retail outlets now accept credit cards.

Oganes Sarkisov in BISNIS Bulletin, February 2002, (website: www.bisnis. doc.gov/BISNIS/BULLETIN/02febbull7.htm) gives the following useful advice:

Ways of getting cash from abroad while you are already in Russia exist, but they are limited and costly:

- One can withdraw cash from one's own bank account in a foreign bank by using cash machines that are available in Moscow and other big cities. Usually such transactions are subject to a fee of 1-4 percent of the sum of the transaction. A number of cash machines or Bankomati are to be found in central Moscow.
- Traveller's cheques can be cashed at selected Russian banks and their regional branches for a fee (for example, the Russian Savings Bank and Alfa Bank charge a two percent flat fee and Vneshtorgbank charge 1 percent). The representative office of American Express in Russia does not cash traveller's cheques, but cash operations are handled by the Delta Bank located in the same building.
- International money transfer agents, such as Western Union, MoneyGram, and (in the near future) RIA Express can transfer money from the United States or Europe almost instantly, but such services are relatively expensive.
- Wire transfer to a bank account requires having an account in a Russian bank and cannot be considered as a good alternative for short-term visitors. Incoming wire transfer fees are 1-3 percent of the amount wired and can take several days to clear.

7.9   Organised crime

Certain forms of business venture, as in other countries, may be prone to organised crime. Whilst each situation should be considered on its own merits, advice on the potential risks, identifying the counter-parties or the structure of the company and establishing how to proceed with greater confidence, can be obtained, prior to travelling, from:

- Foreign and Commonwealth Office (FCO): The FCO provides country-specific Travel Advice notices aim to ensure that British travellers are well prepared before their departure. Information can be obtained directly from the FCO on Tel: 0870 606 0290, or see website: www.fco.gov.uk/servlet/Front?pagename=OpenMarket/ Xcelerate/ShowPage&c=Page&cid=1007029390590
- Security and risk assessment firms such as
  - Control Risks Group, Tel: 0207 970 2100; Website: www.crg.com/-
  - DRUM Resources Ltd Tel: 0207 929 2473; Website: www.drumresources. com/

See section 9.13 on street crime

7.10   Hotels

For non-resident business representatives and those in the process of establishing an office, good hotel accommodation can be difficult to find, especially in Moscow. As large Soviet-era hotels have been torn down, the pace of new construction has not kept up, and there is currently a shortage of mid-range hotel rooms in the city, especially during large conferences and exhibitions.

Published prices for single and twin rooms, in Western standard, business class (4 and 5 Star) hotels, range upwards from US$200 and US$400 per night, respectively. A specialist travel agent will try to obtain a discounted price, which may be as high as 60% off the published price. Luxury hotels are still a rarity outside Moscow and St Petersburg but can be found in areas such as Tiumen in Western Siberia or Ekaterinburg in the Urals. St Petersburg tends to be more expensive than Moscow and at times – especially June during the White Nights Festival – it can be very difficult to get a room.

There are some conveniently situated, independent business class hotels in Moscow and many budget-grade establishments where rooms are clean, functional and with private facilities. Many businessmen, however, looking at cost and value for money use serviced apartments. Moscow has a well developed market for temporary apartments, and this avenue is particularly popular with business travellers coming here for longer stays, who do not want to be confined to a hotel bedroom. Most properties are based within the city centre, with modern furniture and fittings, high speed internet, and good access to the Metro.

On the outskirts of Moscow and St Petersburg, cheaper hotel accommodation can be found. While adequate, standards and service will be quite low, and these hotels may be some distance from the nearest metro station. Caution is necessary, with unfriendly staff, unsanitary rooms, and an unsavoury clientele, hotels located off the beaten track can sometimes be dangerous. In addition, it is wise to be wary of hotel ratings. A property holding 2-3 bunk beds per room would be classified as a hostel in the UK, but is deemed to be a hotel in Moscow. The Hotel Druzhba, with 360 rooms has over 1000 beds.

In regional cities, cheaper hotels can be found with rooms available for about US$60 per night. These are generally less comfortable, but perfectly adequate. In the last few years, small private hotels have opened in most of the main regional cities, and international chains are now starting to expand out of the two capitals as well.

Prospective Russian clients will receive an impression of you from the hotel where you are staying. One British businessman insisted on the new Hyatt Park Ararat Hotel in Moscow because he knew his Russian contact would definitely come to dinner there. The extra cost of this hotel was therefore worth the price to get the meeting.

Most hotel rooms can now be booked directly from the UK through specialist travel agents or increasingly directly over the internet or by phone. 2 useful websites are www.hotels-moscow.ru and www.moscow-hotels.net , although for the international chains such as Holiday Inn or Marriott, it is better to use a site such as www.expedia.com or their own corporate sites. For serviced apartments, www.troikarelocations.com is helpful. Remember visas are needed for trips to Russia (see 7.2).

When visiting the regions particularly, it is recommended you take the following with you:

◆ Adaptors – standard voltage in Russia is 220 volts A/C. Sockets take 2-pin plugs;

◆ A travel alarm clock;

◆ large bath towel;

- first aid kit (see 9.6.2);
- list of main contact numbers (a copy should be left with main family/business contacts in the United Kingdom). A copy of contact addresses in Cyrillic, and especially your hotel, may be helpful;
- a photocopy of your passport and visa;
- suitable clothing, which may include thermal underwear and especially socks, for Northern Russia. Business suit for meetings
- Good walking shoes or thermal boots. Leather soled and patent shoes are likely to be spoilt owing to salt on roads, the poor condition of many Russian streets and adverse climatic conditions. However, if you are going to any-where smart, well polished shoes are the norm. Shoe polish, although readily available, is also worth taking.
- Business cards written in Cyrillic. These may be obtained through the Russo-British Chamber of Commerce (see 10.26).

7.11   Restaurants

Moscow restaurants fall into and out of fashion regularly. To find the "in" place to eat check the free magazine, eXile. This may be found in most hotel lobbies. Restaurants open late in Moscow. For many, 11 o'clock in the evening is a perfectly normal hour to start eating.

7.12   Interpretation Services

Assistance with language training is discussed in more detail in Chapter 12. Private arrangements can be made for interpreters. The quality of the interpreter can vary enormously. A rough guide to payment is between US$30 – 60 depending on the experience of the interpreter and the intensity of the work. Organisations such as the Russo-British Chamber of Commerce (See 10.26) can pre-arrange an interpreter for you.

Most non-budget hotels offer interpretation services, which can be booked either in advance or on arrival in Moscow. There are also a number of specialist agencies offering interpreters and translation. These include:

- Eurologos. Tel: 007 495 268 7677; Fax: 007 495 268 7677; Website: www.eurologos.com/
- Mark Business Translations. Tel: 007 495 737 7161; Fax: 007 495 166 4521; Website www.netcheck.com/mbt.shtml
- Max Sidorov Tel: 007 495 130 0987; Website: translate.max.ru/eng/index.htm

Using an interpreter will increase the time you need for any conversation. A useful tip is to check that your interpreter understands precisely what you are trying to state. Even good interpreters can misinterpret terms such as a "credit check" and "cheque". Additionally, agree that you will speak first and then pause for the interpretation. This allows for continuity and counters any possible confusion that may arise from simultaneous translation.

7.13   Cyrillic

Learning Russian is always going to be a good idea for a frequent visitor or resident. However, it is still useful to familiarise yourself with the Russian alphabet (see annex) to undertake simple tasks such as reading a metro map. The Russia House Ltd (Tel: 020 7403 9922) has produced a very good learning guide, which it claims will teach you the Cyrillic alphabet in 3 hours.

7.14   Office space

Western-style office space, complete with adequate communications facilities, used to be very difficult to obtain. As a result of the opening-up of the market during the 1980s, several office-block projects have been completed in Moscow, and more are in the pipeline. Some are refurbishments of existing properties; others are completely new projects.

As with hotels, Western-style professionally managed office space in Moscow is expensive – around US$600 as well as office maintenance costs at $110-$120 per square meter per year and the length of the lease. In St Petersburg, prices range from $250 to $800 per m2.

Serviced offices are also available from several providers with rates in the range of $1,500 to $1,800 per workstation per month. However, these buildings do provide good communications and, usually, security. Be careful if offered part cash rental propositions. All legal rent agreements must be authorised in the local tax inspectorate and Police Department.

An alternative for both office and residential accommodation is to lease and upgrade a property direct from its Russian freeholder. Such property is often advertised in English-language periodicals such as The Moscow Times and Commercial Real Estate (www.cre.ru/index.php). There are a number of Moscow-based joint ventures with experience of refurbishments.

Property agents operating in Russia also provide services to acquire office space.

Office furnishing (see 9.2) and security (see 8.6.8) are other matters that will need to be considered.

7.15   Telecommunications

7.15.1 Telephone system

Office space in the modern joint-venture development should come complete with good international telecommunications systems. This should always be checked in advance.

The International Trade Administration refers to the inconsistent quality and accessibility of the telecommunications infrastructure throughout Russia.

While major population centres are quite well served, large areas of this vast country have extremely poor access or none at all. In rural areas there are 54,000 villages with no telephone access whatsoever. In the country as a whole, there are a mere 21 phone lines per 100 people, and the waiting list for basic services currently has 6 million names.

Consequently, there are a number of joint ventures operating in Moscow installing modern satellite links into offices or homes. Outside Moscow and St Petersburg there is generally no alternative to the Russian system. One British joint-venture company which is often recommended is Comstar Tel: 007 495 956 0000; Fax: 007 495 956 0707; website: www.comstar.ru/en/

Other companies include:

- Combellga International Satellite Communications Tel: 007 495 931 9950; Fax: 007 495 937 3636;
  Website: http://goliath.ecnext.com/coms2/product-compint-0000496371-page.html
- Golden Telecom Tel: 007 495 787 1000; Fax: 007 495 258 7828;
  Website: www.goldentelecom.com/
- Rascom Tel: 007 495 956 0080/1308; Fax: 007 495 303 9171

Website: www.rascom.ru/?cat=en_home&sr=1

♦ Siemens Tel: 007 495 237 6476; Fax: 007 495 737 1001; Website: www.sie-mens.ru/en

7.15.2 Internet and E-mail

Internet and E-mail services have developed rapidly over the past 7 years and are still expanding. There are now a number of internet cafés in Moscow and St Petersburg.

7.15.3. Cellular telephones & pagers

Coverage, whilst improving, is still limited in sparsely populated areas. Large cities are now well served by mobile phone infrastructure.

Providers of the cellular and pager services include:

♦ Mobile Telesystems
Tel: 007 495 766 0177; Website: www1.mtsgsm.com/profile/

♦ Moscow Cellular Communications
Tel: 007 495 744 4444;Website: www.mcc.ru (Russian only)

♦ BeeLine
Tel: 007 495 910 5831; Website: www.beeonline.ru (Russian only)

7.15.4 Telephone booths

Phone booths are available in Moscow and St Petersburg. Telecards, which are available from kiosks, shops and newspaper stands, must be used. There are also hard currency/credit card telephone booths operated by Comstar.

7.16   Postage

The Russian domestic postal service is slow, but is becoming more reliable. International mail to and from the UK may take two to three weeks to reach its destination. If a parcel has to be sent by post, an established mail or express courier service such as DHL, TNT, UPS or Federal Express should be used.

The Russia House Ltd (Tel: 0207 403 9922) operates a personal once a week service London-Moscow-London over the weekend. Apart from parcels documents and letters it will also take cash dollars to and from Russia.

7.17   Staffing

Finding the right employee is sometimes a hit and miss operation. Many companies offer contracts to people with whom they have already come into contact, or pick up staff on the grapevine. There are also recruitment firms who, for a fee of usually 20– 35% of first year gross package, will either provide a benchmark selection of CVs or will run a proactive search of the market – the fee depends on the introduction rather than the amount of time the search takes and the cheapest option is not always the most effective. Where the recruitment firm works on a "fee on success" basis they are often representing good candidates in the market to anybody who is looking rather than working for you exclusively. You may consider engaging a recruitment firm with an upfront financial commitment – in this case the firm will be working exclusively on your behalf.

Recruitment companies fall into two categories, mid-senior level search and selection firms (for professional and management positions) and staffing agencies for clerical and blue collar workers. It is not advised to use recruitment firms who have no physical presence in Russia.

Antal International is British company with western management which has been in Russia since 1993 can advise on all staffing and recruitment issues. Tel: 007 495 935 8606; website: www.antal.com

7.17.1 Russian staff

The Russian labour force is generally highly skilled and well educated, with top calibre recruits able to command similar salaries to expatriate employees. Such staff can be found through recruitment companies such as Antal International.

Low and unskilled labour can be sourced through companies such as Manpower, Adecco and Kelly Services; all of whom have a presence in Moscow.

Labour mobility is problematic due to the under-developed housing and mortgage market, housing shortages, and the need for residency permits and registration. The availability of subsidised housing, family and cultural ties and work place subsidies such as a company cafeteria and grocery shop, will makes lower paid workers reluctant to move.

7.17.2 Employment contracts

Employment contracts can be for an unlimited period, a fixed period of five years or less, or for the duration of a project. If a fixed-term contract expires, the employer may dismiss the employee without giving a reason, but he must do so no later than the last day of the contract otherwise the employment will be regarded as having been confirmed and made permanent. Trial periods cannot, without trade union permission, exceed three months. During the trial period an employee can be terminated easily, exceeding the trial period automatically qualifies the employee as a permanent staff member.

Employees are protected against instant dismissal although drunkenness, embezzlement and long-term ill health are grounds for dismissal. Incompetence is a more difficult issue. There has to be a history of non-performance of duties and an official reprimand must be issued following the correct procedures. The employer should be able to show that there has been a severe and noticeable decline in the standard of work performed during the contract of employment. It is recommended that job descriptions are given to all staff and that they are informed of all company disciplinary procedures.

There is, in Russia, a right to strike. The Labour Trade states: "It is forbidden to reduce the pay of a worker on the grounds of sex, age, race, nationality, religious or voluntary associations."

All employees are entitled to paid sick leave allowances amounting to between 60% and 100% of their salary, depending on the length of their service, number of dependents and other factors. The period of sick leave is dependent upon the employee's doctor. It is therefore prudent that employment contracts stipulate sickness benefit rules and termination policy. It is illegal to pay Russian employees in currencies other than Roubles.

Women are guaranteed 112 days' paid maternity leave and an option to work for up to a year, after the birth of a child, on partial pay. Holidays (see Key Facts), paternity leave, marriage leave and compassionate leave are also obligatory.

7.17.3 Payment of Western staff

Since 16 December 1993 each non-Russian member of foreign staff must have both a valid visa and a work permit (see 7.2.9.1). Work permits must be authorised by the Russian Federal Migration Service. Non-Russian employees have equal employment rights whilst in Russia but may lose their right to stay in the country if the grounds for staying are no longer valid. Foreigners must register with the police within 72 hours of their arrival in the Russian Federation.

7.17.4 Methods of payment

Russian currency law is not concerned with settlement of debts in foreign countries between non-residents if:

♦ payment takes place outside Russia
♦ is made through the Russian bank account of one of the non-residents
♦ transferred to an account abroad, provided the funds so transferred have either been previously imported into Russia or acquired in Russia in compliance with exchange control regulations.

Since 24th April 1996 payment of capital operations, for example, membership fees, insurance premiums, payment for foreign periodicals, pension schemes and alimony, and for goods and services provided abroad are not subject to exchange control regulations.

With the onset of the 13% flat rate income tax many western companies have become more transparent. The vast majority of western multinationals now fully comply on this issue. Although "black" or "grey" payments are still a feature of some organisations you will find it increasingly difficult to attract staff if you continue to use schemes. Employees will find it increasingly difficult to secure bank loans without a formal proof of income and the tax authorities are becoming more vigilant.

Salaries should be quoted gross (as an income tax increase is a real possibility) and there is a growing trend to quote in Roubles. It is however still common to confirm a salary in US$ but pay in Roubles at the Central Bank Rate. In interviews candidates still generally refer to their salaries as a net figure.

On 1st January 2001, the Unified Social Tax came into law. Salaries are taxed at source, on total income (including benefits in kind), with the employer deemed to be the tax agent. In Russia there is a 13% flat rate on income tax. Dividends are taxed at 6%. However, with regard to social security payments, unlike the UK, tax rates are regressive and vary from 35.6% for low paid employees to 5% for employees earning Roubles 600,000 per annum (see 3.3.3). Employers are obliged to make monthly contributions of up to 28% to the Russian Federation Pension Fund on behalf of their employees, including non-Russian staff. These contributions are mandatory from the employer and are not a deduction from salary. Payment of this is tracked through the individual's ID number corresponding to his Pension Fund Account. Persons engaged in personal and professional services (e.g. lawyers) pay five per cent. The employee contributes one per cent of salary to the Fund.

7.17.5 Staff leasing

Many companies try to avoid bureaucracy, paperwork and tax by arranging a service contract with their employees, which technically makes them self-employed and responsible for arranging their own social security payments. The status of such arrangements has yet to be tested in the Russian courts. This can be particularly useful in the process of establishing your entity in Russia or if you do not wish to set up a physical entity. Antal Ltd is able to act as a third party physically employing staff on your behalf in Russia. In this case the third party will handle all payroll calculations, administration, tax and social cost payments and contractual issues. Antal International, Tel: 007 495 935 8606; Website: www.antal.com.

7.18   Salary levels

Russia's manual labour force is generally poorly paid, however candidates with foreign languages, western outlook and professional skills in sales, marketing, finance, HR, procurement, manufacturing with 2 – 5 years experience in a western organisation often command salaries of US$2,000 to $8,000 per month. The official minimum wage in Russia is 20,500 Roubles per month for a maximum 40-hour working week. However, wages and fringe benefits vary widely by industry, position and region. In 2006, the average monthly wage in Russia was 7,500 Roubles ($250) per month. The equivalent of US$500to $1,000 per month is now common for many manual staff and $2000 for senior clerical staff, particularly in areas where there is a concentration of western manufacturers and very low unemployment.

Salaries for well qualified, bilingual, Russian managers in the larger cities are comparable to those of their counterparts in the West e.g. a Russia CEO of a large foreign enterprise could earn as much as $200-300k per year, whereas a local Russian marketing manager could earn $60-120k per year. (See 7.17).

Western staff may also require other support. Employers often pay all or part of relocation and housing costs including customs clearance. Western employees will usually be covered for tax and legal advice, medical insurance, international school fees, car and driver or taxi allowance, club memberships and memberships in networking groups. In addition, they may have housekeeping and cleaning services, cross-cultural and language training and an entertainment allowance.

There is a requirement of 4 weeks fully paid annual holiday after an employee has been in continuous employment for 11 months. They are also entitled to ten days of public holidays. It is customary for Russian manual workers to take all their annual leave at one time however white collar staff now generally conforms to normal western practices. Be aware that generally there is an exodus from work in the first two weeks of January and Russian Easter.

Noting the cost of senior staff, it is recommended that information provided by applicants be confirmed. Applicants should be informed that their information will be checked. This is now normal practice. Established referencing agencies include:

Control Risks Group, Tel: 0207 970 2100; Website: www.crg.com/
DRUM Resources Ltd London Office Tel: 0207 929 2473
Moscow Office Tel: 007 495 721 1131
Website: www.drumresources.com/

7.19   Opening a bank account

Any company operating an office in Russia will need to open a local bank account with a Russian commercial bank licensed to handle foreign currency transactions, if only for the purpose of paying its office expenses. Companies may also open Rouble accounts with these banks. The British banks' representative offices in Moscow all have dealings with other banks in Russia and advise on options available. If they are representative offices, rather than branches, they will not be able to provide any banking services.

Almost 800 banks have a license to deal in foreign exchange, including some 270, which have gained full general licences, allowing them to hold hard currency accounts with foreign banks. Most of the 130 foreign owned banks restrict currently their activities to Moscow, St Petersburg and other cities.

For representative offices wishing to open an account with a Russian bank the following must be completed:

(a) a request, on the bank's form, to open a hard currency current account;

(b) a specimen signature card. Each signatory has to sign the form in front of a bank official. The bank official will want to see further documentation from each individual so that he can verify their identity;

(c) a notarially certified copy of the certificate of accreditation issued by the Russian accreditation organisation (usually, but not always, the Ministry for Foreign Economic Affairs);

(d) an extract from the company's registry confirming registration of the company in its home country. In practice, for British companies this means a copy of the certificate of Incorporation issued by Companies House. This certificate must be accompanied by a translation into Russian, and both documents must be certified as exact by the Russian Embassy or a Russian consulate in the country of registration;

(e) an authority signed by the head of the company, granting power to the authorised signatory/ (signatories) to operate the account. The authority must be in Russian or accompanied by a translation and both documents should have a notary's or consular certification. For the UK, this is most likely to be in the form of a board resolution on opening the account and confirming the signatories. (Confirmation by a company secretary that the authority is a true extract, which is customary practice in the UK, will not be adequate.) The chairman will also need to sign the document;

(f) a copy of the company's statutes (memorandum and articles of association) translated into Russian (may not be required);

(g) copies of the company's registration with the pension and tax authorities. Failure to register with the tax authorities could result in a fine and closure of the account; and

(h) a deposit sum to cover initial charges (between US$10 and $50) and an opening credit amount.

As items (d) and (f) have to be produced for the accrediting body in order to gain accreditation, it is worth having extra copies made at that time for subsequent use when opening a bank account.

7.20   Office bills

For those companies located in Western or UPDK-run offices, all bills for communications, electricity, heating, etc., are in hard currency and are payable to the lessee. Joint ventures may be able, through their partner, to run an office at Rouble costs.

8   RETAIL: SPECIAL CONSIDERATIONS

8.1 Retailing in Russia

The retail market in Russia is both diverse and changing. Department store and retail chains are developing. Mail order is still under developed owing to the slowness and unreliability of the postal, telecommunications, distribution and delivery systems. Some limited catalogue selling does occur in Russia through agents selling via catalogues in industrial units and factories employing large numbers of personnel. Mail order by fax, to non-Russians living and working in Moscow, is a popular purchasing mechanism. At the top end of the market, high quality boutiques exist but are uncommon outside of the larger cities.

At the lower end of the market, kiosks or Chelnoks abound. There are also many flea markets, hawkers and traders from the backs of vans, selling generally cheap goods generally imported from China or Turkey or domestically produced. Occasionally, expensive, branded products may be sold through such outlets. Unorganised trade is estimated as being at least 27% of retail sales. It is estimated that only 6% of Russians shop in supermarkets and trade centres.

Internationally renowned store names are increasingly in evidence although the range may differ from their home market. As high tariffs and margins have to be accounted for, retail prices can be up to four times the price of their Western European equivalent.

Demand for luxury consumer goods produced overseas is increasing. As wealth spreads beyond a handful of oligarchs into a new affluent class and expanding middle class, Russia has become the world's fourth-biggest luxury market after the US, Japan and China. However, increasingly, it is becoming fashionable or even prestigious to buy Russian products, which are slowly becoming more readily available. Many Western products are also "Russified" through use of packaging and labelling, which must be in Russian. It is now usual to see goods advertised and promoted through marketing strategies that focus on local concepts and values.

Western investment, which to date remains limited, is still focused predominantly on the luxury end of the market where there is significant investment in the boutique market. Retailers also have a presence in many of the new Western International hotels. There are relatively few large Western stores, although they are becoming more common, and in Moscow, widespread. Out of centre shopping precincts are also being created.

Retailing is growing apace, especially in the food sector. In April 2001, the Moscow Government approved a general plan to develop 300 shopping centres by 2020, doubling existing retailing space from 8 to 16 million sq. m. Plans include the creation of supermarket space (2-10,000 sq. m.), trade complexes (10-80,000 sq. m.) and trade zones (130,000 – 400,000 sq. m.). The latter will include entertainment centres and wholesale outlets.

8.2. Purchasing Power

Russia has a population of 141.3 million. Some 50 million people (about one third of the population) spend 80% of their income on food, with the balance on inexpensive consumer goods, including clothing. According to the CIA World Factbook, the number of people falling below minimum income levels has declined from 40% in 1997 to 18% in 2007, with real income increasing 12 per cent in 2007 alone. There is a growing middle class in Russia, especially European Russia, and this section of the population, together with the remaining 5% who would be regarded as wealthy, even by Western standards, are the people most likely to regularly buy British goods. Forbes Magazine in 2008 pointed out that there are 87 billionaires in Russia (54 in 2007) with an average wealth of US$5.9bn. This is the second highest number of any country in the world. Several hundred people have assets over $100m, and about 10-20 thousand are worth over $10m. The number of people with assets over $1m is estimated at over 300 thousand, with some 50% living in Moscow.

One of the most interesting sections of the population is the "aspirant" class. This large section of the population would like to buy quality items but have limited income for this. They are increasingly aware of what is available in the marketplace and as the term suggests, "aspire" to own better quality items.

Moscow has an annual retail trade turnover of around $20 billion, or about 30 percent of national retail turnover, even though the city accounts for only 6.5% of the national population.

Income defined by population, in Western Russian cities.

Income per month		Percentage of Population
$75,000+	Wealthy	2%
$30,000 - $75,000	High income earners	3%
$10,000 - $30,000	Emerging middle class	5%
$5,000 - $10,000	Aspirant classes	15%
$500 - $5,000	Average income group	25%
$150 - $500	Below average wage earners	20%
$40 - $150	Low income earners	14%
Less than $40	Poverty level	16%

Based upon figures taken and adapted from the World Factbook 2007 and World Bank review

Income defined by population, outside Western Russian cities.

Income per month		Percentage of Population
$30,000 +	High income earners and wealthy	3%
$500 - $30,000	Aspirant and emerging middle class	22%
$150 - $500	Lower income groups	57%
Less than $500	Below poverty line	18%

Based upon figures taken from the World Factbook 2006

8.3. Opening your own retail outlet

Most foreign-owned shops are registered as 100% foreign-owned companies. In order to set up a shop you should initially resolve your corporate structure. Details of how to organise this are outlined in Chapter 2. There are, however, a number of specific considerations in addition to those mentioned in previous chapters with regard to setting up retail premises and these discussed below.

8.4   Property

Once registered, the company will need to find shop premises. A British company might approach the Moscow Property Management Committee (Moskomimuschestvo) to obtain details of property auctions. Security and documentary compliance issues should also be considered when buying or renting a property (see 8.6.8)

Contact:

Moscow Property Management Committee (Moskomimuschestvo), Karetny Ryad, 2/1, Moscow. Tel: 007 495 299 2048; Fax: 007 495 299 0575.

Alternatively one may use a number of real estate agents in Moscow including Doki Real Estate

Tel: 007 495 500 0001; Website www.doki.ru/en/relocation/

Doki Real Estate agency, started work in the Russian market in 2005. Its senior managers are specialists who acquired their knowledge and work experience in respected Western universities and corporations, and are familiar with the needs of the international businessman. Today Doki employs more than 150 highly qualified professionals. Doki offers a full range of realty services, including renting, selling, buying, mortgage credit lending. It serves individuals as well as corporate clients. Doki is a member of The Russian Guild of Realtors, The Moscow Association-Guild of Realtors, The American Chamber of Commerce in Moscow, The Russo-British Chamber of Commerce.

8.5   Licences

To be able to function as a shop a company will require:

  (a) A local general trading licence: This can be obtained from the local authority: Mossoviet issue them at a cost of US$2,000.

  (b) A hard currency licence: These are issued by the Russian Central Bank.

Contact: the Russian Central Bank, Neglinnaya Ulitsa 12, Moscow. Tel: 007 495 771 9100; Website: www.cbr.ru/eng/

To obtain this licence you will need to show registration documents, and prove that the shop will be using electronic cash tills. Even with a hard currency licence, the shop will still be legally obliged to accept Roubles although each shop is allowed to set its own exchange rate.

  (c) A trading licence: This is issued by the Moscow Licensing Chamber, 121019, Noviy Arbat 15, Moscow Tel/Fax: 007 495 202 2414. A Russian partner in a joint venture would already have one of these.

There is some flexibility with the licence. If, for example, a Russian partner in a joint venture had a trading licence to sell food, it would be legal to sell anything else provided food continues to be sold.

8.6   Running a shop

It is important to review a number of operational matters in the Russian context. Significant points are:

8.6.1   Customs Certificates

Goods entering Russia for sale must have a verified Certificate of Conformity (CoC) (see 5.11). Goods without a valid CoC may be confiscated.

8.6.2.1   Marketing and display

The Russian consumer is used to merchandise being supplied in a strictly functional manner. Little effort has been expended on retail ambience, or on what the

Western retailers would describe as a total shopping experience. All this is however changing, especially in the more cosmopolitan cities. The Russian consumer is becoming increasingly sophisticated and aware of quality.

8.6.2.2 Promotion and advertising

With developing affluence the consumer market is now more exposed to television, radio and press advertising, use of billboards and other road signage, sponsorship and other sales promotional activities. Most major western advertising agencies are active in Russia. Domestic agencies are growing and their professionalism continues to improve. Direct marketing works well. Internet based selling is still in its infancy but growing apace.

8.6.3 Logistics (distribution and systems)

Although systems are often well advanced, particularly in fields such as industry and the military, retailing is behind in terms of the infrastructure required, for example, telecommunications, postal services, roads, stock management and transportation. These are not fully developed in some of the regions and need to be considered when servicing remote geographic locations.

8.6.4 Payment for goods

Stores that sell imported goods are allowed to mark prices in foreign currency; usually in UE (Uslovnye Edinitsy or "Hypothetical Units", roughly equivalent to US Dollars). At the time of purchase clerks convert the price into Roubles. Many exceptions exist, especially in tourist and international business areas where retail sales in foreign currency using other means of payment such as credit and debit cards are allowed.

Retailers, unlike manufacturers, find it more difficult to operate through joint ventures and there is a tendency to establish operations either through franchises or through a 100% owned subsidiary.

8.6.5 Selling in foreign currency

Since 1 January 1994, cash sales to the public of goods and services for foreign currency have been banned.

8.6.6 Personnel and training

Greater regard is being given to the importance of customer care and other sales techniques. There are two typical solutions to this particular issue:
   (i) Training based in Western countries. For staff with management potential this may often take place over an extended period.
   (ii) Recruitment of new, often younger personnel. (See 7.17).

8.6.7 Taxation

Goods imported into Russia are now subject to three separate taxes:
- Import Duty (see 5.15)
- Excise Duty (see 5.15)
- VAT (see 3.4).

Import duties are, on average, 15% although a number of foods are taxed at only five per cent. The excise tax on goods is high (for example: on spirits = 90%, vodka = 80%, beer and cars = 25%, cigarettes = 50%, tyres = 30%). VAT on imported goods is, on average, 20% of the invoice value (certain foodstuffs and children's clothes are exempted). A paper on import and export taxes is available from the Commercial Department of the British Embassy in Moscow (see 10.10). Retailers are obliged to have on hand certificates for all imported products sold in their stores. Violation of this regulation can result in a fine of up to $10,000.

Additional taxes, relevant to retailers, are VAT, Corporate Profits Tax and the employment tax. VAT is levied at 20%, with a lower 10% rate for foodstuffs and children's clothes. Corporate Profits Tax is 24%, paid in advance on the basis of an estimate for the next three months turnover. Employment related taxes may be as high as 26% of the payments to staff (to cover National Insurance, pensions, etc.) for lower paid workers, with a regressive scale payable for higher paid employees.

There is also a dividend/withholding tax. This is 15% on the final dividend repatriated to the UK. However under the UK/Russian Double Taxation Agreement this can be paid either in the UK or in Russia.

British companies are recommended to seek professional advice from specialist consultancy firms, details of which are available from UK Trade & Investment Russia Unit Tel: 020 7215 4891; Website: www.uktradeinvest.gov.uk/ukti/appmanager/ukti/countries?_nfls=false&_nfpb=true&_pageLabel=CountryType1&navigationPageId=/russia

8.6.8   Security

There is a great deal of press comment about the influence of the so-called Mafia in commercial operations. This is not always unfounded: any major cash-producing venture is certain to attract attention. However, according to a number of foreign business residents in Russia, it seems that the "Mafia" tends to focus on Russian rather than foreign businesses, or on those businesses that are not operating wholly within the law. Shoplifting and credit card fraud are also growing problems in Russia. It is of course important to agree on a security policy with your Russian partner, who might be approached. Advice on security can be obtained from:

◆ Control Risks Group, Tel: 0207 970 2100; Website: www.crg.com/
◆ DRUM Resources Ltd London Office Tel: 0207 929 2473
           Moscow Office Tel: 007 495 721 1131
           Website: www.drumresources.com/

8.6.9   Insurance

The Russian insurer with the longest history and experience in handling insurance for foreign entities is Ingosstrakh Limited. The company Ingosstrakh operates in 214 cites of the Russian Federation. It has 26 sales outlets in Moscow and 87 regional branches.

Contact:
Ingosstrakh Limited
Bolshaya Tulskaya, 10 building 1, Moscow
Tel: 007 495 956 5555 or 007 495 232 3491, Fax: 007 495 959 4518
E-mail: ingos@ingos.ru
Website: www.ingos.ru/en/about/ingo_group/russia/ingos_m/

In addition, there are many other Russian owned companies well able to handle most lines of business and a growing number of foreign-owned companies are present, including AIG, ACE, Zurich, Allianz, Vienna Insurance Group to name the largest. Details of these may be found on:
www.ins-union.ru, www.allinsurance.ru

9   RESIDENTIAL ISSUES

9.1   Residential accommodation

It remains more difficult to find good quality residential accommodation than to find suitable office space. Many representatives spend their first months in Moscow and St Petersburg in hotels waiting for accommodation to become available. In other centres the problem is more severe.

"In choosing an apartment based on its location, one always makes a compromise between work, school, shopping, and transport." (Primacy Relocation) As to the building itself, well lit common areas, secure parking and a secure main entrance, equipped with a videophone are critical.

Your own apartment should be fit with a door with 180° peep-hole and a videophone and secure windows. Ensure it is wired and has sufficient plug and socket outlets to handle a range of equipment including a TV, DVD, VCR, MP3, microwave, cordless phones, hair dryer, mobile chargers, laptop, internet and various items of kitchen equipment. It is prudent to check the operability of the apartment's boiler, air conditioning, and gas supply and to know who is responsible for repairs and maintenance. The landlord will pay usually for security and some utilities, whilst electricity, long distance phone charges and satellite TV incur extra charges. Telephone calls within Moscow are free.

A four-room or three-bedroom apartment would typically cost between US$1,800 – $4,500 per month, the latter price being a premium rate for being in the most prestigious parts of Moscow. Upgrading property is often a consideration but renovation processes are often slow. Accommodation can also be found considerably more cheaply. The Classified Pages in Moscow Times and Residential Property News list apartments available for rental. Property agents, such as Doki Real Estate Tel: 007 495 500 0001; website www.doki.ru, can also offer advice and contacts.

Rental terms are typically one to three years. Rental agreements lasting one year or more must be registered with the local authorities. Therefore, it is common practice to sign agreements that are 364 days in length. As far as tax issues are concerned, landlords are obligated to pay a 13% tax on all income generated via rental of their property. This figure can be reduced to 6% if they register as a private individual. Furthermore, the rental can be broken up into two separate parts in order to minimise taxes. For example, if the total rental amount for an apartment is $2,000. One agreement can be for say $700 that will cover the rent of an apartment, and the other agreement can be for the amount of $1,300. This will cover the rental of furniture and other accessories inside the apartment. This way the tax is only paid on the $700 figure. The other amount is not subject to tax.

Early lease termination by tenant requires a one to three month notice. Early terminations by the landlord are rare – usually implemented when the tenant is in breach. Rent is usually measured in US dollars or Euros, but is actually paid in roubles. Payment is monthly or quarterly, usually by bank transfer to local or foreign accounts. Rent reduction is usually offered for pre-payments. A usual one-month's rent security deposit should be applied to the last month of rent as there is no legal procedure in Russia to guarantee fair deposit return. Cash payment for budget apartments is common.

9.1.1 Property prices in Moscow

MOSCOW RENTAL PRICING				
BED-ROOMS	AVERAGE SIZE (SQ. M)	BUILDING CLASSIFICATION		
		CLASS A	CLASS B	CLASS C
1	60–115	$2,500–6,000	$1,500–2,000	$800–1,900
2	100–150	$5,000–8,500	$2,800–5,500	$1,500–2,500
3	130–220	$7,000–15,000	$5,500–9,000	$3,500–5,500
4	160–250	$8,000–18,000	$7,000–12,000	$5,000–7,000
5	180–350	$11,000–25,000	$7,500–12,500	$6,000–7,500

Russian Apartment Building Classifications

Class A: Modern Development/Ministerial Building/Secure Gated Developments
Today's elite residential complexes usually offer all modern amenities, such as underground garages, gyms, swimming pools and management. These are impressive buildings with elaborate entrances, high level of security, independent infrastructure (heating, phone lines, internet, etc), and many apartments are decorated with expensive fixtures and furniture.
Class B: Stalin Skyscrapers
There are seven such skyscrapers in Moscow; three of them are residential. They are outstanding examples of Stalinist architecture with great views, balconies and magnificent entrances, giving them premium edge in the property market.
Class C: Post Stalin Blocks
These reduced Stalinist style buildings have lower ceilings and smaller floor plans. They are usually six to eight stories with ageing lifts and un-renovated entrances and communal areas.

Taken from "Relocating to Russia: Current issues facing companies and expatriate staff", Primacy Relocation, Sarah Collins, Charles Hecker and Olga Todorenko; Website www.primacy.com

9.1.2 Serviced apartments

Serviced apartments are available from one night to six months, saving up to 40 percent compared to hotel rates. Usually situated in premium locations such as Tverskaya and Arbat, the units tend to have more space than hotels, fully fitted kitchens, on-site property management, and housekeeping services. Nightly rates for a one-bedroom unit range from $110 to $190 US. A two-bedroom unit can cost $150 to $190, depending on length of stay.

9.1.3 Professional help

Help from a tenancy management service (TMS) and lawyer is often crucial. A TMS is a popular form of expatriate staff support that assists tenants throughout the complete term of the lease. Typically, TMS representatives handle all communications with the landlord, monitoring compliance with contractual obligations, and provide 24/7 English-fluent telephone support. Like any corporate-class relocation related service, a good TMS provides one point of contact for all property related issues. Some TMS companies even provide an optional concierge service.

9.2.1. Furnishing (home)

Western furniture for one's home can be purchased from a number of Moscow outlets. There are a number of local furniture boutiques that sell everything from classical type furniture to modern, high-tech and eclectic type of furniture. In addition, there are huge furniture outlets such as IKEA and the new GRAND Furniture centre.

Furniture outlets in Moscow include:

◆ English Interiors, Chistoprudniy Blvd 12a Tel: 007 495 937 7021
◆ Intermebel, UI.Botanicheskaya 35-1 Moscow Tel: 007 495 903 8082
◆ Prego Furniture Salon, Chistoprudny Blvd 2, Moscow Tel: 007 495 924 1566
◆ Queen-Mosmebel, UI. Garibaldi 26/3, Moscow Tel: 007 495 128 7835.

9.2.2 Furnishing (office)

There is a variety of outlets that sell office furniture. Both SOLO (Tel: 007 495 126 4510) and Kabinet (Tel: 007 495 363 0891) have wide ranges of items. A useful website for most Moscow office furniture outlets is www.infoservices.com/moscow/683.htm

9.3. Other personal effects

Both Russians and non-residents may bring personal belongings into the country. Duty, however, has been payable since 01 August 1996 on luggage brought in separately. This is the lower of either:

◆ the first 50 kg is duty free, but any additional amount up to 200 kg is taxed at €7 per 1 kg and on the amount over 200 kg at €4 per 1 kg; or
◆ 50% of the cargo's cost is payable as duty.

Currently individuals may bring in goods up to a value of $2000 to $5000 and, subject to certain restrictions (see 5.7).

9.4 Cars and car registration

Registered companies are permitted to import one foreign car per foreign employee plus an extra foreign car for an employee's family for up to one year.

They can also have Russian cars registered with foreign plates. Registration of cars is time-consuming, but there are numerous car dealers operating in Moscow who will import cars for the Western community. For details contact: Moscow Regional Customs (Tel: 007 495 136 9600) or see the local press.

Imported cars purchased by Russians or residents suffer excise tax of up to 70% (See 5.15 and 8.6.7.) and acquisition tax of 20%. These taxes must be paid before the vehicle is registered.

9.4.1 Driving licence

The rules for obtaining a Russian driving licence change at frequent intervals. Currently, if visiting the Russian Federation on a tourist visa, you will need your personal passport with a valid visa, an international driving licence or a national driving licence with an authorised translation.

If you are intending to drive for a longer duration you are required by law to hold a Russian driver's licence. A British driver's licence cannot be exchanged for a Russian one. To obtain a Russian driving licence you must take Russian theory and practical tests. Once you have passed your test, your Russian driving licence will be valid up until the end of your visa registration period.

Moscow driving schools include:

◆ Auto-online: Melnikova Str. 2 Tel: 007 495 276 4675

- Cabriolet: Shmitovskiy Proezd, 16 Tel: 007 495 256 1574
- Central Driving School: Kashirskoe Highway, 24 Tel: 007 495 725 2207
- Losinka: Olonetskiy Proezd, 6 Tel: 007 495 470 0643
- TCHAIYKA: Kalashnyiy Per., 10 Tel: 007 495 290 2162

9.4.2. Road Tax

This tax is levied on the sale price of the vehicle and ranges up to 2.5% dependent upon where the purchase is made.

9.4.3 Car insurance

Motor third party liability insurance is mandatory. This will have to be bought at the border until Russia joins the international Green Card system (expected 2009). Local obligatory liability limits are low but it is possible to buy higher limits from most companies and serious consideration should be given to this.

Motor physical damage insurance can also be bought locally, subject to inspection of the vehicle, but it may be possible to arrange this abroad before a vehicle is taken into the Russian Federation. For example, most British car insurers will quote for insurance cover in Russia.

While there has been a recent boom in opening private insurance companies, Ingostrakh, the Russian State insurance company, remains the largest and most experienced in this area.

Contact:
Ingosstrakh Limited
Bolshaya Tulskaya, 10 building 1, Moscow
Tel: 007 495 956 5555 or 007 495 232 3491, Fax: 007 495 959 4518
E-mail: ingos@ingos.ru
Website: www.ingos.ru/en/about/ingo_group/russia/ingos_m/

9.4.3.1 Road accidents

In case of an accident, contact the nearest traffic inspection officer and make sure all participants fill in written statements, to be witnessed by a militia inspector. All repairs will be at the foreign motorist's expense.

9.4.3.2 Car breakdown

An emergency breakdown service is offered by:
- RAC (Registration tel: 0800 028 7210;
  Breakdown No – Russia Tel: 33 472 435245 810
- GAI (Government Automobile Inspectors) Tel: 007 495 923 5373.

9.4.4.1 Car parts and supplies

A grave shortage of spare car parts on the internal Russian market means that theft of parts is a perennial problem. Car alarms and steering wheel locks are recommended. Spares can be bought for Russian cars at open-air markets or outside various shops. A more reliable source of parts and accessories in Moscow is Stockmann's Car Supplies shop on Lyusinovskaya Ulitsa70/1 or Sovinter autoservice at Institutsky Pereuluk, 2/1. Several companies, including Mercedes, Saab, Audi/VW, BMW, Toyota and Volvo, also have service centres in Russia.

Should you be driving during the winter months, you should ensure your car is fitted with studded tyres.

9.4.4.2 Motorcycles

The wearing of crash helmets compulsory. Children under twelve are not permitted as passengers. Motorcycles must use dipped headlights at all times.

9.4.5 Petrol

92 or 95 octane petrol and diesel (Solyarka) are relatively easy to purchase in Moscow, St Petersburg and a number of other major cities. However, it is still advisable to keep tank topped up whenever possible. Russian petrol is not suitable for cars fitted with catalytic converters. These should be removed before the car is imported.

Ideally, buy petrol from BP or TNK petrol stations. All BP petrol stations are well lit, safe, have car washes and a mini market. Alternatives to BP and TNK are Yukos, Lukoil and AGIP. It is not recommended to purchase fuel from petrol stations that are not associated with major oil companies. It is not unknown for petrol to be mixed with water or other additives. Credit cards are accepted at some but not all filling stations.

9.5 Schooling

There are number of schools suitable for expatriate children in Moscow. These include:

9.5.1 The British International School

The British International School was founded in Moscow in April 1994 and is situated at nine locations. Some 240 children, mostly of English-speaking backgrounds, are now being educated in this establishment.

Most school programmes are based upon the English & Wales National Curriculum. Alternatively, at the British International School's Nakhimovski site provision is made for students to follow the Russian national curriculum supplemented with some elements of the National Curriculum for England & Wales. Older pupils are prepared for the University of Cambridge International GCSE examinations.

Contact:
Tel: 007 495 987 4486, Fax: 007 49) 159 0139
E-mail: admissions@bismoscow.com, Website: www.bismoscow.com/
Other schools include those managed by Nord Anglia Education Plc, 10 Eden Place, Cheadle, Cheshire SK8 1AT.
Tel: 0161 491 4191; Fax: 0161 491 4409/4410.
Another option is the Anglo-American School
Beregovaya 1, Moscow
Tel: 007 495 231 4488; Fax: 007 495 231 4477
Website: www.aas.ru/
Prior to moving to Russia, you may wish to teach your children some Russian. The London School of Russian Language and Literature can help with this. It also teaches Russian as a Foreign Language, conversational and Business Russian to adults.

Contact
London School of Russian Language and Literature
59A Oakwood Road, London NW11 6RJ
Tel/Fax: 020 8458 6077
Website: www.russianschool.fsnet.co.uk

9.6   Medical advice and facilities

9.6.1   Drinking water

Water in all cities, other than St Petersburg, is generally safe to drink, despite the high iron content that affects its colour, smell and taste. St Petersburg's water supply is infected by a diarrhoea-causing parasite, giardia lamblia.

9.6.2   Medical insurance

There are reciprocal healthcare agreements between Russia and the UK.

However, the agreements cover treatment in state hospitals for accident and emergencies only.

The management of serious accidents and illnesses can be haphazard, confusing and very expensive. All foreign residents and visitors are therefore advised to have full medical travel or out-of-country insurance including evacuation coverage. Most such providers will have 24 hour emergency lines to take charge of the situation with contacts in Russia able to support and advise the casualty.

Those on longer-term assignments in Russia may find it useful to take consultancy from companies such as DRUM Resources or Control Risks.

DRUM Resources:
Gazetny Pereuluk 9, Street 2 Office 36, Moscow 103009
Tel: 007 495 721 1131; Fax: 020 721 1135;
E-mail: info@drumresources.com; Website: www.drumresources.com
Control Risks
Ulitsa Zoologicheskaya, 2, Office 28, Moscow 123242
Tel: 007 495 232 5690, Fax: 007 495 232 5692
Email: crmoscow@control-risks.com; Website: www.crg.com

You should ensure that you have inoculations prior to travel; recommended inoculations include: diphtheria, polio, typhoid, hepatitis A and B, encephalitis (May-September). If travelling to Russia for extended periods, you may be required to produce a certificate confirming that you do not suffer from the HIV virus.

When visiting Russia it is advisable to take a good first aid kit. This should contain disinfectant, disposable syringes, needles and sutures, dressings, antihistamines and medication for diarrhoea, constipation, indigestion and pain. In addition take any special drugs that you require, for example, penicillin, Amoxil, birth control pills and any preparatory brands of medicine you prefer, for example, Aspirin, Dispirin or Paracetamol.

9.6.3   General medical and health services

There are several clinics that employ American and British trained staff. Information on some of these may be found on website: http://moscow.usembassy.gov/consular/files/List-Doctors.pdf

9.6.4   Medical emergencies

Ambulance and emergency facilities are offered by
SOS International, International SOS Clinic Sakhincentr
Ground Floor Office 19
32 Komunisticheskyi Prospekt Yuzhno-Sakhalinsk, Russia 693000
Clinic Tel: 007 424 272 7550
Website: www.internationalsos.com

Clinical and Diagnostic Centre, 6 Michurinsky Prospekt, Moscow. Tel: 007 495 143 2503 (24 hours). Supervisor: Dr Evgeny F. Zakharov.

9.6.5 Other clinics for foreigners

(a) International Medical Clinic: Grokholsky Pereuluk 31 (10th Floor), Moscow 129010. Tel: 007 495 937 5760. The centre offers all kinds of medical services including dental and full pre-natal care and on-site pharmacy. Emergency hospitalisation and evacuation are also provided. Access to the centre is 24 hours per day. Insurance can be obtained from the centre to cover medical visits, tests and X-rays and hospitalisation.

(b) Mediclub Moscow Ltd (Canadian): The Construction Workers' Hospital, 56 Michurinsky Prospekt, Moscow 117192. Tel: 007 495 931 5018; Fax: 007 495 932 8653. Access by subscription.

(c) US Global Health: Medicentre, 4 Dobryninsky Pereuluk 4, Moscow 117049. Tel: 007 495 237 5335; Fax: 007 495 237 8475.
Opened October 1994. Access by subscription.

(d) European Medical Centre: Spiridon`evskiy Pereuluk, 5-1
Tel: 007 495 933 6655, Fax 007 495 933 6650 (24 h)
Website: www.emcmos.ru/en/about-e.cfm

(a) American Medical Centre: Groholskiy Pereuluk 1;
Tel: 007 495 933 7700/7701;
Website: www.amcenter.ru/en
In St Petersburg, clinics that can be contacted are:

British-American Family Practice	Euromed
Grafskiy Pereulok 7	Suvorovskiy Prospekt 60
St Petersburg	St Petersburg
Tel: 007 812 327 6030	Tel: 007 812 327 0301
Fax: 007 812 327 6040	Fax: 007 812 327 0301
	Website: www.euromed.ru/en/

9.6.6 Pharmacy

There are hundreds of licensed pharmacies located throughout Moscow. Many of them are open for 24 hours a day.

It is usually safe to buy medicines from these pharmacies. In addition, large supermarket chains such as the Seventh Continent have in-store pharmacies. Medicine may also be obtained from internet based pharmacies such as www.apteka.ru. Do not buy drugs from small pharmacies or "palatki".

9.6.7 Optical services

Optical services are widely available in Moscow

9.6.8 Dental services

A wide range of reliable dental services are available. These include:
◆ European dental centre Konushkovskaya Ulitsa 34
Tel: 007 495 933 0002/6655
◆ Intermed, Durova Ulitsa 26/5, Moscow 129090 Tel: 007 495 284 7403.
◆ Masterdent, Vostochnaya Ulitsa 2-3 Tel: 007 495 274 1001

9.6.9 Other health considerations

The following should be noted:

(a) Vaccines: none are mandatory for entry: polio, diphtheria and tetanus boosters are recommended every ten years.

(b) First aid: emergency travel kits should be carried at all times (see 8.6.2). These should contain disposable syringes, needles and sutures. Know your blood group.

(c) Food and water-borne diseases: Hepatitis A; tapeworm and trichinella from pork; fish tapeworm (Baltic Sea); episodic diarrhoea. Do not eat raw or undercooked meat or shell fish: freshly cooked hot food is safest. Peel or scald fruit and vegetables. Salad, fruit salad, juices and ice are only as safe as the source and the water used. Where possible drink boiled water, canned and bottled drinks, especially in St Petersburg as there are often parasites in the water supply.

(d) Rabies: endemic in rodents in rural areas and sometimes reported in dogs in cities. Report bites. Vaccines may be effective.

(e) Hepatitis B and AIDS: Insist on your own syringes, needles and sutures being used. Avoid blood transfusions, but if necessary use blood substitutes. Adhere to safe sexual practices.

(f) Cold weather: fingers, face, lungs and toes need special care. Use body heat to warm frostbite. Mittens give better frost protection than gloves. A scarf worn over the nose and mouth warms inhaled air. Always wear a hat outside in winter.

(g) Radioactivity: there is no risk to residents other than in the exclusion zones. Iodate tablets block radioactive uptake by the thyroid in the event of a nuclear accident.

(h) Spectacles and dentures: spares are advisable. Pollution and freezing temperatures make contact lenses hazardous.

(i) Medical evacuation: insurance may be taken out, in advance, to cover medical evacuation, usually to Helsinki.

Visitors are subject to the laws of the territory in which they are travelling. Penalties for possession, use, or trafficking in illegal drugs are severe in Russia, and convicted offenders can expect jail sentences and fines.

9.7   Personal insurance

Personal insurance is the most rapidly developing segment of the domestic insurance market. It is dominated mostly by Russian insurance companies although large foreign insurance companies are gaining a greater market share.

For greater protection against contingent risks such as Kidnap and Ransom, the more specialised UK brokers will be able to give advice and arrange coverage.

AIG Russia Insurance Company is able to offer a number of insurance products designed for foreign expatriates.

Contact
AIG Russia Insurance Company
16/2 Tverskaya Street, Moscow 125009
Tel: 007 495 9358950
E-mail: Vadim.Lishinsky@aig.com, Website: www.aigrussia.ru

9.8   Social and cultural activities

Leisure activities in Moscow and St Petersburg are readily available. Unless specifically designated, all ventures in Russia are legally bound to accept only Rouble or credit card payments.

There are many shops, restaurants and bars to choose from. Food to suit all tastes, dietary and religious requirements and cost are becoming increasingly accessible. There are also casinos and several nightclubs.

Many of these entertainment facilities may be found in tourist guides, such as Fodor's Guide. A good restaurant guide is www.menu.ru, on which you can find restaurant addresses and even menus with prices. The website www.welrus.com/moscow/restaur/ is well worth viewing for its lists of restaurants, places of interest, entertainment and leisure guides.

Other sources of information for eating out and social life include the local English-language press.

Moscow and St Petersburg are two of the world's great cities for heritage and culture. Museums, palaces and art galleries of world renown are situated there. Music, ballet, circus and cinemas showing English language films are available for both residents and tourists.

9.9 Religious Worship

Places of worship for all religions are available in Moscow and St Petersburg. Other cities are less cosmopolitan.

9.10 Sport

Sporting activity is accessible but expensive. There are a large number of high-class health clubs in Moscow. Examples include Planet Fitness, World Gym, World Class Fitness and Petrokva Sports. Membership fees range usually from $1400 to $2000 per annum, with the most expensive clubs costing as much as $4000 to $5000 per annum. Both the Penta and the Slavyanskaya Hotel have health clubs. There are also tennis clubs run by UPDK and the Chaika Joint Venture. There is a squash court at the Indian Embassy. This is open daily from 7.00-23.00.

9.11 Shopping

There is considerable choice as to where to shop in Moscow. It is easy to buy all consumer goods for Roubles in the State shops or the markets. A visit to GUM Department Store in Moscow is worthwhile.

9.12 Dry cleaning

Many non-budget hotels in Moscow offer dry cleaning services for non-residents. Dry cleaning firms that offer a pick-up and delivery service include:
◆ California Cleaners outlets Tel: 007 495 497 0005/0011
◆ Diana: Tel: 007 495 467 1422
◆ Vladikino Zao: Tel:007 495 401 3765; Fax: 007 495 401 8744

9.13 Street crime

Crime, and particularly mugging, is on the increase in Moscow and St Petersburg. However, it is important to keep this threat in perspective. In Russia, as elsewhere, fear of crime is often worse than the reality. Crime in Russia often has a violent edge, but most people are as unlikely to be the victim of a crime there as they are in other US or Western European cities. To reduce the risk of trouble, business-men should use their common sense.

As anywhere, the best way to avoid problems, including pick pocketing, is to be prudent, for example, by not wearing ostentatious jewellery or carrying large sums of money. It is both comforting and sensible to pre-arrange for transportation when going out, and where possible, to be accompanied by someone who speaks Russian.

Particular care should be taken with under-passes. Over the past three years there have been many incidents of the "dropped wallet" which a visitor may instinctively pick up to return to the individual who dropped it. This results in a group forming, stating that they witnessed the foreigner remove some of the cash.

9.14   Emergencies

In the event of emergencies, businessmen should contact the duty officer in the British Embassy in Moscow or the Consulate in St Petersburg.

Contact:

British Embassy

Sofiiskaya Naberezhnaya 14, Moscow.

Tel: 007 495 956 7200. or:

British Consulate

Ploshad Proletarskoi Dictatury 5, St Petersburg.

Tel: 007 812 320 3200 (24 hours). or:

British Consulate General in Ekaterinburg

15a Gogol Street, 4th Floor, 620075, Ekaterinburg

Tel: 007 3432 55 4931

For more immediate help call: Fire 01 Police 02 Ambulance 03.

More legroom to Moscow.

That's bmi time.

bmi operate three direct flights a day from London Heathrow to Moscow

- operated in conjunction with Transaero
- convenient connections from regional airports
- 41" legroom in business class
- personal DVD players for all business passsengers
- complimentary food and drink for all passengers

flybmi.com ✈

A STAR ALLIANCE MEMBER

10 ASSISTANCE FOR MARKET RESEARCH AND ANALYSIS

10.1   Introduction

Russia offers tremendous potential for exporters of goods and services from the UK and for the establishment of joint venture operations for both internal and outward trade. As with any market, it is important to develop a strategy leading to market entry. There is no short cut into conducting market research although it is possibly reassuring to note that much relevant information can be obtained easily and often at no cost from a number of governmental and commercial sources. The principal support agency is UK Trade & Investment.

UK Trade & Investment is the Government organisation that supports companies in the UK doing business internationally and overseas enterprises seeking to set up or expand in the UK.

With commercial teams based in over 100 offices around the world, and a network of specialists throughout the UK, UK Trade & Investment provides a unique operational and strategic resource for British exporters and overseas investors.

Whether you are venturing into selling overseas for the first time, or an experienced exporter trying to break into new markets, UK Trade & Investment's advice, information and support will provide you with a significant advantage when doing business internationally.

Wherever in the world you want to sell your goods and services, UK Trade & Investment can be your international trade specialists; helping you gain the necessary skills, identify the best opportunities, make the right introductions and then help turn them into real business.

UK Trade & Investment offers three main areas of help for British companies:

♦ Advice and support: Tailored, experienced, impartial advice and training to new and inexperienced exporters, maximising their chances of sustained success overseas.

♦ Information and opportunities: Essential, unique and trusted information from our commercial staff overseas, helping companies make the most informed and profitable business decisions.

♦ Making it happen: To be a successful exporter you need to travel overseas and build lasting commercial relationships with your clients and partners. We provide practical assistance before you go and ongoing help, reassurance and introductions whilst you are there. For further information about how UK Trade & Investment can help your business visit.
Tel: 020 7215 4891; Website: www.uktradeinvest.gov.uk/ukti/appmanager/ ukti/countries?_nfls=false&_nfpb=true&_pageLabel=CountryType1&naviga tionPageId=/russia

In addition, UK Trade & Investment liaises with:

♦ Business Links
Tel: 0845 600 9006; Website: www.businessadviceonline.org

♦ WalesTrade International
Tel: 0292 082 5097; Website: www.ibwales.com/

♦ Invest Northern Ireland
Tel: 0289 023 9090; Website: www.investni.com

♦ Scottish Development International
Tel: 0141 228 2828;
Websites: www.sdi.co.uk/pages/index.asp?e=scottishdevelopmentinternational.com

Free help may also be obtained from other sources including business libraries, banks, trade organisations and the embassies, High Commissions and consulates of overseas governments in the UK.

10.2   UK Trade & Investment Russia Unit

UK Trade & Investment's Russia Unit can provide general knowledge and advice to firms interested in trading in Russia. This includes information on political, economic and commercial changes. There are two Desk Officers dealing with Russia. Advice and general information is available on:

(a) The political and economic scene;
(b) specific regions and sectors;
(c) local conditions for doing business;
(d) market prospects and product suitability;
(e) local tariffs and other import regulations;
(f) local competition; and
(g) business contacts.

The data may be tailored to the needs of the inquirer. In addition, details of opportunities for Trade & Investment will then be disseminated whenever they become available.

Contact:
UK Trade & Investment Russia Unit
Bay 949, Kingsgate House, 66-74 Victoria Street, London SW1E 6SW
Tel: 020 7215 4891;
Website: www.uktradeinvest.gov.uk/ukti/appmanager/ukti/countries?_nfls=false&_nfpb=true&_pageLabel=CountryType1&navigationPageId=/russia

10.3   Sector advice

In addition to the UK Trade & Investment country desks, there are now a number of sector desks covering different industries, professions and services. When making an enquiry select the sector heading required and ask for the appropriate sector desk, e.g. the sector desk for the automotive industry.

Contact:
Tel: 020 7215 4891;
Website: www.uktradeinvest.gov.uk/ukti/appmanager/ukti/countries?_nfls=false&_nfpb=true&_pageLabel=CountryType1&navigationPageId=/russia

10.4   Caspian and Turkey Business Group (CATBIG)

Russia is one of the countries covered by the Caspian and Turkey Business Group. The group meets at the Department for Business Enterprise and Regulatory Reform bi-annually. It provides an opportunity for business people to hear about recent developments in the market and to exchange market information.

Contact:
Tel: 020 7215 4741
E-mail: james.key@ukti.gsi.gov.uk, Website: www.uktradeinvest.gov.uk

10.5   Overseas Trade

UK Trade & Investment supports the publication of Overseas Trade, the UK's leading export title. It includes much useful export advice and covers Russia frequently, highlighting business opportunities particularly in the oil and gas sector. It is published ten times a year and is free. For inclusion on its mailing register online at www.overseastrade.co.uk/

10.6 The British Library

This free service provides:

- in depth company information including financial and statistical information on UK and overseas companies;
- UK and international company product and patent information, and market data competitor information and improving market position;
- company annual reports and house journals from UK, Europe, USA and Japan;
- business and trade journals with international coverage of companies and markets;
- training courses on sources of company and market information;
- free access to 30 business information databases.

You will need to obtain a reader pass to use the collections. This may be obtained from website: www.bl.uk/services/reading/admissions.html

Contact: The British Library & IP Centre,

96 Euston Rd, London, NW1 2DB. Tel: 020 7412 7454; Fax: 020 7412 7453; Email: bipc@bl.uk;

Website: www.bl.uk/bipc

10.7.1 The National Statistics Information and Library Service (NSILS)

The NSILS holds domestic information on economic statistics including business, macro-economic and micro-economic statistics; social statistics including census data, population, health and the labour market; and general economic and social surveys. International statistics held include data published by international bodies such as the UN, OECD and Eurostat and from many national statistical offices.

Contact:

Office for National Statistics Library

Government Buildings, Cardiff Road, Newport, South Wales NPIO 8XG

Tel: 0845 601 3034; Welsh-speaking line 01633 813381; Minicom: 01633 812399

Website: www.statistics.gov.uk

10.7.2 Federal State Statistics Service

The Federal State Statistics Service provides a similar function to the NSILS (See above), meeting the information requirements of the state authority and administration, media, general public, scientific community, commercial and international organisations. The system of state statistics covers district, regional and federal levels, as well as Moscow and St. Petersburg. It comprises 89 regional committees and 2,200 district departments.

Contact

39, Miasnitskaya Street, 103450, Moscow

Tel: 007 495 207 4902

Website: www.gks.ru/wps/portal/english

10.8 HM Revenue and Customs Statistics and Analysis of Trade Unit (SATU)

Statistical information on UK trade with Russia may be obtained from the HM Revenue and Customs Statistics and Analysis of Trade Unit (SATU), which was designed, developed and is now maintained by Forvus Computer Services (See Website: www.forvus.co.uk). The service is fee based.

Contact:
SATU
5th Floor, Alexander House, 21 Victoria Avenue, Southend on Sea, SS99 1AA
Tel: 01702 367485; Fax: 01702 367331; Website: http://customs.hmrc.gov.uk/channelsPortalWebApp/channelsPortalWebApp.portal?_nfpb=true&_pageLabel=pageImport_TradeStats

10.9   International Trade Advisors

International Trade Advisors, through Business Links provide advice on export development to companies in their area to assist them in developing export strategy.

International Trade Advisors are appointed on the basis of their extensive personal experience of working in export. Each councillor has over 20 years' hands-on practical experience in exporting goods and services to over 120 markets around the world. They know the markets, have carried out the fieldwork, travelled to the customer and taken the orders. International Trade Advisors will usually help enquirers draw up export and marketing plans. Their key role will be to help you:

◆ Find overseas agents/distributors;
◆ Help you with market research;
◆ advise you on trade missions;
◆ help you with overseas publicity for your products and services;
◆ advise you on tariffs and regulations.

Contact:
UK Trade & Investment Russia Unit
Bay 949, Kingsgate House
66-74 Victoria Street
London SW1E 6SW
Tel: 020 7215 4891;
Website: www.uktradeinvest.gov.uk/ukti/appmanager/ukti/countries?_nfls=false&_nfpb=true&_pageLabel=CountryType1&navigationPageId=/russia

10.10   British Embassy in Moscow

The Embassy's Commercial Department welcomes enquiries from those doing business in Russia wishing to do so in the future. It can offer advice on the problems of doing business in Russia and functions as a co-ordinating point for matters of common interest, holding monthly meetings for the residents of the business community.

Contact:
British Embassy, Smolenskaya Naberezhnaya 10, Moscow 121099.
Website: www.britaininrussia.ru
Consular Office:
Tel: 007 495 956 7200, Fax: 007 495 956 7201
E-mail: moscow@britishembassy.ru
Commercial Department,
Tel: 007 495 956 7477, Fax: 007 495 956 7480
E-mail: commercial.moscow@fco.gov.uk;
Help may also be sought from:
British Consulate General in St Petersburg
Sq. Proletorskay Diktatury 5, St Petersburg 193124

Tel: 007 812 320 3200, Fax: 007 812 320 3211
E-mail: bcgspb@peterlink.ru, Website: www.britaininrussia.ru
British Consulate General in Ekaterinburg
15a Gogol Street, 4th Floor, Ekaterinburg 620075
Tel: 007 3432 55 4931, Fax: 007 3432 59 2901
E-mail: brit@sky.ru, Website: www.britaininrussia.ru

10.11   Business opportunities

The Business Opportunities service is a free internet-based system, matching UK
businesses with international Business Opportunities gathered by the Government's
network of British Embassies, High Commissions and Consulates worldwide.

To benefit from this service, UK businesses need to register on the UK Trade
& Investment website (www.uktradeinvest.gov.uk/) and profile themselves to
receive opportunities relevant to their products/services from specific markets
around the world. They can then see the opportunities when they have logged-on
to the website. UK customers have the added option of being alerted by E-mail, if
they wish, when new opportunities come in to match their profile.

10.12   The Moscow Delegation

The Moscow Delegation is one of over 130 European Commission Delegations
around the world. It is a fully accredited diplomatic mission, which represent the
European Commission, the executive arm of the European Union. The Moscow
Delegation monitors, analyses and evaluates the development of Russian policies and follows bilateral relations in the political, economic, commercial as well
as financial and technical cooperation areas. It also conducts negotiations in all
spheres of commerce, industry, regulation and governance on behalf of the EU in
accordance with approved mandates. Since 1 February 2002, the Delegation has
also become responsible for the management of the EU's technical cooperation
programmes (European Neighbourhood Policy, European Initiative for Democracy and Human Rights). Additionally, the Delegation provides logistical support
to all EU institutions and the EU Presidency.

All officials serving in the Delegation are administratively attached to the
European Commission's Directorate General for External relations and serve in
principle for four years in Moscow.

Contact:
Moscow office of the Delegation
Kadashevskaya nab., 14/1, Moscow 119017
Tel: 007 495 721 2000, Fax: 007 495 721 2020
E-mail: Delegation-Russia@ec.europa.eu
Website: www.delrus.ec.europa.eu/en/index.htm

10.13 Other business contact information

Business contacts can be obtained from trade directories such as:

(a) Kompass Russia   Tel: 007 495 737 6157
    Infogroup Kompass   Fax: 007 495 737 6157
    Malaya Tulskaya St 25   E-mail: info@kompass.ru
    Korpus 5   Website: www.kompass.ru
    Moscow

(b) Moscow Business Telephone Guide Tel: 007 495 788 0545
    (Published 10 times per year)   Fax: 007 495 788 0566

OOO Infocom Izdat
12 Oktyabrsky Pereulok
127018 Moscow

E-mail: info@mbtg.ru
www.mbtg.ru

(c) Yellow Pages Moscow
B Tatarskaya Ulitsa 35
Moscow 113184

Tel: 007 495 951 6371
E-mail: Bdd@bdd.ru
Website: www.yellowpages.ru/eng/nd2

(d) Adres Moskva
(Published each autumn)
ZAO Izdatelstvo "Evro-Adres"
Office 204,
20, 1st Schipkovsky Pereulok
Moscow 113093

Tel: 007 495 787 1787
Fax: 007 495 787 1788
E-mail: Info@euroadress.ru
Website: www.euroadress.ru

10.14   Export Control Organisation – Public Enquiry Unit

Export controls are in place for a variety of reasons, including:

◆ the collective security of the UK and its allies;
◆ national security;
◆ foreign policy requirements;
◆ international treaty obligations and commitments;
◆ the UK's non-proliferation policy;
◆ concerns about terrorism or internal repression and other human rights violations.

If goods or technologies are subject to UK export controls, you will need a licence to export them.

The BERR's Export Control Organisation's Helpline acts as a first point of contact for any export control enquiry from an exporter. The section provides advice on many issues including how to establish whether or not specific goods need an export licence, the different types of export licences, how to complete export licence application forms and how long they take to process.

The service is contactable by E-mail or fax only at E-mail eco@dti.gsi.gov.uk; Fax: 020 7215 0531; Website: www.berr.gov.uk/europeandtrade/strategic-export-control/index.html

Other information on export controls may be obtained from:

◆ The Department for Culture, Media and Sport. Tel: 020 7211 6200, Website: www.culture.gov.uk on the export of antiques and work of art
◆ BERR's Action Single Market. Tel: 020 7215 4212, Website: www.berr.gov.uk/europeandtrade/europe/problemstradingsolvit/page9922.html on European Union/European Economic Area trade barriers or illegal state aids
◆ HM Revenue and Customs National Adviceline. Tel: 01702 367485, Website: http://customs.hmrc.gov.uk/channelsPortalWebApp/channelsPortalWebApp.portal on customs procedures dealing with regulations and costs of compliance

10.16   Government Departments

Many other government departments provide advice and assistance to companies wishing to establish trade links overseas. Some are particularly relevant to Russia in view of the high volume of exports to that country.

10.17   International Agriculture & Technology Centre (IATC)

The International Agriculture & Technology Centre promotes and develops international business in the agro-food sector matching overseas buyers with UK suppliers. It undertakes this through programme of events and activities both at home and overseas including exhibitions, road shows, conferences and seminars.

Contact

International Agriculture & Technology Centre

Stoneleigh Park, Warwickshire CV8 2LZ

Tel: 08707 200275; Fax: 08707 200285; Website: www.theiatc.org/

10.18 Department for Children, Schools and Families (DCSF)

The DCSF has an International Relations Division that can advise companies and educationalists on issues in supplying goods and services, including inspection and examination support, to schools overseas.

Contact

Tel: 0207 273 4910

10.19 Knowledge Transfer Networks

Knowledge Transfer Networks aim to make information on new technology and innovation policy easily accessible to business and to help firms find suitable, collaborative partners. Such information could include news, patents, reports and debates, at multi-regional, national and international levels, and involve many relevant stakeholders from academia and business to Regional Development Agencies, devolved administrations and government departments. See Website:

www.businesslink.gov.uk/bdotg/action/detail?type=RESOURCES&itemId=1075067605)

10.20 UKWatch magazine

UKWatch is a quarterly magazine published jointly by science and technology groups of the UK Government. Highlighting UK innovation and promoting inward investment opportunities into the UK, the publication is available free of charge to UK and overseas subscribers.

Contact: subscriptions@ukwatchonline.com; Website: www.britishembassy.gov.uk/servlet/Front?pagename=OpenMarket/Xcelerate/ShowPage&c=Page&cid=1151077696977

10.21 Templeton Thorp (TT-TOTAL)

TT-TOTAL – political, business & financial intelligence service is a unique system using cutting-edge technology and journalistic insight to monitor and collate the output of over 200 regional, national and international news providers into a single, multi-perspective, flexible online and email subscription package.

Bringing in around 4,000 new articles every day, the system allows subscribers to track 24/7 business, political and financial developments in 29 countries from C&E/SE Europe to Russia, the Caucasus and Central Asia. TT-TOTAL's Russia coverage is further broken down by economic region.

TT-TOTAL's flexible interface allows users to configure their own accounts to view only the information they need. The service tracks 21 sectors from Agribusiness to Real Estate, and can be set up to provide specific coverage of over 450 companies and 300 business and political figures.

TT-TOTAL can be used both as a searchable media-archive, and as a flexible alerting/reporting system, with the option of real-time email alerts, or regular twice-daily, daily, bi-weekly or weekly email reports.

TT-TOTAL key features:
– 24/7 on-line website access, updated every 5 minutes
– 'Cache' facility for an outstanding specialist research archive of over 1.7 million articles
– Automatic Russian-English translation facility
– Concise profiles on all business and political figures covered by the service
– Government lists detailing the political structure of all countries covered

TT-TOTAL is provided by Templeton Thorp, the definitive independent market specialist for intelligence, business and political information, and due diligence services in Russia, the CIS, and Central and South Eastern Europe.

Contact:
TEMPLETON THORP
7-10 Adam Street, The Strand, London WC2N 6AA
Tel: 020 7520 9380, Fax: 020 7504 8180
Email: enquiries@templetonthorp.com,
Websites: www.templetonthorp.com, www.tt-total.com

The information contained herein is confidential and is intended solely for the addressee(s). Any unauthorized access, use, reproduction, disclosure or dissemination is prohibited. If it has been received in error, please notify the sender immediately and delete it.

10.22   Web based Information

10.22.1 Country information:

www.cia.gov/library/publications/the-world-factbook/geos/rs.html   –   general country profile

www.government.ru – Russian government website (Web pages in Russian)
www.ru/eng/index.html – Russia on the net
www.usrbc.org/russianregions/ – general information with good links to the Regions

10.22.2 Business information:

www.uktradeinvest.gov.uk/ukti/appmanager/ukti/countries?_nfls=false&_nfpb=true&_pageLabel=CountryType1&navigationPageId=/russia   –   general business information

www.users.globalnet.co.uk/~chegeo – Import – export website
www.russiaexport.net – Import – export website
www.ceebd.co.uk/ceebd/business.htm – central and Eastern Europe business directory

www.kasna.com/bin/index.php?q=russia&q_type=sx&domain_name=kasna.com&token=aA6AuZ4rX3wKEwiI2MqliIKOAhUc_IYKHRBKFxoYAyAA-MOTaxAk4DQ – general business information and business opportunities

10.22.3 News reports:

♦ www.russiajournal.com/taxonomy_menu/1 – The Russian Journal website
♦ www.prime-tass.com – Prime-Tass.com website
♦ www.britishembassy.gov.uk/servlet/Front?pagename=OpenMarket/Xcelerate/ShowPage&c=Page&cid=1089123734028 – Russia: Monthly Economic Report

- www.eiu.com/index.asp?layout=country&geography_id=1750000175&rf=0 – Economist Intelligence Unit reports on Russia
- www.newslink.org/euruss.html – Links to online Russian newspapers
- www.bisnis.doc.gov/ – General country information
- www.moscowtimes.ru/ – online daily newspaper
- www.rferl.org/newsline/index.html – Daily reports on events in Russia and Eastern Europe
- www.russiatoday.com/ – Daily news and information resource from Russia
- http://en.rian.ru – News reports from Russia

10.23 Books and directories

One excellent publication is "Living and Working in Moscow" – a PricewaterhouseCooper's guide for ex-patriots. This is user-friendly book that provides much useful information for both the visitor and foreign resident. Euromonitor plc. (Tel: 0207 251 8024; Fax 0207 608 3149) also publish a number of books relating to conducting business in the Russian Federation and neighbouring countries. Other useful publications include: Kogan Page's (Tel: 0207 278 0433) The Essential Guide for the Business Traveller by John Mattock.

Travel guides may be purchased from The Travel Bookshop, 13 Blenheim Crescent, London W11 2EE, Colletts, Foyles and many branches of W H Smith & Sons Ltd also stock travel guides.

10.24 Newspapers and Magazines

10.24.1 RBCC Bulletin

A key and exclusive benefit of RBCC membership is the monthly Bulletin. The full-colour Bulletin comprises up-to-date summaries of economic and business news from Russia, Chamber news, and features on a wide cross-section of subjects in English and Russian.

Each issue contains articles on legal and regional affairs, industry sector reports, comment and analysis by leading figures in business and politics, and listings of major conferences, seminars and exhibitions in (or related to) Russia throughout the year.

The Bulletin, with a readership of approximately 6000, goes to UK and Russian members, to Russian regional and Federal Chambers of Commerce, British and Russian Embassies, Consulates and British Council offices. It is also available at events to potential members, is distributed on BA, and at various hotels and corporate locations in Moscow and London.

As this is a publication for Chamber members, there is also broad scope for member companies to have input, and contributions in the form of articles are welcome. They also offer free "advertorial" for new member companies. The transformation of the Bulletin, has resulted in more and more companies – members and non-members alike – seeing it as an effective means of advertising.

For contact details and further information see 10.29

10.24.2 Business Monitor International

Established in 1984, Business Monitor International is a leading print and online publisher of specialist business information on global emerging markets. Our range of daily, weekly, monthly and quarterly services covers political risk, finance, macroeconomic performance, outlook and forecast, industry sectors and the business operating environment. Business Monitor International also publishes directories and CD-ROMs profiling multinational companies active in emerging markets.

Contact:
Business Monitor International
Mermaid House
2 Puddle Dock
Blackfriars
London
EC4V 3DS
Tel: 020 7248 0468
Fax: 020 7248 0467
Website: www.businessmonitor.com

10.24.3   Other English-language sources

Other up-to-date English language sources of information include:

10.24.3.1   Press

- Kommersant – www.kommersant.com/
- Moscow News – http://english.mn.ru/english/
- Novaya Gazeta – http://en.novayagazeta.ru/
- Russia Beyond the Headlines – http://rbth.rg.ru/
- Russia net –www.russia.net/
- St Petersburg Times – www.sptimes.ru
- The Moscow Times – www.themoscowtimes.com/indexes/01.html
- The Moscow Tribune – www.tribune.ru
- The Russia Journal Daily – www.russiajournal.com
- The Russia Journal Weekly – www.trj.ru

These newspapers all aim to give information on Russia. Magazines available in English include Delovie Lyudi.

Information may also be obtained from the Russian TV Magazine Russian Hour see website: www.russianhour.tv/index_en.php

10.24.3.2   Television

- Russia Today – www.russiatoday.ru/

10.24.3.3   Radio

- Voice of Russia – www.ruvr.ru/index.php?lng=eng

10.25 Seminars and Conferences

Many organisations now organise seminars and conferences relating to Russia. Details of these may be obtained from the Russo-British Chamber of Commerce (see 10.26).

10.26 Russo-British Chamber of Commerce

The Russo-British Chamber of Commerce, founded in 1916, is a private company, limited by guarantee, and a non-profit making entity. The Chamber has offices in London and Moscow.

Chamber services include general assistance and business advice from bilingual British and Russian staff, with a broad base of business experience. The

Chamber can for example find partners for companies, set up commercial programmes, organise "UK Trade & Investment" sponsored trade fairs, missions and seminars. It also offers publications including its Bulletin (see 10.26.1), a regular electronic newsletter, and various directories.

The Chamber offers members business consultancy, training, market research, logistics, presentations, help with communications, use of Moscow office, regular events in Russia and the UK, corporate promotions, advertising, database search, mail shots and many other services. Some of these are free, others chargeable, but with substantial reductions for members. There are also discounts available in Moscow and London hotels, and on travel, translation, product certification, etc.

Russo-British Chamber of Commerce Website: www.rbcc.com
RBCC London
42 Southwark Street, London, SE1 1UN
Tel: 020 7403 1706; Fax: 020 7403 1245;
E-mail: office.manager@rbcc.co.uk
RBCC Moscow
Galereya Aktyor Business Centre, 4th Floor,
Tverskaya Street 16/2, Moscow 125009
Tel: 007 495 961 2160, Fax: 007 495 961 2161
E-mail: russiadirector@rbcc.com
RBCC St Petersburg and NW Russia
Office 4, 36 Liteiny Prospekt, St Petersburg 191104
Tel: 007 812 336 5080, Fax: 007 812 279 0336

10.27 The British Chambers of Commerce

The BCC represents the interest of exporting business in the UK nationally, regionally and locally. We ensure that exporters' views are clearly expressed and delivered to all the relevant Government and private bodies and that action is taken to ensure exporters' needs are met today and in the future.

The BCC supports and advises businesses in all areas of International Trade development and intelligent exporting, and in the promotion and awareness of language skills.

The BCC supports its accredited network in the provision of international trade services such as:

- Training in all aspects related to World Trade
- Export Documentation Services
- Market research and online intelligence
- Credit checks and Letters
- Export Planning
- Translation services and multilingual marketing material
- Inward / Outward Trade missions and fairs
- Export clubs and international networking
- Consultancy Projects
- Tender advice and opportunities
- Specialist Advisory Service
- Letters of Credit
- Credit checks
- Market focused Programmes
- Events and Seminars
- Introduction and contacts with local and central players in Government

The BCC enjoys a close and productive relationship with UK Trade & Investment, the government organisation which supports UK companies trading internationally and overseas enterprises seeking to locate in the UK.

On behalf of UK Trade & Investment, the BCC manages and delivers two of their key services; the Export Marketing Research Scheme (See 10.31.1), which encourages UK businesses to conduct research before entering a new overseas market, and the Export Communications Review (See 12.13.1), which aims to reduce the instances in which cultural and language barriers come between UK businesses and success overseas.

With a worldwide Network of bilateral and International Chambers the BCC can provide UK exporters with a unique added dimension, beyond the existing roles of Embassy Post.

The British Chambers of Commerce
4 Westwood House, Westwood Business Park, Coventry, CV4 8HS
Tel: 02476 694484; E-mail: enquiry@britishchambers.org.uk
Website (General): www.chamberonline.co.uk/
Website (Russia): www.link2exports.co.uk/regions.asp?lsid=1431&pid=1213

It should be noted that the following Chambers of Commerce claim special expertise in Russia:

Derbyshire & Nottinghamshire Chamber of Commerce Tel: 0845 6011 038
Greater Manchester Chamber of Commerce Tel: 0161 236 3210
London Chamber of Commerce Tel: 020 7248 4444
North Staffordshire Chamber of Commerce Tel: 01782 202222

10.28   Confederation of British Industry (CBI)

The CBI's Initiative Central and East European Department runs a comprehensive programme of events and produces a number of publications to promote business opportunities in the area. These include missions, seminars with eminent speakers and conferences and workshops on the market.

Contact: The Central and East European Department, Confederation of British Industry, Centre Point, 103 New Oxford Street, London WC1A 1DU. Tel: 0207-379 7400; Fax: 0207 836 1972/240 1578 Website: www.cbi.org.uk

10.29   Passport to Export Success

Through Passport to Export Success, UK Trade & Investment is able to advise and offer financial help to British businesses looking to be more proactive in their exporting activity. Through this programme exporters may receive up to £3,000 in matched funding towards expenditure on implementing an agreed export plan and up to £500 towards training and development. The maximum funding available is £5,000 per company.

For further information, contact your local Business Link: Tel: 0845 6023 709

10.30   Overseas Market Introduction Service (OMIS)

The Overseas Market Introduction Service (OMIS) provides UK companies with a wealth of practical support and advice to guide them through the process of breaking into a new overseas market. It can provide them with all the help they will need at every stage of the process from initial research to making their first visit.

As each company will have its own individual requirements, five levels of service are offered. The levels vary in price from £225-£1800 depending on the amount of help required. The levels needed to achieve a similar result may differ from country to country and depend on the product or service involved. Examples of what might be provided for each level are:

Level 1 – this basic level is designed for smaller but significant pieces of work, e.g. where a company has conducted some research of its own but needs help in contracting potential customers.

Level 2 – this can be used for pieces of work to supplement previous OMIS activities, or to support other market-entry activities, e.g. Trade Missions and visits supported by UK Trade & Investment Market Visit Support.

Level 3 – this level is designed to give companies essential information based on local in-country market research. It would suit those preparing to enter a new market and requiring more comprehensive market information, contact details and itineraries for visits to local partners.

Level 4 – this level is likely to include more in-depth research on a particular sector, in-market help and mentoring from trade officers and accompanied visits.

Level 5 – the level offers the most comprehensive help, e.g. assistance organising a seminar, presentation or event, including identification of potential delegates, marketing, invitation mailing and all round support.

Contact:

UK Trade & Investment

Bay 817, Kingsgate House, 66 – 74 Victoria Street, London, SW1E 6SW

Tel: 020 7215 4891; Website: www.uktradeinvest.gov.uk

10.31.1 Export Marketing Research Scheme

This grant is designed to encourage small to medium established British companies (i.e. employ fewer than 250 people), to undertake or commission marketing research based on sound methods. Companies may apply for up to ten marketing research projects with a maximum of two projects in any one year. Only one study can be supported for Russia.

The scheme is open to those British companies offering products or services, primarily of UK origin. Commission agents are not eligible for support. It is not anticipated however that companies less than two years old or employing less than five people will have the resources to make appropriate use of the scheme.

Support available

Support of up to £20,000 per study may be offered. No more than £60,000 is available to any one firm.

Assistance is available towards the costs of:

(a) conducting in-house research;

(b) employing market research agencies;

(c) buying published market research; and

(d) participating in multi-client studies;

If you were to directly visit a country on a marketing research (not selling) trip, on behalf of your own company, you may be awarded grant support towards the costs of all travel expenses including, air fare, hotel, subsistence, car hire and interpreter's fees.

A company commissioning a marketing research agency may receive a grant of up to 50% towards their fees and expenses. Applications for consultancy projects must be accompanied by detailed and fully costed proposals from three independent marketing research agencies, together with one copy of the brief prepared by the applicant.

Information required

In order to apply for a grant the following information will be required on the application form:

- the year the business started;
  company registration number
- the number of employees;
- your annual turnover and your export turnover;
- which countries will be researched;
- turnover in respect of sales to the countries you will be researching;
- list of products you are currently selling to the countries you wish to research;
- list of other products you have sold to this country;
- proposed date of departure and date of return;
- number of nights to be spent in each country;
- economy air fare to the market. You must state route to be taken;
- internal overseas travel costs. Specify whether air, ferry, car or other means is to be used;
- estimated interpreter's fees in each country; and
- the name of the researcher, together with a brief c.v.

Applications for in-house projects must be accompanied by a detailed proposal that sets out the terms of reference for the project. A full set of printed guidance notes is available from the Scheme Managers on request.

All applications must be submitted at least 28 days prior to the proposed commencement of the study.

Prior to the commencement of fieldwork, the applicant is required to carry out desk research. This may include referencing published reports and contacting UK buying offices, trade organisations, Chambers of Commerce, the British Embassy or Consulate in the country to be visited, library research, and UK Trade & Investment services such as country and sector desks

10.31.2 Payment of grant

The grant monies will be paid after the research trip:

    (a) on provision of a satisfactory marketing research report; and

    (b) the production of receipts and invoices for expenses.

Contact:

Export Marketing Research Scheme

British Chambers of Commerce, 4 Westwood House, Westwood Business Park, Coventry, CV4 8HS

Tel: 024 7669 4484; Website: www.chamberonline.co.uk

11 PROMOTIONS AND MARKET ENTRY

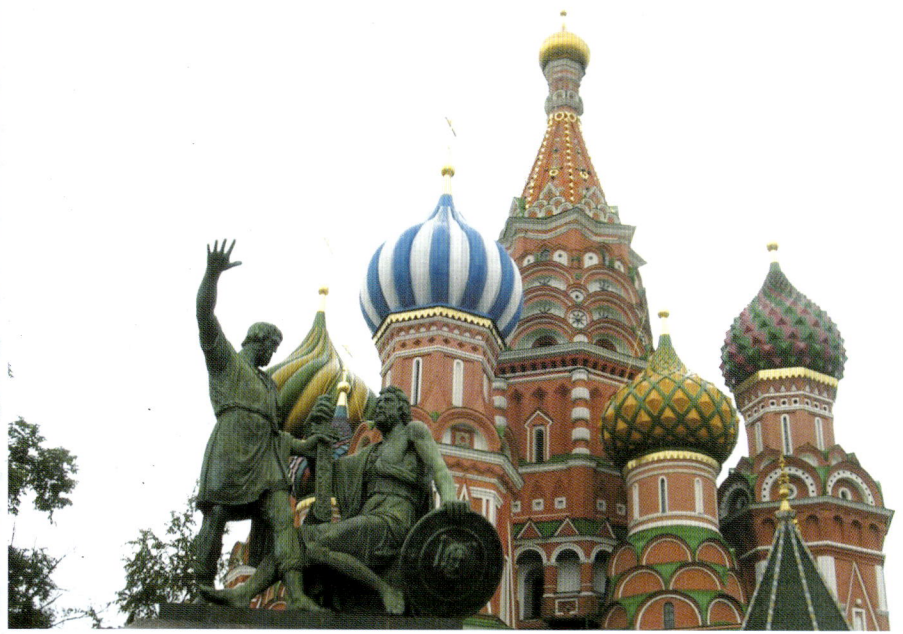

RUSSIA: Practical Solutions

Annual November Conference on Russia

The Event:

The event takes the form of a debate, luncheon, round tables and reception. Its remit is to provide practical help to companies doing business or considering doing business in Russia. We have organized this annual event since 2005.

Opportunities:

- Meet specialists in law, travel, certification, freight, taxation, recruitment, crossborder trade, insurance, language, branding and more
- Obtain discounts on products and services
- Mingle with other companies doing business in Russia, and swap experiences with them

Testimonials:

- "Thank you for the event last week. It was good to make some contacts and hear more about some of the practical difficulties (and solutions!) with working in Russia."

  Paxton & Whitfield

- "This was a real opportunity to mix with companies like ours, which export to Russia, and to help each other!"

  John Crane UK Ltd

ALBION (OVERSEAS) LTD

ELLION HOUSE
6 Alexandra Rd
Tonbridge TN9 2AA
United Kingdom

Tel: +44 (0)1732 769 003
Fax: +44 (0)1732 353 373
Website: www.albionoverseas.com
E-mail: david@albionoverseas.com
Skype: albionoverseas

11.1   Introduction

Having identified sources of help and possibly researched the market, establishing a permanent presence may on your agenda. In support of this UK Trade & Investment and other departments and agencies provide a range of initiatives to businesses to help them to find and to safely secure export orders. Much of this support is free or subsidised.

11.2   Tradeshow Access Programme (TAP)

UK Trade & Investment's Tradeshow Access Programme (TAP) provides grant support for eligible Small & Medium Sized Enterprises to attend trade shows overseas.

Participation is usually as part of a group of UK businesses led by an Accredited Trade Association that has agreed to help deliver TAP support.

There is normally a great advantage for inexperienced businesses when they exhibit as part of an organised group. Additionally, working with Accredited Trade Organisations, UK Trade & Investment will seek to raise the profile of the UK group and the UK sector at specific "key" exhibitions.

However, TAP can also accommodate a smaller number of participating businesses wishing to exhibit at trade shows where there is no ATO led group, on an independent or "solo" basis. Grant rates are set at £1,800 or £1,500 for "solo".

For trade events in Russia the following should be considered:

1) The need for a professional interpreter;
2) The display of your goods;
3) A basic knowledge of export procedures, tariffs and regulations;
4) Knowledge of the Russian customer;
5) If it is not your first exhibition, use the event to re-establish and consolidate existing contacts.

Potential customers will not always be smartly or conventionally dressed when they visit a trade fair. As a result, serious and substantial buyers have sometimes been ignored at some trade stands, owing to their casual appearance and clothing. Such neglect has resulted in orders going to companies more attuned to the Russian market.

Details of exhibitions where an Accredited Trade Organisation will be recruiting a group of UK businesses and organising their grant support are published on the UKTI website www.uktradeinvest.gov.uk This website also contains links to many connected sources of advice and help for new exporters.

Other useful sources of information include:

◆ www.exhibitions.co.uk is a BERR sponsored site that offers a comprehensive and free listing on all consumer and trade exhibitions held in the UK.
◆ The UK Trade & Investment sponsored publication, Overseas Trade (Tel: 020 7368 9622) includes details of planned overseas trade fairs.
◆ Trade journals
◆ The British Chambers of Commerce (Tel: 020 7654 5800; Website: www.chamberonline.co.uk
◆ The Year Ahead Directory (Tel: 0207 190 7814; Fax: 0207 190 7797; Website: www.yearahead.co.uk).
◆ www.expo24-7.com is an exhibition industry portal that publicises exhibitions in over 120 countries.

11.3   Trade Associations

Many trade associations provide export intelligence as well as invaluable advice on selling overseas to potential customers. They are often also the main organisers of buyers' visits to the United Kingdom, trade fairs, inward and outwards missions and other export related schemes, many of which are supported by government grants.

A list of trade associations can be accessed through websites www.brainstorm. co.uk/TANC/directory/welcome/html and www.martex.co.uk/taf/

11.4   Partenariat programme

The Partenariat programme is a European Commission scheme which aims to encourage and promote business 'partnering' opportunities and co-operation between small- and medium-sized enterprises in the EU and other countries. Usually there are one or two events held somewhere in the world each year. Each event normally lasts two days. Meetings are pre-arranged with the Host companies from the target region, and last about 30 minutes each. There is no charge to take part in a Partenariat. Delegates will need to pay for travel and accommodation. These costs are usually at a reduced rate owing to prices negotiated by the host or chamber with airline companies and hoteliers.

It has been demonstrated that those companies that prepare well in advance and follow up initial contacts once the event is over achieve success.

Full details of the programme of events is available from the British Chamber of Commerce

Contact:

Portsmouth and South East Hampshire Chamber of Commerce & Industry Regional Business Centre

Harts Farm Way

Havant

Hampshire PO9 1HR

Tel: 023 924 49449

E-mail: info@chamber.org.uk

Website: www.chamber.org.uk

11.5   Overseas Seminars

Overseas seminars help exporters promote the quality of their goods and services to an invited foreign audience. Accredited Trade Organisations may receive significant financial help from UK Trade & Investment to organise events. This in turn may be used to subsidise up to 50% of a participant's costs up to a maximum of £2,300.

Occasionally, seminars involve a ministerial presence, which increases the overall profile of the event.

Contact:

Trade Associations, Chambers of Commerce or Business Support Agencies, such as Business Link

11.6   Overseas Stores Promotions

Overseas stores often stage promotions of British goods where there is potential for volume sales. UK Trade & Investment supports the store by providing financial assistance towards the expense incurred in promoting the event.

Promotions with a UK theme may include demonstrations, displays, entertainers and other attractions with a British flavour. The main aim is to increase sales of UK goods in the longer term. UK Trade & Investment and Diplomatic Service commercial staff works closely with the store to ensure that the event achieves maximum exposure for the UK and its products. The UK Trade & Investment also liaises with stores, buying offices and supplies on the merchandising aspects of a promotion. Details of these events are given in the Overseas Trade magazine's quarterly Promotions Guide and via trade associations and Chambers of Commerce.

Contact:

Trade Associations, Chambers of Commerce or Business Support Agencies, such as Business Link

11.7   Inward Missions

UK Trade & Investment organises a number of Inward Missions bringing those who are in a key position to influence the purchase of UK goods and services to visit the UK to see for themselves what is available from UK industry. If you are interested in participating please get in touch with your UK Trade & Investment sector contact or contact the UKTI enquiry line TEL 020 7215 8000.

11.8   Trade-Related British Ministerial Visits Overseas

Each year British government ministers participate in a large number of trade-related overseas visits, sometimes accompanied by representatives from British business. The 'Unclassified List of Trade-Related Ministerial Visits' forward plan can be obtained from UK Trade & Investment Russia Unit (See 10.2).

11.9   Albion (Overseas) Limited

Set up in the mid-nineties, Albion (Overseas) Limited is an established consultancy, trading organisation and exporter with long experience of working in Russia and with Russian companies overseas. Albion operates throughout the Russian regions, and has offices and warehousing in Russian and the United Kingdom. Albion offers the following services:

◆ Consultancy:

Albion assists companies to start a business in Russia. This is usually, but not exclusively, for companies which want to sell goods into Russia. Where a company has already conducted some initial research, for example by commissioning an OMIS report (See 10.30) we can set up a programme of accompanied meetings, and more importantly, follow these meetings up. We can also assist with areas such as travel, certification, tax and legal issues, and so on, working with other companies, which are specialists in their field. Help might be needed from making just one or two phone calls, to getting a company its first order.

On a longer term basis, we can help companies by offering them a low cost Moscow office with use our warehouse. Within this office is an individual who reports exclusively to you the client. This has the benefit of our consultancy support, at no charge, which is especially useful when moving products across the border, which is where problems can often occur. This has a further, major advantage, or allowing you to sell your goods for Roubles, whilst still receiving payment in the hard currency of your choice.

◆ Training:

Russia is very different to many markets, and needs a specific style of business psyche. Albion conducts training for UK companies, preparing them for this. Albion also offers consultancy and training services to Russian companies, and to Russians within western companies. This may include preparing companies for a first visit to the market. Training may be on an individual basis or in groups. Training clients have included: Dirol Cadbury, Gillette, METRO stores, Michelin, Chevron Texaco, Alfa Laval, Dunlop, CSG, TRW, Dixons stores and others. (See 12.11)

♦ Trading:

Albion is distributor for a number of companies selling into Russia. These are mainly industrial products. Please contact us if you are interested in our distribution services.

♦ General Assistance:

Albion is the organiser of the annual conference "Russia: Practical Solutions", held for the first time in 2005, and hosted by the BBC's Bridget Kendal. This conference has become popular for its direct, pragmatic objectives. The conference is a gathering of companies interested in doing business in Russia, and a variety of companies which have been operating there for many years in sectors such as travel, freight, certification, law, tax, training and others. A morning debate and look at issues featuring in the Russian business landscape of today is followed by gloves-off, confidential individual discussion and networking stands for more open chat.

Contact:

Albion (Overseas) Ltd, UK

Ellion House, 6 Alexandra Rd, Tonbridge, TN9 2AA

Mob: 07801 961866

Skype: albionoverseas

E-mail: david@albionoverseas.com, Website: www.albionoverseas.com

Or

Mikhail Kondrashov

Albion (Overseas) Ltd, Russia,

Ul. Skakovaya 9, 4th floor, office 529, 125040 Moscow

Tel: 007 495 945 2795, Fax: 007 495 945 2781

E-mail: mikhail@albionoverseas.com

11.10 Other firms providing strategic and implementation services

These include:

Central European Trust Co Ltd (CET), Tel: 020 7258 7100;

Fax: 020 7258 710; Website: www.cet.co.uk/

CET Moscow Tel: 007 495 788 6867; Fax: 007 495 788 6865

The Russian Business Cooporation Network Corporation (RBCNet-Corp), Tel: 007 495 973 0287; Fax: 007 495 973 0088; E-mail: rbcnet@rbcnet.ru; Website: www.rbcnet.ru/

SociumInfopolis, Tel: 007 495 158 9681; Fax: 007 495 158 9971; E-mail: Socium@mbt.ru; Website: www.dpmexpo.ru/2006/eng/participants/direct/218680.stm

11.11 Distributors, consultants, sales agents and representatives

A number of firms offer representative services to UK manufacturers. Details of these may be obtained from a trade association, the British Embassy and other organisations involved in promoting trade between the UK and Russian Federation. Members of the RBCC (see 10.26) have automatic access to these companies.

11.12 Scottish Development International

Scottish Development International provides a full range of export support to firms based in Scotland. It runs a number of grant assisted schemes including:

- SDI Learning Journeys – SDI Learning Journeys provide companies, who are new to the Russian market, with the opportunity to access a wide range of experts in all aspects of doing business, learn from Scottish companies or organisations already set up there, gain first-hand experience of market conditions and meet potential customers. The participating companies normally spend two-three days in the Moscow area and are introduced to:
- Doing Business in Russia – Presentations from various speakers covering incorporation, taxation, visas, employment laws, accounting, marketing, local business networking & community and Scottish company case-studies.
- Networking Reception with local business people hosted by SDI Moscow
- Major market participants: group visit.
- Individual meetings with potential clients or partners (Individual company research completed by Scottish Development International's Moscow office to identify potential clients/suppliers).
- Research information supporting your business interest.
  Contact:
  Scottish Development International
  Atlantic Quay
  150 Broomielaw, Glasgow, G2 8LU
  Tel: 0141 228 2828, Fax: 0141 228 2089
  Website: www.scottishdevelopmentinternational.com
  Office 13 "V"
  Koroviy Ulitsa Val 7117049, Moscow
  Tel: 007 495 937 3773, Fax: 007 495 937 3770

12   HELP FOR TRAINING

12.1   Introduction

A number of initiatives are available, throughout the United Kingdom and in Russia, to improve the quality of staff engaged in a joint venture and to build up a level of expertise with potential business associates.

12.2   British Council

The British Council creates, through education, training and cultural programmes, a climate favourable to British trade and contributes to the promotion of British goods and services worldwide.

The Council promotes technical, educational and cultural co-operation between Britain and overseas countries. Its work is designed to develop worldwide partners and improve international understanding.

Through its offices in over 100 countries, the British Council has created a unique network of contacts with government departments, universities, professional bodies and locally based business and industry.

The British Council can provide a number of services to British education exporters working in Eastern Europe, including:

(a) Providing information on the demands for education and training;

(b) Enabling British specialists to teach, advise and establish joint projects; and

(c) Securing contracts for overseas consultancy projects involving British enterprise.

It can also be of service to British industry and commerce, helping to raise the international profile of British companies through:

- the management of sponsored activities; and
- linking their interests to its education and training activities, including industrial attachment.

Through its offices in Central and Eastern Europe, the British Council gives access to British skills, expertise and talent by:

(a) providing information about British expertise through library and information services;

(b) providing access to British education and training resources; and

(c) providing language and business skills training in situ.

The British Council have representation in Russia. Details can be found at website: www.britishcouncil.org/russia

Contact:

- General information: Tel: 0161 957 7758
- Management of Sponsored Events. Tel: 020 7389 4940. Fax: 020 7389 4058
- Language, Business and Management Training In-Country.
  Tel: 020 7389 4374. Fax: 020 7389 4140.
- Education section: Tel: 0207 389 4383

12.3   BOND

BOND is a UK Trade & Investment initiative, managed by the British Council, which provides UK companies with low-cost introductions to potential business partners in key developing international markets. High quality professionals, selected through the worldwide network of British Council offices overseas, are assigned to UK companies for up to twelve months. BOND placements are an enriching experience for all concerned – your company gains cultural and business insights into overseas markets, and the participants gain experience of UK business that will enhance their career prospects. At the end of the placement when the professional returns home they are ideally placed to raise awareness of your company, products and services in their own country, paving the way for positive trade links in the future. The flexibility of the Scheme ensures that it can be tailored to suit most business needs.

12.3.1 How BOND works

The BOND team processes the required work permit and visa, provides return airfares for each professional and conducts pre-departure briefings on living in the UK. It arranges 'meet and greet' at port of entry and accommodation for the first few nights. In addition it:

- provides ongoing support, and participants have access to our emergency 24/7 welfare service.
- arranges for BOND hosts and their professionals to meet other local businesses at networking events arranged by UK Trade & Investment.
- monitors the impact of the Scheme, both with host organisations and the participants through our British Council Alumni register overseas.

12.3.2 Costs

BOND operates on a self-financing cost recovery basis. The costs to the host organisation are an agreed monthly stipend for the professional and a modest monthly management fee to cover costs. The only additional cost is a one off charge made by the Home Office for a work permit, which is passed on at cost. There are no headcount issues or tax implications, other than VAT on our management fee. Bills are invoiced quarterly.

12.3.3 Funding

SME's using the UKTI Passport to Export Success Initiative (see 10.29), may be eligible for funding towards the cost of a BOND placement.

If your company is based in England, Wales or Northern Ireland contact:
BOND
The British Council
Bridgewater House, 58 Whitworth Street, Manchester M1 6BB
Tel: 0161 957 7684, Fax: 0161 957 7488
E-mail: bond@britishcouncil.org
Website: www.britishcouncil.org/bond
If your company is based in Scotland contact:
Scottish Networks International
British Council Scotland
The Tun (3rd floor), 4 Jackson's Entry, Holyrood Road, Edinburgh EH8 8PJ
Tel: 0131 524 5740, Fax: 0131 524 5701
E-mail: Scottishni@britishcouncil.org
Website: www.scottishni.org/sni_v4/sni_display_wide.jsp?pContentID=50&p_applic=SNI_CCC&p_service=Content.show&

12.4 Chevening Scholarships

Chevening Scholarships are named after Chevening House, the official country residence of the British Foreign Secretary. The Scholarships are aimed at overseas graduates wishing to spend a period of study in the UK. They are open to:

- Russian graduates currently residing in Russia who intend to work in Russia following completion of scholarship
- Have a clear vision of how your period of study in the UK will benefit Russian society and economy
- Be able to show at interview that they possess the personal qualities to benefit from their scholarship and use it to succeed in their chosen career.
- Excellent English language skills with a minimum International English Language Testing System (IELTS) score of 6.5 IELTS. The IELTS can be taken by contacting The British Council or British Embassy.
- Excellent grades from a recognised Russia University
- A minimal of 2 years work experience in the area related to your chosen career

  Priority fields of Study include –
- Public Administration (including Public Health and Urban Planning as well as Governance issues)
- International Relations (including International Security)
- Political Studies
- Public, Constitutional, International and Human Rights Law; Law Enforcement
- Journalism (Print and Broadcasting media)
- Sustainable development and environmental studies (including climate change, environmental protection; planning and management issues; Energy Security; Energy efficiency and renewable energy)
- Innovation
- Economics
- Exceptional candidates in other fields

  There are basically two types of scholarships;
- Fully funded scholarships – these are full scholarships that cover tuition fees, monthly stipend and various one-off allowances;
- Part funded scholarships – these vary from award to award and cover part/full stipend and/or allowances.

  To participate in the scheme applicants must apply to The British Embassy, Moscow

  British Embassy
  Smolenskaya Naberezhnaya 10
  Moscow 121099.
  Tel: 007 495 956 7200
  Fax: 007 495 956 7201
  E-mail: moscow@britishembassy.ru
  Website: www.britaininrussia.ru

12.5   Management training courses

No-one has ever questioned the high standards of education in Russia, the ability of Russians to cope with change, or the perseverance and determination of the Russian people. However, it has been recognised, both within Russia and outside, that there was little management perception of how to run a business in a mature market economy. To assist in this many countries, both individually and collectively, as well as Russia itself have embarked on a variety of training programmes to teach the ablest of Russian managers how businesses, within the market economy, work. In addition, there are an increasing number of management training courses available from independent organisations such as multi-national companies.

12.6   The Vladimir Potanin Foundation

The Vladimir Potanin Foundation was established in 1999 for the implementation of socially significant projects in the sphere of domestic education and culture. It is a competitive scheme, aimed at high calibre students from Russia's major state educational institutions, talented teachers and museum employees. The Foundation annually awards over 400 grants and 2,300 scholarships. There are five scholarship and seven grant programs currently under way.

Contact:

Vladimir Potanin Foundation

ul. Bolshaya Yakimanka, 9, Moscow 119180

Tel. 007 495 726 5764, Fax 007 495 726 5754

E-mail: info@fond.potanin.ru

12.7   Norwegian scholarship programme (2007–2010)

The Norwegian government has initiated a scholarship programme for studies and research at institutions of higher education located in Northern Norway with at least half of the scholarships available being granted to Russia students in higher education. Students are recruited by Norwegian institutions in cooperation with Russian partner institutions. The scholarships are granted for a maximum duration of two terms.

Priority areas include:

♦ Tourism

♦ Subjects related to natural resource management, including fisheries and aquaculture

♦ Subjects in technology; natural resources; social sciences relevant to the oil and gas sector

♦ Subjects related to business development in the Arctic or High North, including business administration

♦ Environmental studies

♦ Other subjects with a special relevance to the High North

Contact:

Arne Haugen

Tel: 00 475 530 8840, Fax: 00 475 530 8801

Email: arne.haugen@siu.no

Ragnhild Solvi Berg

Tel: 00 475 530 8833

Email: ragnhild.berg@siu.no

Website: http://siu.no/en/konferanser_og_publikasjoner/nyheter_fra_siu_2007/nytt_stipendprogram_for_studier_i_nordomraadene

12.8   Samsung MBA Program

The Samsung Group, a world leader in the area of information technologies, is keen to attract high calibre students from top Russian universities, (such as Business Schools at the Academy of National Economy, Moscow State University, Higher School of Economics, Russian Economic Academy, MIRBIS, etc.) majoring in various areas of business administration (such as marketing, economy, management, finances, decision sciences), to join its MBA Global Scholarship Program.

The goal of this program is to develop the future Samsung leaders. The MBA course is taught at the Samsung Graduate School of Business (GSB) of the Sungkyunkwan University.

The Samsung Group pays for all educational expenses including the tuition, admission, two round-trip plane tickets, medical insurance and registration fees for the students. Dormitory support may also be provided. Moreover, each GSP-SKK member is granted scholarship in the amount of around US$ 800 per month. After completing the MBA course and receiving the MBA Degree, the GSP-SKK Program's member is provided with an opportunity to work at Samsung in South Korea for 2 years and then in Russia for the following 2 years.

See Website: http://edu.samsung.ru/mba/

12.9 TEMPUS IV (2008 – 2113)

Tempus (trans-European mobility scheme for university studies) is the European Commission's trans-European cooperation scheme in higher education. Tempus IV builds on previous Tempus programmes, which were limited to higher education, extending across the spectrum of lifelong learning to include schools, vocational education and training and adult education. This grant programme significantly contributes to and reinforces regular academic exchanges between the EU and Tempus partner countries, including Russia, supporting them in their efforts to update higher education and training systems. There is a wide range of priority areas including law, economics, environmental studies, agriculture, social work and modern languages. Tempus IV aims to bring out common cultural values, allow for the fruitful exchange of views to take place and to facilitate multinational activities in the scientific, cultural, artistic, economic and social spheres.

Grant support available includes Individual Mobility Grants (IMGs) to individuals working in Higher Education institutions, helping them work on specific projects in other countries.

Contact
The European Commission
Directorate General for Education and Culture
Directorate A – Education
Rue de la Loi 200, B-1049 Brussels
Tel: 00 322 296 6319, Fax: 00 322 295 5719
Website: http://europa.eu.int/comm/education/tempus/home.html

12.10 Albion (Overseas) Limited

In undertaking business in Russia, be prepared for the different culture, especially because Moscow particularly may appear to be an extension of Europe. It is not. Even the style of conducting meetings is very different, when compared to Western Europe. Business can quite literally be won or lost, depending upon how you lead a meeting, irrespective of whether your product or service is the best, the cheapest, or the biggest brand. Albion conducts training for companies, so that they are prepared for all of this. Subjects covered can include travel and accommodation, security, conducting meetings, language, women in business, payment issues, partner difficulties, alcohol, bureaucracy, etc, etc.

Contact:
Albion (Overseas) Ltd, UK
Ellion House, 6 Alexandra Rd, Tonbridge, TN9 2AA

Mob: 07801 961866
Skype: albionoverseas
E-mail: david@albionoverseas.com, Website: www.albionoverseas.com
Or
Mikhail Kondrashov
Albion (Overseas) Ltd, Russia
Ul. Skakovaya 9, 4th floor, office 529, Moscow 125040
Tel: 007 495 945 2795, Fax: 007 495 945 2781
E-mail: mikhail@albionoverseas.com
Website: www.albionoverseas.com

12.11 Kingston Business School

Kingston Business School offers management tuition courses aimed at Russian management trainees. The courses are preceded by preparatory work in Russia. The courses include presentation skills, business planning, managing information, financial and human resource management, operations management, marketing and business simulation. These would be followed by secondment with a company for between two and six months.

One programme offered is a Moscow-based MBA programme, run in partnership with Russia's Academy of National Economy. It is delivered through a combination of video-conferencing and tuition from Kingston staff who regularly visit Russia.

Contact: Kingston Business School, Kingston University, Kingston Hill, Kingston-upon-Thames, Surrey KTU 7LB. Tel: 020 8547 2000; Fax: 020 8547 7029; website: http://business.kingston.ac.uk/index.php

12.12 TNG

TNG, part of the Avanta Group, has worked actively in Russia since 1991.

TNG's services include the development and delivery of training programmes and distance learning materials and training via e-learning in both English and Russian languages. Study tour programmes in the UK for Russian organisations are arranged in conjunction with educational establishments throughout Russia and private and public sector organisations in the UK.

TNG also provide Project Management services and can advise on strategies for obtaining and managing funds from international donors.

Contact
Paul Wolstencroft, Director
TNG
196 Great Cambridge Road, Enfield, Middlesex EN1 1RP
Tel: 020 8367 0647, Fax: 020 8367 3582
E-mail: paul@tngconsulting.co.uk
Websites: www.tng.uk.com/ and E-learning site: www.advance365.com

12.13 Language and Cultural Training

Governments now recognise that the ability to understand and communicate in languages other than English is increasingly important in the global economy. In the most simple of terms, the business people who are able to speak the language of the company they wish to sell to will be more likely to win business. Accordingly, the government supports may initiatives to help British schools and business people learn second languages.

The National Centre for Languages (CILT) offers free advice and information on language training cultural consultants, interpreters and translators.

Contact:

CILT

20 Bedfordbury, London WC2N 4LB

Tel: 020 7379 5101, Fax: 020 7379 5082

Website: www.cilt.org.uk

The Regional Language Network London (RLN), supported by CILT, promotes language and cultural skills for London businesses. It offers a free database of translators, interpreters, language trainers and cultural consultants. Website: www.rln-london.com

Chambers of commerce and trade associations are able to put you in touch with language service providers. Grants may also be available for training in these areas through Learning and Skills Council (LSCs), Local Enterprise Companies (LECs) and Local Authority Business Development Units.

12.13.1 Export Communications Review

The Export Communications Review provides companies with impartial and objective advice about how to overcome the language and cultural barriers that arise when trading with foreign markets. Companies are eligible if they meet the following criteria:

a) UK based;

b) trading for a minimum of 2 years;

c) currently exporting or have plans to export in place;

d) less than 250 employees

In a review, a company learns where they are strong, where they are weak and how they can improve their current systems for communicating with overseas customers and representatives, reviewing, amongst other things, letters, E-mails, faxes, phone calls, packaging, exhibitions, presentations, literature and websites. The review itself will vary in time according to the size of the company and the extent of its product range and export activity, a review may involve up to three visits by the consultant.

Review Level	Consultancy Cost	Total Grant Value	Cost to Company
One visit	£400 (+VAT)	£350	£50 (+VAT)
Two visits	£800 (+VAT)	£550	£250 (+VAT)
Three visits	£1200 (+VAT)	£750	£450 (+VAT)

The BCC maintains a register of Export Communications Consultants who are experienced in the language and cultural needs of international trade and who are specifically trained in the skills of export communications reviews. The information gathered by the consultant is presented with their analysis and recommendations for improvement in a report, listing appropriate providers and an estimate of costs to implement the recommendations.

Contact: Export Communications Review,

The British Chambers of Commerce,

4 Westwood House, Westwood Business Park, Coventry, CV4 8HS

Tel: 024 7669 4484; Fax: 024 7669 5844;

E-mail: ecr@britishchambers.org.uk

Website: www.chamberonline.co.uk/c0aoX_to2c5pNA.html

12.13.2 Institute of Linguists

The Institute of Linguists offers a free internet-based short-listing service for firms seeking professional, interpreters, translators, language tutors and consultants. It undertakes translation, interpreting and other services through its subsidiary Language Services Ltd at the same address.

Contact:

The Institute of Linguists

Saxon House, 48 Southwark Street, LONDON, SE1 1UN

Tel: 020 7940 3100, Fax: 020 7940 3101

E-mail: info@iol.org.uk, Website: www.iol.org.uk

12.13.3 Other sources of help

These include

♦ Institute of Translation and Interpreting. Tel: 01908 325250; Website: www.iti.org.uk

♦ Association for Language Learning. Tel: 01788 546443; www.all-languages.org.uk

12.13.4 The Russian Language Centre

The Russian Language Centre offers a comprehensive and flexible range of Russian language services, including Evening classes. Established in 1992, The Russian Language Centre was the first school in Britain dedicated entirely to Russian language and culture. Clients include multi-nationals and other corporate bodies, law firms and private individuals.

Contact:

The Russian Language Centre

5A Bloomsbury Square, London WC1A 2TA

Tel: 020 7831 5330

Website: www.russiancentre.co.uk/

12.13.5 Other training schemes

Many UK government bodies, and the EU, provide funding for schemes which train youths and graduates for projects in the commercial and voluntary sector. Both vocational and professional training schemes may be funded. Cross-border projects and exchange programmes are particularly favoured.

Contact:

The British Council

10 Spring Gardens, London, SW1A 2BN

Tel: 020 7389 4076/4151, Fax: 020 7389 4090

Website: www.britcoun.org/

or:

Local Government International Bureau (LGIB)

Local Government House, London, SW1P 3HZ

Tel: 020 7664 3100, Fax: 020 7664 3128

E-mail: enquiries@lgib.gov.uk

Website: www.lgib.gov.uk/

Meetings with Russia
–they can be difficult

NOVOSTI LIBRARY

So make sure your mind is free to concentrate on your business.

Let

THE RUSSIA HOUSE
Est 1970 – 38 years experience

arrange your:

* **TRAVEL** – Best flight deals to within and from Russia.

* **ACCOMMODATION** – Reservations available at over 300 establishments from the Baltic to the Pacific.

* **VISA** – Successful procuration, on time, every time.

* **COURIER** – A discreet and secure service once a week to and from Moscow. First courier on line to Moscow in 1975 and still the best. Documents, parcels and cash.

and more:

INTERPRETERS / TRANSLATORS / TRANSPORT / SECURITY
SEMINAR ARRANGEMENTS
Call: 020 7403 9922

RUSSIA – EXPERIENCE COUNTS

LONDON OFFICE:
The Russia House Ltd, Chapel Court, Borough High Street, London SE11HH.
Tel: 020 7403 9922 or 0700 4 RUSSIA. Fax: 020 7403 9933.
E-mail: russiahouse@btinternet.com Web site: www.therussiahouse.co.uk

MOSCOW OFFICE:
BM Terra, Building No. 1, D. 3/9 Stanislavskovo, Moscow 109004, Russia.
Tel: 911 2609. Fax: 911 9232. E-mail: bmterra@col.ru

SOCHI – ADLER – KRASNAYA POLYANA

These three areas are going to be the build up of Russia's successful bid for the 2014 winter Olympics.

There's going to be enormous business opportunities in the restructuring of the area for British business, to cope with the Winter Olympics 2014 and to make the area an international mountain winter and summer resort and to expand Sochi into a Black Sea Riviera paradise for the 21st Century.

The "Ice" events stadium will post Olympics be turned into International Sports Events Arena including the home for the Russian National football team.

A British initiative has been formed to go for business gold over the next 6 years, with UKTI and RBCC support, seminars, trade missions and exhibitions are going to be held.

Full details: www.therussiahouse.co.uk
                      email russiahouse@btinternet.com
                      Tel 020 7403 9922

The British initiative: The Russia House, Albion (Overseas) Ltd, O'Grady Air Services, The PBN Company, Paul Forrest Research, RBCC.

Opportunities

STADIUM & SPORT FACILITIES BUILD • ENERGY, WATER, SEWAGE • COMMUNICATIONS • ROADS • TRANSPORT/VEHICLES • HOUSING • HOTELS • PLEASURE PARKS • RESTAURANTS • BARS • SHOPS • DISCO • ENTERTAINMENT • CONSUMER SUPPLIES • EDUCATION • INSURANCE

13 EU AND OTHER FUNDING

13.1　Introduction

The importance given to the Russian Federation by both the British Government and the European Union cannot be understated. It is 1the EU's fifth trading partner (after the US, Switzerland, China and Japan). In turn, the EU is Russia's main trading partner accounting for above 50% of its total trade. Russia with its huge resources and large population is, therefore, one to be cherished as a partner. Partnership, however, requires understanding. To this end the European Union and its individual members – not forgetting the USA, Canada, Japan and other countries – have and continue to provide financial support to help it develop its infrastructure and to bolster political reform and the country's progress as a market economy.

13.2　The EU and the Russian Federation

Overall, the EU's main objectives are to foster political and economic stability in Russia; to contribute to the strengthening of the rule of law through the development of efficient institutions as well as effective legislative, executive and judicial systems; to support measures for a better investment climate in Russia and enhance legislative harmonisation with the EU, and to co-operate in combating "soft" security threats in the fields of justice and home affairs, environment and nuclear safety and Russia's relations with bordering nations. It expedites this through a number of instruments including:

13.3　European Neighbourhood and Partnership Instrument Eastern Region (ENPI)

The European Neighbourhood and Partnership Instrument Eastern Region (ENPI) is a seven year strategy project covering the period 2007-2013. ENPI defines EU support for Armenia, Azerbaijan, Belarus, Georgia, Moldova, the Russian Federation and Ukraine. The regional programme operates at a bilateral level, through Action Plans agreed with each partner country, each of which has its own Country Strategy Paper (CSP) and in the case of Russia, four Common Spaces. The underlying theme of ENPI is "To facilitate and advance cooperation in areas of mutual interest and benefit between the partner countries themselves, and between the EC and the partner countries. This complements the objective of the individual national strategies of developing increasingly close relationships with ENP partner countries, going beyond past levels of cooperation, towards gradual economic integration and a deepening of political cooperation…" achieving economies of scale and/or through avoiding the duplication of efforts. Russia's country Strategy Paper includes a Multi-Annual Indicative Programme stating which type of individual projects can be undertaken and the processes for putting them out to commercial tender.

ENPI builds on the former Tacis (Technical Assistance for the Commonwealth of Independent States) programme, much of which was specific to bringing countries under that scheme to parity economically, socially and politically with countries of central Europe. Its emphasis is to develop an increasingly close relationship and good neighbourliness with countries within the region and with the EU. The projects that brought the greatest regional benefit under Tacis were those that from the outset attracted high level political support. By contrast, projects implemented through a bottom-up approach, i.e. as a result of demand from individual partner countries, rather than within a well defined political multi-lateral framework, have tended to remain isolated, even when successful, and in general have not succeeded in fostering a genuine regional spin-off.

ENPI offers support in five strategic categories:

i) Networks, in particular transport and energy networks;

ii) Environment and forestry;

iii) Border and migration management, the fight against international crime, and customs;

iv) People-to-people activities, information and support;

v) Anti-personnel landmines, explosive remnants of war, small arms and light weapons.

EU Relations with the countries of the region encroach on other areas too; including the EU's foreign and security policy; justice; human rights; trade; nuclear safety; information and communication technology.

13.3.1 ENPI cross-border cooperation (CBC)/ Neighbourhood and Partnership Programmes (NPP)

Neighbourhood and Partnership Programmes (NPPs) have been set up to promote cross-border cooperation between ENPI partner countries, EU Member States, and the candidate and potential candidate countries wishing to join the EU.

NPPs are based on two types of programme: bilateral programmes (involving typically two countries sharing a border) and multilateral programmes (e.g. for the Black Sea). The specific objectives and issues addressed in each programme are set out from a local perspective, by the NPP partners themselves reflecting their local priorities.

13.3.2 ENPI Interregional Programme

The ENPI Interregional programme includes activities that, to ensure coherence, visibility and administrative efficiency are best implemented in the same way for all the neighbouring countries, including those in the ENPI South and East regions. Examples are the Technical Assistance and Information Exchange (TAIEX), TEMPUS and the new Scholarship Programme.

13.3.3 ENPI Thematic programmes

There are five thematic programmes under the new instruments. These include

♦ Human rights and democracy

♦ Migration and asylum

♦ Quangos and local authorities, particularly with regard to civil society cooperation.

♦ Food security

♦ Environment and sustainable use of natural resources including energy

These programmes will only apply provided they do not duplicate strategic programmes.

13.3.3.1 How to get involved

♦ For an overview of the ENPI and its priorities look at the Commission's Q&A website at http://ec.europa.eu/world/enp/faq_en.htm .

♦ Check out the Country Strategy Papers and Multi-Annual Indicative Programmes to find out about the EU's priorities in specific countries. These will also give you an idea of the sectors and types of projects that are likely to be put out to tender.

♦ Look at the Commission's EuropeAid website for forecasted and current tenders and project information at http://ec.europa.eu/comm/europeaid/cgi/frame12.pl.

207

♦ Check out UK Trade & Investment's website at http://www.uktradeinvest.gov. uk for multilateral aid-funded business opportunities in the ENPI region. This service is free of charge to UK registered companies.
Contact:
Commercial Section
UK Permanent Representation to the EU
Avenue d'Auderghem 10, 1040 Brussels, Belgium
Tel: 00 322 287 8387
E-mail: jan.soeltenfuss@fco.gov.uk, Website: www.ukrep.be

13.3.4 Democracy and Human Rights Instrument

Since 2007, the new Democracy and Human Rights instrument has provided support to promote freedom of expression and association, and the protection of human rights defenders; anti-torture measures; promote human rights, conflict protection; democratic reform; improving the international human rights framework and election observation.

13.3.5 Nuclear Safety Instrument

Since 2007, EC assistance in the area of Nuclear Safety has been provided under a new dedicated instrument. This continues to cover improvements to nuclear plants, regulation of nuclear capacity and emergency management and projects to rehabilitate the Chernobyl site in the Ukraine.

13.3.6 Stability Instrument

The main goal of the Stability Instrument is to provide an effective, timely, flexible and integrated response to situations of crisis, emerging crisis or continued political instability.

13.3.7 Technical Assistance and Information Exchange (TAIEX)

The Technical Assistance and Information Exchange Instrument of the Institution Building unit of Directorate-General Enlargement of the European Commission aims to provide to the New Member States, acceding countries, candidate countries, and the administrations of the Western Balkans and Neighbouring countries, including Russia, with short-term technical assistance, in line with the overall policy and legislative objectives of the European Commission.
Contact:
Phone: 00 322 296 7307, Fax: 00 322 296 7694
E-mail: elarg-taiex@ec.europa.eu

13.3.8 The Common Spaces

EU cooperation with Russia is conceived in terms of, and is designed to strengthen, a strategic partnership. At the St. Petersburg Summit in May 2003, the EU and Russia agreed to create four 'common spaces':
♦ a Common Economic Space;
♦ a Common Space of Freedom, Security and Justice;
♦ a Space of co-operation in the field of External Security; and
♦ a Common Space for Research and Education, including Cultural Aspects.

The St Petersburg Summit of May 2005 set out the programme to reach these objectives. Notwithstanding, the conflict in Chechnya has provoked widespread humanitarian problems with the continuing crisis threatening to tip the wider Northern Caucasus into disarray and conflict. The EU is thus concerned to support the stabilisation, recovery and ultimately the development of the North Caucasus.

13.3.9 Country Strategy Paper (CSP)

The Country Strategy Paper is based on the premise that the Common Spaces are the bedrock of EU and Russian understanding and collaboration.

The main interests of the EU in Russia lie in:

- ◆ fostering the political and economic stability of the Federation;
- ◆ in maintaining a stable supply of energy;
- ◆ in further co-operation in the fields of justice and home affairs, the environment and nuclear safety in order to combat 'soft' security threats; and
- ◆ in stepping up cooperation with Russia in the Southern Caucasus and the Western NIS for the geopolitical stability of the CIS region, including for the resolution of frozen conflicts.
- ◆ in ensuring that the socio-economic potential of the Kaliningrad Oblast, which is an enclave in the EU, is fulfilled.

Funding allocated by the EU to help Russia implement the CSP is €30 million per annum over the period 2007- 2010.

13.4 New Neighbourhood Instrument and Neighbourhood Programmes

In 2003, the European Union launched its "Wider Europe – New Neighbourhood" initiative, which aims to address chal0ourhood Policy is to share the benefits of the EU's enlargement with neighbouring countries in strengthening stability, security and well-being for all concerned, and hence prevent the emergence of new dividing lines between the enlarged EU and its neighbours. In practical terms, the initiative is aimed at helping neighbouring countries improve conditions for the free movement of goods, services, capital and persons as well as developing a zone of prosperity and friendship. It does this through:

- ◆ Promoting sustainable economic and social development in the border areas;
- ◆ Working together to address common challenges, in the fields such as environment, public health and the prevention of and fight against organised crime;
- ◆ Ensuring efficient and secure borders;
- ◆ Promoting local, "people-to-people' actions.

Through integration and partnership, the New Neighbourhood Policy sets out the ways and means by which partner countries can participate progressively in key aspects of EU policies and programmes. The European Neighbourhood Policy provides additional support including financial support, through technical assistance and "twinning" schemes for those partners that wish to meet EU norms and standards. The Commission is also examining the possibility of allowing partner countries to participate gradually in certain Community programmes that promote cultural, educational, environmental, technical and scientific links.

Programmes to date have commenced in:

- ◆ Nord (Kolarctic) – Murmansk and Archangelsk oblasts, Nenets okrug
- ◆ Euregio Karelia – Republic of Karelia
- ◆ South-East Finland / Russia – Leningrad oblast, City of St Petersburg
- ◆ Baltic Sea Regional Programme – Republic of Karelia, City of St Petersburg, Murmansk,

- Leningrad, Pskov, Novgorod, Kaliningrad and Archangelsk oblasts, Nenets okrug
- Estonia / Latvia / Russia – Leningrad and Pskov oblasts, City of St Petersburg
- Lithuania / Poland / Russia – Kaliningrad
  Contact:
  Kadashevskaya nab., 14/1; 109017, Moscow
  Tel: 007 495 721 2000; Fax: 007 495 721 2020
  E-mail: Delegation-Russia@cec.eu.int
  Websites: http://europa.eu.int/comm/world/enp/faq_en.htm
  www.delrus.ec.europa.eu/en/index.htm

13.5   UNIDO Investment and Technology Promotion Office

The United Nations Industrial Development Organisation (UNIDO), established 1n 1966, is the specialist agency of the United Nations with the mandate to promote industrial development and co-operation, and to act as the central coordinating body for industrial activities within the United Nations system.

It assists both Governments and the public and private sectors through technical cooperation, policy advice, investment promotion and technical support. It provides services to developing countries and to countries in transition to a market economy wishing to strengthen their industrial base.

Through partnership with development financial institutions, governmental and non-governmental agencies, public and private industry, and industrial associations, UNIDO makes technology and expertise more readily available to developing countries.

The agency also promotes industrial investments. Through industrial investment programmes for four developing regions and a global investment promotion network, UNIDO mobilises investment resources for developing countries by assisting sponsors of industrial development projects and their foreign or local partners to co-operate in business ventures. There are Investment & Technology Promotion offices in Moscow and Warrington.

Technical co-operation projects have benefited 172 countries and regions over the last 40 years. The estimated volume of UNIDO operations for the biennium 2006-7 is €356 million, drawn from the regular budget (€151m), the operational budget (€20m) and voluntary contributions (€185m). The top five contributors to the regular budget accounted for some €90million, as follows Japan (33m); Germany (19m); United Kingdom (13m), France (13m); Italy (10m).

In the UK, UNIDO is a business led and business focused organisation, hosted and operated by the Northwest Development Agency (NWDA). It makes a practical contribution to helping UK businesses make the most of the opportunities arising from economic growth in developing countries, but doing this in a way that is consistent with sustainable industrial development.

What sets UNIDO ITPO (UK) apart from other organisations is its close association with Governments in developing countries, a relationship that has been developed over 30 years. Central to this is the understanding of investment practices in emerging markets, projecting UNIDO as a key partner in the worldwide delivery of new technology and restructuring services.

13.5.1 Introduction to services

UNIDO – UK provides a complete package to companies based in the North West of England. Its services range from project appraisal to implementation and funding support. The office operates in three distinct areas:

a) Technical Assistance

b) Industrial programmes

c) Investment Services

a) Technical Assistance

UNIDO deploys technical experts in developing countries to identify, profile and vet investment and technology opportunities for UK companies. Through the evaluation of new and restructured industrial projects and connections to local finance institutions UNIDO can offer UK companies a flow of screened investment and manufacturing opportunities.

b) Industrial Programmes

UNIDO can use its financial analysis skills and management support packages to help UK companies bring their investment/manufacturing projects in emerging markets to completion.

The following projects can be facilitated:

A. In country manufacturing

(i) New build-New Start-up

(ii) Acquisition or investment

(iii) Joint venture

B. Licensed manufacture overseas

C. Outsourcing/Direct purchase

On each project UNIDO can offer finance, management and technology expertise to:

♦ Assist on strategy formulation

♦ Advise on funding options

♦ Offer in-country implementation support

c) Investment Services

UNIDO has close links to both finance houses and private investors who are a recognised source of funds for developing countries and respect UNIDO as a source of new opportunities. By utilising these relationships UNIDO is able to introduce companies to potential fund providers with the aim of sourcing finance for proposed international investments.

UNIDO can also assist in services to management before and post investment by advising on:

♦ In-country due diligence processes

♦ In-country business and market sector practices

♦ Management structures post acquisition to include personnel incentives

♦ Information reporting mechanisms to facilitate structured growth

Most importantly, UNIDO seeks to build long-term relationships with companies, which it has assisted such that, by gaining an understanding of their ambitions, opportunities can be identified and appraised for further investments that meet their specific investment criteria.

Contact:

United Nations Industrial Development Organisation Investment & Technology Promotion Office

UK

PO Box 37, Renaissance House, PO Box 37, Centre Park,

Warrington, Cheshire, WA1 1XB
Tel: 01925 400399; Fax: 01925 400402; E-mail: itpo.uk@unido.org
Russia
Ulitsa Kuusinena 21B, 125252 Moscow
Telephone: 007 095 9430021; Fax: 007 095 943 0018; E-mail: office@unido.ru
Website: www.unido.ru/eng/frameSet_e.html

13.6   Britain-Russia Development Partnership

The Britain-Russia Development Partnership, run under the auspices of the Department for International Development (DFID) works in partnership with federal
and regional state authorities, non-governmental organisations, academic institutes, the private sector and international agencies to help build strong economic,
political and social institutions in a stable market economy in Russia. Support, by
way of grants, focuses on the provision of technical assistance – i.e. consultancy
advice, seminars and training carried out in Russia, the UK and occasionally in
third countries. Projects include those concerning:

- Governance
- Health
- Social Protection
- Public Finance
- Enterprise Development
- Rural Livelihoods
- Environment
- Global Issues such as trade and conflict prevention

Bilateral projects are largely concentrated in the above sectors and in the following cities and regions: Moscow, St Petersburg, Leningrad Oblast, Samara,
Sverdlovsk, Kemerovo, Ruston and Nizhny Novgorod.

Contact:
In the UK:
Eastern Europe & Central Asia Department (EECAD)
DFID, 1 Palace Street, London SW1E 5HE
Tel: 020 7023 0041; Fax: 020 7023 0019; Website: www.dfid.gov.uk
and in Russia:
Development Section, British Embassy, Moscow Tel: 007 495 956 7200;
Website: www.britembmsk.ru
British Consulate General, St Petersburg Tel: 007 812 325 3200
British Consulate General, Ekaterinburg Tel: 007 343 256 4931

14   GRANTS FOR RESEARCH AND TECHNOLOGY

14 Grants for Research and Technology

Scientific and humanitarian research is regarded as a means to improve not only relationships between Russia and the rest of the World but also the well-being of the Russian people in a time of transition to a market economy and democracy The European Union and a number of institutions in both the UK and Russia, work towards this end.

14.1 Seventh Framework Programme (2007–2013) – FP7

The EU's seventh R & D Programme for 2007 – 2013 (FP7), which has a provisional budget of €67.8bn, is similar to the preceding Sixth Framework Programme (FP6 – 2002–2006). FP6 provided €17.5bn for research and innovation projects (including Euratom energy and nuclear waste programmes) covering the period 2002–2006. Both FP6 and FP7 emphasise the importance of partnership between European organisations, from different countries, leading to integrated research efforts and to the strengthening of Europe's scientific and technological dynamism on an increasingly global stage. Any legal entity throughout Europe may take part in and receive financial support under the programme. Small and Medium Size Enterprises are particularly encouraged to take part with 15% of the budget reserved for their participation. See website: http://ec.europa.eu/research/fp7/

14.2 EUREKA

EUREKA is a pan-European initiative that aims to facilitate collaborative research and development projects between European companies, research and technology organisations and higher education institutions. It is a flexible and non-bureaucratic way of getting lucrative international projects off the ground.

In addition to the important benefits arising from any collaborative R&D (cost and risk sharing, access to new skills, increased or wider market presence), pursuing projects via the EUREKA route offers extra benefits:

◆ Networking: The EUREKA office, no matter how specialised your technology area, can help you to find suitable partners overseas;
◆ Publicity: EUREKA projects receive Europe-wide publicity and participating organisations are likely to attract the attention of those either looking to join the project or offering new business opportunities;
◆ Project Status: EUREKA participants are eligible to carry the EUREKA seal – an internationally recognised hallmark of excellence;
◆ Contacts with government: participation in EUREKA provides direct contact with governments, offering the opportunity to discuss, for example, issues which may affect the market success of your project;
◆ Funding: The EUREKA office may be able to help with the cost of putting projects together although across the member states there may not be dedicated Eureka funding pots. It may also help small firms, research and technology organisations, or higher education institutes, with actual project costs.

Priority is given to smaller firms for assistance towards actual project costs. Availability of funding will depend on the nature and scope of the project. As a general guide applicants should not expect to get a grant of more than 35-40% of their total project costs.

For further information contact: EUREKA NPC, Technology Strategy Board, B1 North Star House, North Star Avenue, Swindon SN2 1JF; Tel: 01793 442750; email: EurekaUKNPC@tsb.gov.uk, Website: www.eureka.be

14.3　The Russian Academy of Sciences (RAS)

The Russian Academy of Sciences, established in 1724, was reinstated by the Decree of the President of the Russian Federation dated November 21, 1991 as the supreme scientific institution of Russia.

Its principal aim is research on natural, social and human development themes that will promote technological, economic, social and cultural development in Russia.

Contact
14 Leninskii Prospekt, Moscow, 119991
Tel: 007 495 237 2822; Fax: 007 495 938 1844;
Website: www.ras.ru/index.aspx?_Language=en

14.4　Russian Scientific and Technical Information Institute of Russia (VNTIC)

VNTIC is a nationwide information institution responsible for maintaining a database of all Russians scientific research and development reports and dissertations.

It provides the following services:

♦ 7 million documents covering the main results of R&D activities undertaken in Russia and the former Soviet Union (FSU)
♦ publication of abstracts of research reports;
♦ dissemination of information into foreign languages;
♦ information on over 3,000 R&D institutions in Russia and the NIS;
♦ Information on over 14,000 Russian scientists.

Contact VNTIC, 17 Presnensky Val Street, Moscow, 123557, Russia. Tel: 007 495 737 0174; Website: www.vntic.org.ru/eng/engdefault.htm

14.5　InterTec

InterTec in cooperation with Russian Scientific and Technical Information Institute (See 14.4) provides on-line access to databases with scientific and technical information. Its Database Directory presents a list of existing databases in the sphere of economy, industry, science and education, culture and social life of Russia.

Contact:
InterTec Ltd
Austria, Brahmsplatz 8/3, A-1040, Vienna, Austria
Tel: 00 431 504 4091, Fax: 00 431 504 4094
E-mail: info@intertec.co.at, Website: www.intertec.co.at

14.6　SISTER (Support for International Science, Technology and Engineering Research)

The British Council SISTER resource is an online funding route map which aims to encourage and facilitate international scientific collaboration. The resource provides links to the relevant web pages of all national and multilateral bodies that provide significant funding for international collaboration in science and technology.

Contact
British Council Science
Bridgewater House, 58 Whitworth Street, Manchester M1 6BB
Tel: 0161 957 7030, Fax: 0161 957 7029
Website: www.britishcouncil.org/sister

14.7   The Royal Society

The Royal Society, as the national academy of science for the United Kingdom promotes international scientific collaboration through a range of scientific exchange programmes. It works collaboratively with The Russian Academy of Sciences (See 14.3 above)

Contact
The Royal Society
6-9 Carlton House Terrace, London SW1Y 5AG
Tel: 020 7451 2500, Fax: 020 7930 2170
Website: www.royalsoc.co.uk/

14.8   Research Councils UK

Research Councils UK unites seven Research Councils focusing on research in medical and biological sciences, astronomy, physics, chemistry and engineering, social sciences, economics, and the arts and humanities. Collaborative projects with Russia, including the exchange and secondment of staff are often undertaken. See website: www.rcuk.ac.uk/default.htm

14.9   The Royal Society of Chemistry

The Royal Society of Chemistry offers a number of travel grants, research and education initiatives support schemes, science journalism fellowships, and other funding options to its members. See website: www.rsc.org/index.asp

14.10 The NATO Science Programme

The NATO Science Programme offers support for international collaboration between scientists from the NATO countries and Russia.

Contact:
Public Diplomacy Division (PDD)
NATO
Bd. Leopold III
1110 Brussels
Belgium
Fax: 00 322 707 4232
Website: www.nato.int/science/index.html

14.11 The Wellcome Trust

The Wellcome Trust offers a variety of schemes for funding research and collaboration in the fields of biomedical science, technology transfer, medical humanities and public involvement.

Contact:
Wellcome Trust
Gibbs Building, 215 Euston Road, London NW1 2BE, UK
Tel: 020 7611 8888, Fax: 020 7611 8545
E-mail: contact@wellcome.ac.uk, Website: www.wellcome.ac.uk/funding

14.12 The Novartis Foundation

The Novartis Foundation awards bursaries covering 12 weeks travel expenses and board and lodging for researchers aged 23–35 to attend its international scientific symposia. All applicants must be actively engaged in research on the topic covered by the symposium.

Contact:
The Bursary Scheme Administrator
The Novartis Foundation
41 Portland Place, London W1B 1BN, UK
Tel: 0 20 7636 9456, Fax: 0 20 7436 2840
Email: bursary@novartisfound.org.uk, www.novartisfound.org.uk/bursary.htm

14.13 Russian Foundation for Basic Research

The Russian Foundation for Basic Research is a state organisation created to support for basic scientific research in all areas of fundamental science and the development of scientific links across nations. Its work includes:

- the publication of research papers and science proceedings within the Russian Federation and elsewhere;
- holding of scientific events (conferences, seminars, etc.);
- organising Russian participants of scientific events in the Russian Federation and abroad;
- projects for the development of the experimental base of scientific research, including the development and acquisition of information support devices, means and technologies in areas supported by the Foundation;
- the provision of funding to selected projects including the funding of joint research projects;
  Contact
  Russian Foundation for Basic Research
  Leninsky prospect, 32A, 119991, B-334, GSP-1
  Moscow
  Tel: 007 495 938 5532, Fax: 007 495 938 1931
  Website: www.rfbr.ru/eng/default.asp?section_id=0

14.14 Other Sources of Information

- Business Eastern Europe (Economist). Tel: 01708 381444; Fax: 01708 371850
- ConCISe – Aerospace News from CIS; Fax: 01706 828300
- Eastern European Reporter. Tel: 020 7559 4800; Fax: 020 7559 4825
- FT Profile, Fitzroy House, 13-17 Epworth Street, London EC2A 4DL. Tel: 020 7825 8000; Fax: 020 7825 7999; Website: www.ft.com
- InterFax: Tel: 007 495 250 0022, 250 3171; Fax: 007 495 250 1436; E-mail: russia@interFax:com; Website: www.interfax.com/
- Itar-Tass Website: www.itar-tass.com/eng/
- PlanEcon Tel: 020 7073 4600; Fax: 020 7073 4601; Website: www.factset. com/www_1.asp
- Reuters Ltd, East European Briefing, 85 Fleet Street, London EC4P 4HE. Tel: 020 7250 1122.
- Russian Economic Trends. Distributor Tel: 01767 604800
- Russia Express. Tel: 01600 890274; Fax: 01600 890774
- Russian Information Agency – Novosti (RIA-Novosti), 3 Rosary Gardens, London SW7 4NW. Tel: 020 7370 3002; Fax: 020 7244 7875; Website: http:// en.rian.ru
- Russia News Service. Tel/Fax: 001 202 318 8905; Website: www.einnews. com/russia/

15 MULTILATERAL AND OTHER LOANS FOR PROJECT FINANCE

15.1   Introduction

Mention has already been made of the banking system in Russia and methods of opening up hard currency accounts (See 4.12). This chapter concentrates on loan schemes appropriate for businesses wishing to establish operations in Russia. For major funding, i.e. over £5 million, support may be sought from multilateral agencies. Other sources of help such as venture capitalists are beyond the scope of this chapter although some organisations specialising in investments in Russia do now exist. Sources of export credit, trading finance and export risk cover are discussed in Chapter 14.

15.2   World Bank

The World Bank Group consists of a number of agencies with various aid functions. These include

- The International Bank for Reconstruction and Development and the International Development Association. This works with national governments in the Third World by providing loans and credits (i.e. 'soft' loans), which help fund infrastructure improvement projects concentrating on key industrial sectors;
- The International Finance Corporation. This works with companies that are trying to establish a business in a developing country by providing minority financing (i.e. not more than 25% of the overall project cost) and technical support; and
- The Multilateral Investment Guarantee Agency. This provides limited non-commercial risk cover for would-be investors in Third World business ventures.

Queries relating to specific World Bank projects supported by the IBRD and IDA may be referred to the UK Trade & Investment's Development Business Team

Tel: 020 7215 4635; E-mail: graham.hawes@uktradeinvest.gov.uk
Contact:
The World Bank
Milbank Tower, 12th Floor, 21-24 Millbank, London SW1P 4QP
Tel: 020 7592 8400, Fax: 020 7592 8420
Website: www.worldbank.org/
World Bank
36, Bldg. 1, Bolshaya Molchanovka Street, 121069, Moscow
Tel: 007 495 411 7555, Fax: 007 495 411 7556

15.3   European Bank for Reconstruction and Development (EBRD)

The establishment of the London-based EBRD was agreed in May 1990. It has a capital of €10 billion and its members include 57 countries and two institutions. It began its operations on 15 April 1991. The bank finances projects that will help to:

- (a) create a competitive private sector;
- (b) foster entrepreneurial activity and small- and medium-sized enterprises;
- (c) privatise state-owned enterprises;
- (d) encourage foreign direct investment;
- (e) create and strengthen financial institutions;
- (f) restructure the industrial sector;
- (g) create a modern infrastructure for private sector development and transition to a market economy; and

219

(h) improve the environment.

The EBRD provides loans and equity finance for private sector companies already established in the region who wish to either: expand their operations and increase their investment in the area; or create new companies with international strategic investors.

These include:

♦ loans (secured or unsecured, subordinated, convertible or equity-linked) with a maximum final maturity of ten years for commercial enterprises and of 15 years for infrastructure projects;

♦ equity;

♦ debt guarantees;

♦ debt and equity underwriting.

The EBRD does not issue guarantees for export credits or undertake insurance activities.

Loans can be denominated in any of the major currencies or in currency units. The Bank does not accept exchange risk on repayment.

The EBRD's loans to commercial enterprises are not guaranteed by the host government and are typically without recourse to foreign sponsors, if any. Loan financing to state-owned enterprises under privatisation is on a similar basis.

15.3.1 Rapid evaluation

The EBRD aims to be a highly efficient funding source for private sector investments in Central and Eastern Europe. It targets a three-month project cycle. This is achieved through reliance on first class partners; capable industrial companies as equity investors, and experienced financial institutions as co-lenders. The Bank bases its financing decisions partly on the strength of its partners' due diligence.

15.3.2 Working with advisers

The EBRD concentrates on providing direct investment, not advice. It therefore encourages sponsors to use experienced financial advisers: commercial, merchant and investment banks, and accounting and consulting firms. Provided the advisers add value and their fees are reasonable, the sum charged can be included in the loan.

Proposals submitted by private enterprise and companies to be privatised should have strong sponsors or partners and viable business plans based on:

(i) competitive products or services with sound market prospects;

(ii) significant equity commitment in cash or in kind by project sponsors;

(iii) strong management;

(iv) dependable technology; and

(v) sound environmental management.

Forty per cent of the EBRD's funding is directed towards the public sector. An important element of its work will be investment designed to improve the environment. Where appropriate, the EBRD will be willing to take a direct stake in the business by buying shares itself. The Bank will be able to make up to 35% of its investment in equity.

15.3.3 EBRD Venture Capital Funds

The EBRD has also established 11 venture capital funds in Russia.

One fund, the St Petersburg Regional Venture Fund, (RVF) covers both the City of St Petersburg and the Leningrad region. It is specifically intended to assist local medium sized businesses. Other projects include providing finance to

Russian banks to purchase shares in other Russian banks, thereby helping with a process of consolidation in the sector. The fund comprised $30 million from the EBRD and $20 million provided by the German government. The EBRD fund supports projects lasting 3 to 5 years, put forward by enterprises already established in the Russian market.

Excluded activities include tobacco products, alcoholic drinks, defence industry, banking, insurance and financial services, and projects which are not sensitive to the environment.

Contact:

European Bank for Reconstruction and Development

One Exchange Square, London, EC2A 2EH

Tel: 020 7338 6000, Fax: 020 7338 7470

Website: www.ebrd.com/

Russian Federation head office

Ducat Place III, Second floor, 6 Gasheka Street, Moscow 123056, Russia

Tel: 007 495/501 787 1111, Fax: 007 495/501 787 1122

Business Group Director, Russia and CESI: Alain Pilloux

Russian regional office:

25 Nevsky Prospekt, 191186 St Petersburg, Russia

Tel: 007 812 103 5525, Fax: 007 812 103 5526

Head of office: Bruno Balvanera

Russian regional office:

Office 404, 46 Verhnerportovaya Street, 690003 Vladivostock, Russia

Tel: 007 423 251 7766, Fax: 007 423 251 7767

Regional representative: Elena Danysh

Russian regional office:

Office 413, 4th floor, Karla Libknekhta 22, Yekaterinburg, Russia

Tel: 007 343 310 0060, Fax: 007 343 310 0062

Head of Office: Artyom Sitnikov

15.4　The International Finance Corporation (IFC)

15.4.1　General Background

Based in Washington DC, but with 27 offices located around the world, including Moscow and London, the IFC is the largest single source of finance for private sector projects developing countries. While part of the World Bank Group and working closely with that institution, the IFC has a separate capital base, charter, and staff.

The IFC's mandate is to further private sector development by means of equity investments, loans, capital market development activities (largely the creation and/or support of private financial intermediaries) in projects or institutions where IFC's help is fundamental to realising private initiatives. Unlike the World Bank, its Articles prevent it from taking government guarantees so its main business is non-recourse project finance. In addition, it takes on advisory work with respect to privatisation, investment restructuring, foreign investment regimes and promotion, and the legal and institutional framework for the development of capital markets in developing countries.

Operations in Russia commenced in 1992 and have included projects in the energy sector, manufacturing, hotels/offices and financial institutions. A number of projects have been co-financed with EBRD with whom IFC maintains a close and co-operative relationship. IFC has also been heavily involved in privatisation and work in the financial sector. It is also likely to get involved in private sector infrastructure, which now accounts for about 25% of its global commitments.

Contact:
International Finance Corporation
Millbank Tower, 12th Floor; 21-24, Milbank, London SW1P 4QP
Tel: 020 7592 8400, Fax: 020 7592 8420
Website: www.ifc.org/
or:
International Finance Corporation
36, Bldg. 1, Bolshaya Molchanovka Street, 121069, Moscow
Tel: 007 495 411 7555; Fax: 007 495 411 7556

15.4.2 Typical financing guidelines

The IFC usually adopts the following principles in considering an investment.

(i)   Clients must be majority private or in a fixed transition to that end.
(ii)   For its own account, IFC would normally provide about 25% of project cost for new projects. For expansions, that percentage could be higher. Financing can be split between equity and loan, although IFC does not normally take on an equity position greater than 20% of the share capital.
(iii)   IFC mobilises funds in excess of the limits noted above by selling participations in its loans to investors who thereby enjoy a measure of protection against country risks due to IFC's preferential creditor status.
(iv)   IFC expects project sponsors to be qualified in their sector and to have a serious financial commitment to the completion/operation of the project.
(v)   Projects must meet the tests of commercial returns and international competitiveness, and must be environmentally defensible.
(vi)   IFC aims to earn a commercial return on its loan and equity portfolio. It is not a subsidised source of funds except to the extent that it will take country risks and provide long-term maturities not available from others. It can, in some cases, provide grants for the preparation of projects.
(vii)   The average size of IFC's commitment has been about US$11 million. The largest single exposure to date is about US$120 million. IFC provides finance in a broad range of currencies, maturities and at fixed or floating rates depending on investors' preferences. It can provide an array of instruments other than straight loan or equity, for example, subordinated loans, convertibles, preferred shares and income notes. Also, a wide variety of approaches can be used, such as guarantees, underwriting of security issues in either the host developing country or abroad, and risk management facilities for currency, interest rate or even commodity price hedging.
(viii) As an equity investor, IFC sees its role as a catalyst, and in line with its overall mission, it will seek to roll over its equity portfolio when it is profitable and sensible to do so. Operating in the private sector, it takes seriously its role as a confidential, corporate partner.
(ix)   In complex projects where IFC is to have a catalytic financing role, it is willing for a fee to help sponsors develop the entire financing structure drawing from its own group of in-house financial, technical and legal staff.

15.6   Commercial Investment Funds

There are numerous sources of funding available from commercial investment banks. Many of them are specific to a country or region and most of them have eligibility rules. They will invest through the provision of equity capital and are especially interested in financing joint ventures.

Various publications list periodically the investment funds available. It is recommended that companies that approach banks should have a prepared business plan, which should include:

(a) Description of a business project;
(b) Assessment of market opportunities and existing and future competition;
(c) Proposed structure of the business project;
(d) background of any partners, both in terms of finances and experience;
(e) technical feasibility;
(f) investment requirements from the bank;
(g) timescale; and
(h) financial assessment, both present and estimated.

The following commercial investment houses are active in the Russian Federation:

15.6.1 J P Morgan Fleming Russian Securities plc

The aim of JPMorgan Fleming Russian Securities plc is to achieve capital growth by investing in Russian Securities. The Trust invests principally in the shares of companies active in oil and gas, telecommunications, energy generation and distribution and mineral extraction sectors.

Contact:
JP Morgan House
Grenville Street, St Helier, Jersey, JE4 8QH
Tel: 01534 626232
E-mail: info@jpmorganfleming.com, Website: www.jpmfrussian.com
Or
JPMorgan Fleming Emerging Markets Investment Trust plc
Finsbury Dials, 20 Finsbury Street, London, EC2Y 9AQ
Tel: 020 7742 6000

15.6.2 Moscow Investment Corporation

A Moscow Investment Corporation (MIC) has been established by order of the Moscow City government.

The corporation aims to implement priority investment projects, the examination of privatised businesses' investment programmes, and the placing of blocks of shares owned by privatised businesses on the city's stock market. Furthermore, the city government has authorised the MIC to finance the city's investment projects, to extend guarantees to Russian and foreign investors and creditors, and to allot foreign investment credits on terms of tender. MIC is also set to issue securities; allotted mostly to operating investment organisations. Some 25% of the corporation's authorised capital is held as blocks of shares of privatised businesses, held by the Moscow City government.

Contact:
Moscow Investment Corporation
125319, Moscow, B.Koptevsky proezd 6
Tel: 007 495 935 8718, Fax: 007 495 926 5228

E-mail: galmed@galmed.com
Website: www.tns-global.ru/rus/group/russian/mic/index.wbp

15.7   Commercial banks

The state of banking in Russia, and the methods and means of opening a bank account have been commented on in sections 1.6 and 8.16. Several banks, due to their long-standing history in dealing in and with Russia, are mentioned below.

15.7.1 Moscow Narodny Bank Ltd

Moscow Narodny Bank was incorporated in London in 1919. It remains the only Russian-owned bank authorised by the Bank of England. It provides a full range of domestic and international banking and support services including the drafting of letters of credit, payment/performance guarantees and tolling. The Moscow Narodny Bank is unique among the British banks in possessing a countertrade team, which actually takes title to goods. It provides a comprehensive service for its customers in handling such transactions and is able to respond quickly to any proposals put forward.

One other great benefit in using Moscow Narodny Bank is its long experience in dealing with other Russian banks and in being able to ease the documentation procedures that may be required in inter-bank dealings.

Contact:
Moscow Narodny Bank Ltd
81 King William Street, London EC4N 7BG
Tel: 020 7623 2066; Fax: 020 7283 4840
Website: www.users.globalnet.co.uk/~chegeo/mnb2.htm
or:
CB Mosnarbank
1st Troitsky Pereulok 12, Building 5, 129090 Moscow
Tel: 007 495 792 5000; Fax: 007 495 755 5990
Website: www.mosnar.com

15.7.2 Mosbusinessbank

Mosbusinessbank has 40 branches in all the largest cities in Russia. It provides a wide range of international operations and is one of the largest clearing centres in Russia. It provides the full range of banking facilities. It is noteworthy that international money market operations account for 40% of the bank's foreign currency profit.

Contact
Mosbusinessbank
15 Kuznetsky Most, Moscow 103780
Tel: 007 495 924 4430
Website: users.crocker.com/~ial/russia/business/sponsors/mosbank.html

15.7.3 International Moscow Bank (Mezhdunarodny Moskovskiy Bank – MMB)

ZAO International Moscow Bank, established in October 1989, is a Russian commercial bank with international capital. It specialises in providing services for corporate and private clients, as well as in corporate financing and treasury operations. It is listed among the top ten national banks and finance houses in Russia. Its shareholders are made up of a number of the world's leading banks including the German HVB Group, which owns 53% of the equity. At present UniCredit, the second largest bank in Italy is in process to buy HVB Group and to create the "First Truly European Bank" by the end of 2005. Nordea, the largest financial group in the Nordic countries holds 26%, BCEN, the French subsidiary of the Russian Central Bank 16% and the EBRD 5% of common stock in IMB. The bank has one of the highest Standard & Poor's and Fitch Ratings international credit ratings amongst Russian commercial banks. The bank's central office is located in Moscow. Services are provided at eleven branches in Moscow, two in St Petersburg, two branches in Chelyabinsk and Rostov-on-Don, and at a number of regional offices in Archangelsk, Voronezh, Volgograd, Ekaterinburg, Krasnodar, Nizhny-Novgorod, Perm, Samara, Saratov, Ufa, Omsk, Novosibirsk and Stavropol.

Contact:
International Moscow Bank
Prechistenskaja embankment, 9, Moscow 119034
Tel: 007 495 258 7200; 007 495 956 8575; Fax: 007 495 258 1524
E-mail: imbank@imbank.ru, Website: www.imb.ru/en/

15.7.4 Other Banks dealing in foreign exchange

Alfa Bank
9 Mashy Poryvaevoy Street, Moscow 107078
Tel: 007 495 925 9191,
Website: www.alfa-bank.com
Avtovazbank – Business Bank
117218, Moscow, Nahimovsky prospekt, 32
Tel: / fax: 007 495 124 0800, 007 495 124 8383, 007 495 332 4596
E-mail: web@avbm.rmt.ru, Website: www.avbank.ru (only Russian)
Bank of Russian Federation Foreign Trade – VTB Bank
Pljushchiha, .37, Moscow, GSP – 2, 119992
Tel: 007 800 200 7799 or 007 495 739 7799,
E-mail: info@vtb.ru, Website: www.vtb.ru/rus/web.html?l=2
Bin Bank
121471 Grodnenskaya 5a
Tel: 007 495 755 5060, Fax: 007 495 440 0975
Website www.binbank.ru
Citibank
125047 Moscow St. Gasheka, 8-10,
Tel: 007 495 725 1000, Fax: 007 495 725-6700
Website: www.citibank.ru
Deltabank
121099 Moscow, Pereuluk Kamennoy Slobodi 11
Tel: 007 495 258 0400, Fax: 007 495 258 6296
Website: www.deltabank.ru
Gazprombank
Tel: 007 495 913 7900, Fax: 007 495 913 7548
Website: www.gazprombank.ru/eng/index.wbp
HSBC
107031 Dmitrovskiy Pereuluk 9
Tel: 007 495 721 1526, Fax: 007 495 721 1527
Website: www.hsbc.com

HypoVereinsbank
Trade Finance Team at HVB Group
41 Moorgate, London, EC2R 6PP
Tel: 020 7638 2728, Fax: 020 7573 8304
Website: http://profile.hypovereinsbank.de/cms/profile/
or
Prechistensky Pereuluk 14, 5th floor, Moscow 119034
Tel: 007 501 937 18 98, Fax: 007 501 937 18 97
INGBank
123022 Krasnaya presna 31
Tel: 007 495 755 5400, Fax: 007 495 755 5499
Website: www.ing.ru/main.asp?lang=eng&tid={F3488E2D-B3ED-11D4-A6DB-00508B8B783F}
MDM bank
115035 Sadovnicheskaya 3
Tel: 007 495 797 9500, Fax: 007 495 797 9501
Website www.mdmbank.com
Vozrozhdenie Bank
Moscow, Luchnikov Pereuluk, 7/4 bild.1
Tel: 007 495 777 0888, Fax: 007 495 913 7548
E-mail: vbank@co.voz.ru, Website: http://eng.vbank.ru

16   EXPORT CREDIT, INSURANCE AND RISK

16.1   Introduction

Whether you wish to engage in permanent business in Russia or conduct ad hoc case transactions you should consider the financial and other risks. Payment uncertainties are greater now than they were previously under the command economy, despite more encouraging political and socio-economic developments. Insurance against political risks, although not impossible, was initially difficult to obtain following the Yukos affair and trial of Mikhail Kordokovsky. However, the situation has normalized. It should also be remembered that legislation is in place to protect foreign interests in Russian industry and that this one incident, whilst highlighting potential issues, has not blunted international optimism in the Russian economy and developing political system.

Export credit insurance is offered for exports made on short-term payment terms, typically for consumer goods or raw materials by a number of private sector companies and banks. The cover provided by such companies will usually protect the exporter against failure of payment and against political risks that may arise in the buyer's country. A bank or insurance broker should be able to advise on which company they deem most suitable for an exporter's needs.

16.2   ECGD

ECGD is the UK's official export credit agency. It provides credit insurance and support for the 'heavy duty' capital goods, construction and services sectors, where exports are generally on long credit terms (two years' credit or more, although it can also insure 'cash' contracts for such goods).

All ECGD facilities are available for business with Russia. It is likely that Russian Sovereign guarantees will only be available for non-commercially viable projects of a social nature. ECGD is prepared to consider corporate risks on a number of major banks and well-founded corporate entities. It is also prepared to consider sub sovereign risk for the Cities of Moscow and St Petersburg.

Companies with potential business in Russia are advised to check the current cover position with ECGD at the address given below.

ECGD offers three basic services to the UK exporting community:

(a) Insuring exporters against non-payment risk such as default/ insolvency, war/civil war, and countries running out of foreign exchange;

(b) providing 100% guarantees of payment to UK banks providing export finance, enabling exporters to receive payment once the goods are exported; and

(c) helping exporters to offer their buyers the certainty of fixed interest rates by providing UK financing banks with interest rate support.

16.2.1 Finance facilities

ECGD supported lending is provided by United Kingdom banks with the benefit of ECGD's guarantee. ECGD is not a direct lender.

ECGD offers three types of finance facility:

(i) Buyer Credit: for the larger, more complex deals, with a typical minimum contract value of £5 million, or the foreign currency equivalent. A form of the Buyer Credit is used for Limited Recourse, or Project Financing, projects, e.g. Build, Operate, transfer (BOT schemes).

(ii) Supplier Credit Finance Facility (SCF): normally for smaller value, more straightforward exports.

(iii) Lines of Credit: ideal for smaller, medium-term contracts, typically entered into by SMEs, with a minimum value US$25,000, or the sterling or foreign currency equivalent.

Each facility gives UK companies the benefit of effectively cash contract terms while allowing buyers time to pay. In addition, they allow the buyer access to fixed interest rates. If the buyer fails to repay any loan amount or interest, ECGD pays the bank providing the finance facility in full under its unconditional guarantee.

16.2.2 Insurance policies

ECGD offers a range of export insurance policies to exporters, protecting them against the risk of non-payment arising from commercial and political risks that they are likely to encounter:

(i) Export Insurance Policy (EXIP): provides, stand-alone cover for pre-credit risk and credit risk loss.

(ii) The EXIP can also be used in conjunction with a Buyer Credit or SCF to cover elements of a contract excluded from finance under the loan, or to cover the exporter against loss during the manufacturing period for elements eligible for finance under the loan until payment is made to the exporter from the loan.

The cover offered may be up to 95% on approved transactions

In addition, a number of special facilities are available, including:

(iii) Overseas Investment Insurance: insures new, long-term, equity and loan investments against the political risks of war, expropriation, and restrictions on repatriating capital and profits. The maximum initial period of cover is 15 years. Bond Insurance Policy (BIP): insures exporters against unfair calls and fair calls attributable to political causes, on performance bonds and other bonds. BIP cover is only available in conjunction with Buyer Credit, SCF or EXIP cover.

16.2.3 Premium

ECGD's rates are tailored to match the risks on each individual case. Generally, the exporter is responsible for paying the premium.

Details of all ECGD's services are available on its website: www.ecgd.gov. uk

Contact:

ECGD Help Desk

PO Box 2200, 2 Exchange Tower, Harbour Exchange Square, London E14 9GS.

Tel: 020 7512 7887

16.3 Atradius

Atradius, which is headquartered in Amsterdam, provides tailored solutions for multinationals and larger companies and more convenient solutions for smaller ones. Its services also include worldwide debt collection and innovative online services for customers including a company information service.

Around 80% of risks covered by Atradius are for goods sold on credit terms of up to 180 days. Cover for business on longer terms is also available, subject to individual discussion.

Atradius' core product insures against the risk of non-payment for exported goods sold on credit terms of up to two years.

16.3.1 Buyer risks covered

(i) The insolvency of the buyer.

(ii) The buyer's failure to pay within six months of due date for goods accepted.

(iii) The buyer's failure, or refusal, to accept goods dispatched which comply with the contract.

16.3.2 Country risks covered

(i) Delays in transferring money from the buyer's country.

(ii) Any action of the government of a foreign country which wholly or partly prevents performance of the contract.

(iii) Political events or economic, legislative or administrative measures occurring outside the UK which prevent or delay transfer of payment.

(iv) War, civil war and the like, outside the UK preventing performance of the contract. This provision may be circumscribed.

(v) Cancellation or non-renewal of an export licence or the imposition of new restrictions on exports, after date of contract.

(vi) When Atradius agrees that the public buyer cause of loss applies Ñ the failure or refusal to fulfill any of the terms of contract.

You are normally covered for 90% of loss in cases of buyer default or insolvency and 95% for the country risks.

16.3.3 Claims

The time at which claims are paid varies according to the cause of the loss, but provided a fully documented claim is submitted promptly and is accepted, payment is normally made:

(i) Immediately on proof of your buyer's insolvency;

(ii) Six months after due date of payment for a protracted default on goods accepted;

(iii) One month after resale if the original buyer has failed to take up the order;

(iv) Four months after due date for most other causes of loss.

Contact

Atradius, Harbour Drive, Capital Waterside, Cardiff CF10 4WZ

Tel: 02920 824951

Website: www.atradius.co.uk

Or in Russia

Ingosstrakh Insurance Company

Credit insurance department, Lesnaya, 41, Moscow

Tel: 007 495 725 7338; Fax: 007 495 234 3601

16.4 Euler Hermes UK

Selling your product, whether in the UK or exporting overseas, is a risky business. One of the biggest risks is that of non-payment so it makes sense to insure against this. Euler Hermes is one of the few leading export credit risk insurers in the UK to thoroughly research its clients' customers. This reduces the risk for both client and insurer. Euler Hermes is in possession of crucial management information that enables it to underwrite a greater level of cover for their clients than the buyers' published accounts would seem to justify. In a recession client companies can therefore feel confident to trade, secure in the knowledge that should any customer go under, Euler Hermes will secure the debt. At the same time Euler Hermes' regular research allows it to monitor not only general economic trends but also all those sectors where it has a number of policyholders. A team of Country Risk Underwriters constantly monitors countries around the world for changing economic and political situations. These results are published in two different reports, each of which is issued quarterly.

Euler Hermes' tailor-made policies use the common pricing factors of turnover, industry (and sector), financial situation, past bad debt losses, strength of credit control, quality of customers and geographical destination. Constant monitoring by Euler Hermes' Economics and Risk Analysis teams ensures its policies are cost effective. Being part of the Euler Hermes group, the world's largest credit insurer, provides greater opportunity to service multi-national clients by sharing commercial data. This will strengthen Euler Hermes' underwriting operation enabling it to provide its clients with accurate global business information.

The table below briefly sets out the key products available for exporters. These can be built into other policy structures as required.

	Scheme	Scheme
What kind of cover do you need?	Your company has an annual turnover up to £10million	Your company has an annual turnover above £10million
Cover on UK and/or overseas customers for the whole sales ledger against insolvency, protracted default or political risks	Trade Builder	Trade Credit Manager
Cover in respect of selected top customers. This is particularly suitable for larger companies where a substantial proportion of business is with key accounts	Please contact EHUK to discuss your needs	Trade Flex
Exceptional loss cover This is ideal for larger companies with excellent credit management looking to protect themselves against an exceptionally high level of bad debts	Please contact EHUK to discuss your needs	Trade Secure
Cover for multinational businesses with multiple international locations		EHUK offers tailored solutions to suit individual needs. Please contact EHUK to discuss your needs

All EHUK policies now come with exclusive access to First Source, the company's credit information service on UK and Irish companies. Included in the policy is a domestic and international collection service that is provided by Euler Hermes Collections UK Limited, the leading UK commercial debt collection agency.

Contact
Euler Hermes UK
1 Canada Square, London E14 5DX
Tel: 020 7512 9333; Fax: 020 7512 9186
Website: www.eulerhermes.com

16.4.1 Other credit insurance

Details of other credit insurers may be obtained from the Association of British
Insurers
Tel: 020 7600 3333; Fax: 020 7696 8999; website: www.abi.org.uk/

16.5   Commercial banks

Many banks provide credit insurance for exporters. The NatWest has a scheme
open to exporters with an export turnover of over £200,000. Under this scheme
exporters can borrow up to 80% of the amount needed for a transaction, subject to
negotiation between the bank and the customer. Barclays Bank allows exporters
to select the markets that they wish to have covered by insurance. Minimum turnover required by the exporter is £250,000. The HSBC provide insurance facilities
allowing for payments over periods of the transaction, e.g. over 60 or 90 days,
depending on the insured company's trade terms.

All the major banks are also involved in export factoring which can provide
facilities through exporters to cover increasing overseas trade and allow for both
slow payments and risk.

Banks may also provide services for invoice discounting. By this means, the bank
will pay for goods after proof of dispatch with a small retainer of usually 10%-20%
being held against the featured remittance. It should be noted that payment is in good
faith against the quality specification of goods and services provided.

Banks will also provide insurance against currency fluctuation if required.

16.6   Credit referencing

The short trading history of many businesses and access to up-to-date information
may pose difficulties to companies wishing to find out about prospective Russian partners. Should a company not have a credit reference the vendor needs to
be cautious. Where a Russian is serious in conducting business, he will provide
bank references, trade references and references from city authorities. The latter
of these, if available, would be encouraging. Prepayment for goods, when first
dealing with a customer, is an accepted norm.

The following companies can provide help in this.

16.6.1 DRUM Resources Limited.

DRUM Resources Limited is a UK based provider of risk management services
in Russia and throughout former Soviet countries. A core part of DRUM's work
is the safekeeping of physical assets on behalf of clients and the provision of a
range of services for identifying, assessing and managing risks to assets and investments. DRUM tailors services to clients' needs to ensure the best protection
for investors:

♦ Manufacturers – Pre-investment intelligence to identify the structure of the
company, history,
♦ specific risks both Regional and Federal and how to control goods / payments.

- Banking – pre-deal intelligence focused on Structured Trade / commodity
- finance, Project finance, Mergers & Acquisitions and Private equity. As part of compliance, FSA and money laundering legislation.
- Law Firms – working as part of the due-diligence process.
  Contact DRUM
  Moscow Tel: 007 495 721 1131 / Fax: 007 495 721 1135
  London Tel: 020 7706 2203 / Fax: 020 706 2208
  website: www.drumresources.com

16.6.2 Dun & Bradstreet International

Dun & Bradstreet International is the world's largest business information supplier, with operations in more than 60 countries and a database of 35 million companies. Dun & Bradstreet can collate and verify information required by joint venture partners when seeking to set up a business within the Russian Federation. Services include:

(a) Business marketing intelligence to identify target companies and market sectors;

(b) commercial risk assessment to evaluate and manage risk levels, make financial
   decisions, select suppliers and develop new markets;

(c) receivable management services including debt recovery; and

(d) International Risk & Payment Review, a monthly publication
   providing an overview of the political and economic situation in 120 markets.

Contact: Dun & Bradstreet Ltd, Holmers Farm Way, High Wycombe, Bucks HP12 4UL Tel: 01494 422000; Fax: 01494 422260; website: www.dnb.com

16.7   Security referencing

Information on the validity of potential Russian joint venture partners may be provided by a number of firms who have, over the years, built up contact with police, armed forces and security networks (see 8.6.8). Advice on security can be obtained from:

Control Risks Group, Tel: 0207 970 2100; Website: www.crg.com/
DRUM Resources Ltd London Office Tel: 0207 929 2473
   Moscow Office Tel: 007 495 721 1131
   Website: www.drumresources.com/

16.8.   Political risk insurance

Political risk insurance would cover:

- confiscation, expropriation, nationalisation and deprivation;
- forced abandonment, selective discrimination and forced divestiture of assets;
- currency and convertibility of profits, dividends, equity, loans, lease proceeds and proceeds of a forced sale;
- removal, destruction or physical damage to assets resulting from war, civil war, strikes, riots, civil commotion, terrorism, sabotage or acts of political violence;
- embargo, blockage, inability to export/import and licence cancellation;

- aggregation of production, concession, tax and other grievance by a host of government or regulatory action which is expropriatory and discriminatory in effect;
- business interruption;
- failure or refusal of a public obligor/guarantor to perform its obligations under a contract or other agreement, including the unfair calling of guarantees;
- aircraft repossession; contract frustration.

The below companies will insure such risks in Russia. However, the availability of insurance may be limited and a high premium may be demanded.

Contacts:

Alexander Forbes Ltd

Alexander Forbes House, 6 Bevis Marks, London, EC3A 7AF

Tel: 020 7933 0000; Fax: 020 7933 1333

Website: www.alexanderforbes.co.uk

P R M Brokers Ltd

129 Crawford Street, London W1U 6BH

Tel: 020 7738 7922; Fax: 020 7924 0390

Website: www.politicalriskmanagers.com

APPENDIX 1

Sample distribution agreement

AGREEMENT

Between (   )
and (   )
(   )hereinafter referred to as the "Supplier" on the one part and
(   ) hereinafter referred to as the "Distributor" on the other part hereby
agree as follows:

1 INTRODUCTION

1.1. The Supplier is engaged in the business of distributing, promoting, marketing and selling the Products.

1.2. The Distributor wishes to purchase the Products for the purpose of marketing and selling the Products in its retail shop located in ( ) and to wholesale within the Territory.

2 DEFINITIONS

2.1. **"Invoice Value"**

means the sums invoiced by the Supplier to the Distributor in respect of any Products, less any taxes, duties or levies and any amounts for transport or insurance included in the invoice;

"Local Regulations"

means all regulations and laws applicable to the manufacture, sale, packaging and labelling of the Products which are in force within the Territory;

"Products"

means the products listed in Schedule 1 and such other products as may from time to time be agreed in writing by the parties;

"Restricted Information"

means any information which is disclosed to the Distributor by the Supplier pursuant to or in connection with this Agreement (whether orally or in writing, and whether or not such information is expressly stated to be confidential or marked as such);

"Sales Contract"

means a written contract between the parties in relation to each order for the Products;

"the Territory"

means (   );

"Year"

means a period of twelve months.

3 APPOINTMENT OF DISTRIBUTOR

3.1. The Supplier hereby appoints the Distributor as its distributor for the resale of the Products in the Territory and the Distributor agrees to act in that capacity subject to the terms and conditions of this Agreement.

3.2. Subject as provided in clause 2., the Supplier shall not:

A) appoint any other individual, firm or company in the Territory as its distributor or agent for the sale of the Products in the Territory or;

B) supply to any other individual, firm or company in the Territory any of the Products, whether for use or resale; or

C) supply to any other individual, firm or company outside the Territory any of the Products which it knows or ought reasonably to know are intended for resale in the Territory.

3.3. If in any Year of this Agreement the aggregate Invoice Value of the Products ordered by the Distributor from the Supplier falls short of the aggregate Invoice Value shown opposite that Year of this Agreement in column (2) of the table given in Schedule 2, then, unless the Distributor pays a sum equal to the shortfall to the Supplier within ( ) days after the end of that Year of this Agreement, the Supplier shall be entitled, by giving not less than ( ) months' written notice to the Distributor within ( ) months after the end of that Year of this Agreement, to:-

A) terminate the restrictions on the Supplier specified in clause 3.2.; or

B) terminate this Agreement.

4   TERM AND TERMINATION

4.1 This Agreement shall be effective from the date of signing stated hereunder. The Agreement shall be in effect for a period of one Year from the date of signing and shall thereafter be automatically renewed for successive renewal terms of one Year each.

4.2 This Agreement may be terminated by either party by six months notice in writing or by the Supplier under clause 3.3.

5   SUPPLY OF THE PRODUCTS

5.1 Each order placed by the Distributor with the Supplier shall be subject to the relevant Sales Contract. No order will be accepted until the relevant Sales Contract has been signed by the authorised signatories of both parties, upon which signing the order will be deemed confirmed.

5.2 All products shall be delivered and sold to the Distributor CIF within the meaning of the most recent edition of the Incoterms published by the International Chamber of Commerce.

6   PRICES

6.1 Products shall be sold by the Supplier to the Distributor at the prices and upon such terms and conditions of sale specified in each Sales Contract.

6.2 The Supplier expressly reserves the right at any time upon at least sixty days prior written notice, to change any or all prices for the Products and their terms and conditions of sale effective on such date as the Supplier shall designate in writing. Any Products invoiced on or after such date shall be at the newly established price.

6.3 The Distributor shall be solely responsible for payment of all charges connected with the shipment of the products, including but not limited to customs fees, documentation fees, brokers fees, forwarder charges, expenses for storage and handling. The Distributor shall also be responsible for obtaining and paying for any warehouse operation permits.

7.   PAYMENT

Payment of the purchase price on all orders for Products, including any charges incurred by the Supplier on behalf of the Distributor in connection with the shipment of Products shall be made by the Distributor in accordance with the "Terms of Payment" clause in the relevant Sales Contract.

8 TAX
Any and all taxes, charges and levies on the purchase or importation of the Products shall be the responsibility of and for the account of the Distributor.

9 ADVERTISING AND MARKETING
9.1 The Supplier shall supply at its own cost such quantities of available advertising, display and marketing materials as the Distributor may reasonably request.

9.2 The Supplier may elect to participate in promotional events in the Territory relating to the Products.

10 RETENTION OF TITLE
Until the Supplier has been paid in full for Products delivered to the Distributor pursuant to orders placed by the Distributor under this Agreement, the Supplier shall retain legal and beneficial title to the Products which shall be held on trust by the Distributor for the Supplier.

11 CONFIDENTIALITY
11.1 Except as provided by clauses 11.2 and 11.3, the Distributor shall at all times during the continuance of this Agreement and after its termination:

A) use its best endeavours to keep all Restricted Information confidential and accordingly shall not disclose any Restricted Information to any other person; and

B) not use any Restricted Information for any purpose other than the performance of the obligations under this Agreement.

11.2. Any Restricted Information may be disclosed by the **Distributor** to:-

A) any customers or prospective customers;

B) any governmental or other authority or regulatory body; or

C) any employees of the Distributor;

to such extent only as is necessary for the purposes contemplated by this Agreement, or as is required by law and subject in each case to the Distributor using its best endeavours to ensure that the person in question keeps the Restricted Information confidential and does not make use of it except for the purpose for which the disclosure is required.

11.3. Any Restricted Information may be used by the Distributor for any purpose, or disclosed by the Distributor to any other person, to the extent only that:-

A) it is at the date hereof, or hereafter becomes, public knowledge through no fault of the Distributor (provided that in doing so the Distributor shall not disclose any Restricted Information which is not public knowledge); or

B) it can be shown by the Distributor, to the reasonable satisfaction of the Supplier, to have been known to it prior to its being disclosed by the Supplier to the Distributor.

12 NOTICES

12.1 A notice given under this Agreement:

A) shall be in writing in the English language (or be accompanied by a properly prepared translation into English);

B) shall be sent for the attention of the person, and to the address or fax number, specified in clause 12.2

C) shall be:

delivered personally; or

sent by fax; or

sent by recorded delivery.

12.2 The addresses for service of notice are:

[SUPPLIER]

name:

address:

for the attention of:

fax number:

[DISTRIBUTOR]

name:

address:

for the attention of:

fax number:

12.3 A notice is deemed to have been received:

A) if delivered personally, at the time of delivery; or

B) in the case of fax, at the time of transmission; or

C) in the case of recorded delivery, at the time of delivery.

12.4 To prove service, it is sufficient to prove that the notice was transmitted by fax to the fax number of the party or, in the case of recorded delivery, by written confirmation of delivery to the correct address.

13. COMPLIANCE WITH LOCAL LAWS AND REGULATIONS

13.1 The Distributor shall have sole responsibility for obtaining any licences or permits required to import the Products into the Territory.

13.2 The Distributor warrants that it has informed the Supplier of all Local Regulations affecting the manufacture, sale, packaging and labelling of the Products in the Territory.

13.3 The Supplier warrants that the Products comply with the Local Regulations in force at the date of this Agreement.

14 FORCE MAJEURE

Neither party shall have liability under or be deemed to be in breach of this Agreement for any delays or failure in performance of this Agreement which result from circumstances beyond the reasonable control of that party.

15 REMEDIES

Each right or remedy of the parties under this Agreement is without prejudice to any other right or remedy of the parties, whether or not such rights or remedies are set out in this Agreement.

16   NO PARTNERSHIP OR AGENCY

This Agreement shall not constitute or imply any partnership, joint venture, agency, fiduciary relationship or other relationship between the parties other than the contractual relationship expressly provided for in the Agreement.

17   ENTIRE AGREEMENT

This Agreement contains the whole agreement between the parties and supersedes any prior written or oral agreements, representations or undertakings between them. The parties confirm that they have not entered into this Agreement on the basis of any representation that is not expressly incorporated into this Agreement. Nothing in this Agreement shall exclude liability for fraud.

18   FURTHER ASSURANCE

The parties shall promptly execute and deliver all such documents, and do all such things, as may be reasonably required for the purpose of giving full effect to the provisions of this Agreement.

19   COUNTERPARTS

This Agreement may be executed in any number of counterparts, each of which shall be deemed to be an original, and all of which together shall constitute one and the same instrument notwithstanding that all parties are not signatories to each counterpart.

20   SEVERABILITY

If a provision of this Agreement is found to be illegal, invalid or unenforceable, then to the extent it is illegal, invalid or unenforceable, that provision will be given no effect and will be treated as though it were not included in this Agreement, but the validity or enforceability of the remaining provisions of the Agreement will not be affected.

21   COSTS

Each party shall bear its own legal and other costs and expenses in relation to the negotiation, preparation, execution and implementation of this Agreement.

22   WAIVER

Any delay or waiver by any party in exercising its rights under this Agreement shall not limit or **restrict the future exercise or enforceability of those rights**.

23   THIRD PARTY RIGHTS

This Agreement does not create any right enforceable by any person not a party to it.

24   ASSIGNMENT

Neither party may assign, delegate, sub-contract or otherwise transfer any or all of its rights and obligations under this Agreement without the prior written consent of the other party.

25   AMENDMENTS

Any amendments, addenda or future appendices to this Agreement are valid only when made in writing and signed by the both parties. This Agreement is made up in two versions (English & Russian) both being authentic. In case of any conflict, the English version shall prevail.

26 AGENT FOR SERVICE

The Distributor hereby undertakes to appoint an agent to receive on its behalf in England or Wales service of any proceedings arising out of or in connection with this Agreement, and to notify the Supplier in writing of such appointment providing details of the agent's name, address and fax number. Such service shall be deemed completed on delivery to such agent (whether or not it is forwarded to and received by the Distributor) and shall be valid until such time as the Supplier has received prior written notice that such agent has ceased to act as agent for the Distributor.

27. GOVERNING LAW AND JURISDICTION

This Agreement and any dispute arising out of or in connection with it shall be governed by and construed in accordance with English law.

28 ARBITRATION

Any dispute arising out of or in connection with this Agreement, including any question regarding its existence, validity, breach or termination, shall be referred to and finally resolved by arbitration under the LCIA Rules, which Rules are deemed to be incorporated by reference into this clause.

ADDRESSES OF THE REGISTERED OFFICES OF THE PARTIES

THE SUPPLIER   THE DISTRIBUTOR

SIGNED:

THE SUPPLIER: THE DISTRIBUTOR

SCHEDULE 1

THE PRODUCTS

SCHEDULE 2

MINIMUM YEARLY INVOICE VALUE

(1)
(2)

Year   Aggregate Invoice Value

1
2
3
4
5 and each year thereafter

APPENDIX 2

Contacts for Intellectual Property Rights

REGISTRATION AGENCIES:

ROSPATENT (RUSSIAN PATENT AGENCY)
30-1 Berezhkovskaya Naberezhnaya
Moscow, Russia 121858
Tel: 007 495 240 0174 / 007 495 240 6015
Fax: 007 495 243 3337
Website: www.fips.ru/ruptoen/index.htm
Registration of inventions, trademarks, industrial models, computer software and databases.

RUSSIAN COPYRIGHT SOCIETY
6/A B. Bronnaya Street
Moscow, Russia 103670
Tel: 007 495 203 3777, 203 3260
Fax: 007 495 200 1263
E-mail: rao@rao.ru
Website: www.rao.ru

LEGAL ADVICE

**INTELLECTUAL PROPERTY PROTECTION
AND REGISTRATION AGENCY**
4 Petroverigskiy pereulok
101990, Moscow,
Tel/Fax: 007 495 921 4728, 921 3158, 928 3174
E-mail: pattrade@commail.ru
Website: www.esp-pat.com/

THE COALITION FOR INTELLECTUAL PROPERTY RIGHTS
Baker & McKenzie
Sadovaya Plaza, 11th Fl.
Dolgorukovskaya St., 7
127006 Baker & McKenzie
Tel: 007 495 787 2700
Fax: 007 495 787 2701
E-mail: eugene.arievich@bakernet.com
Website: www.cipr.org/contact/index.htm

FEDERAL ANTIMONOPOLY SERVICE OF THE RUSSIAN FEDERATION
11 Sadovaya Kudrinskaya Ulitsa
Moscow 123231, Russia
Tel: 007 495 252 7653
Fax: 007 495 254 8300
Website: http://fas.gov.ru/english/
Gennady M. Khodyrev, Minister

ROSPATENT CHAMBER OF APPEALS
24 Berezhkovskaya Nab., Bldg. 1
Moscow 121857, Russia
Tel: 007 495 240 4672
Fax: 007 495 240 3363
E-mail: rospatent@rupto.ru
Website: www.fips.ru/rospatent/index.htm

ASSOCIATIONS
BUSINESS SOFTWARE ALLIANCE (BSA)
Hot line in Moscow: 007 495 258 0928
Website: www.bsa.org
The organization fights with software piracy worldwide.

INTERNATIONAL FEDERATION OF PHONOGRAPHIC INDUSTRY (IFPI) MOSCOW
23, 1st Tverskaya-Yamskaya Street
Moscow, Russia 125047
Tel: 007 495 956 6057/58, 725 6573/74
Fax: 007 495 956 2609
Website: www.ifpi.org
The IFPI, which represents the international recording industry, has its headquarters in London. It aims to combat music piracy and promote adequate copyright laws in the NIS, Asia, Europe, and Latin America. Producers of sound recording and music videos are eligible for membership in IFPI.

RUSSIAN ANTI-PIRACY SOFTWARE ASSOCIATION (RAPSA)
Dmitrovskiy Pereuluk, d. 4, Street 2
103031, Russia, Moscow
Tel/fax: 007 495 246 7442
E-mail: info@elspa.ru
Website: www.elspa.ru/start_e.html
RASPA helps its members, who are largely Russian and foreign software developing and distributing companies, protect their intellectual property rights and copyright in Russia. The association organises raids, jointly with the Regional Department of Organized Crime Prevention, on distributors and vendors of pirated software and assists in settling claims.

RUSSIAN ANTI-PIRACY ORGANIZATION (RAPO)
11/8 Pugovishnikov Lane
Moscow, Russia 119021
Tel: 007 495 245 1938, 246 7393
Fax: 007 495 245 1864
E-mail: rapo@dol.ru
Contact: Mr. Konstantin Zemchenkov, Director
The association's members include the Motion Picture Association of America and Russian film producers and distributors.

INDEX